Aspects of Consciousness

Aspects of Consciousness

Volume 1
Psychological Issues

Edited by
Geoffrey Underwood and Robin Stevens

Department of Psychology
University of Nottingham
England

1979

ACADEMIC PRESS
A Subsidiary of Harcourt Brace Jovanovich, Publishers
London   New York   Toronto   Sydney   San Francisco

ACADEMIC PRESS INC. (LONDON) LTD.
24/28 Oval Road,
London NW1

United States Edition published by
ACADEMIC PRESS INC.
111 Fifth Avenue
New York, New York 10003

British Library Cataloguing in Publication Data
Aspects of consciousness.
    Vol. 1; Psychological issues
    1. Consciousness
    I. Underwood, Geoffrey
    II. Stevens, Robin
    153   BF311   79–41233
    ISBN 0–12–708801–6

Text set in 11/12 Baskerville
Printed in Great Britain by W & J Mackay Limited, Chatham

Contributors

Michael J. Apter, *Department of Psychology, University College Cardiff, PO Box 78, Cardiff CF1 1XL, Wales*

Richard ־A. Block, *Department of Psychology, Montana State University, Bozeman, Montana 59717, USA*

Thomas H. Carr, *Department of Psychology, University of Nebraska, Omaha, Nebraska 68182, USA*

Eric A. Lunzer, *School of Education, University of Nottingham, Nottingham NG7 2RD, England*

Howard R. Pollio, *Department of Psychology, University of Tennessee, Knoxville, Tennessee 37916, USA*

James Reason, *Department of Psychology, University of Manchester, Manchester M13 9PL, England*

Graham F. Reed, *Department of Psychology, York University 4700 Keele Street, Downsview, Ontario, Canada*

Peter W. Sheehan, *Department of Psychology, University of Queensland, St. Lucia, Queensland, Australia*

Geoffrey Underwood, *Department of Psychology, University of Nottingham, Nottingham NG7 2RD, England*

Preface

An era of rigid Behaviourism which concentrated on observable stimuli and responses and their relationships has recently passed, and many of the theories of this period have proved to be sterile. The richness of our thoughts and the knowledge which comes through our self-awareness had no place in the Behaviourist's world and it is not surprising that the knowledgeable layman could see little of relevance to himself in psychological theories. Behaviourism was an appropriate reaction to the psychology of introspection which preceded it, and its most important lesson, the need to link psychological theories with observable behaviour, is implicitly accepted by most contemporary theorists. However, many of the issues concerned with aspects of conscious experience which concerned the introspectionists are once again seen as being of fundamental importance.

Of the several questions relevant to an adequate account of consciousness there are, in our opinion, two which are central. How can an organism, a physical system, give rise to the non-corporeal state of awareness? How can this metaphysical state affect in turn the same physical system on which it depends, or indeed any part of the physical world? Thus we need to explain how a physical organism can become aware of its world and can experience different states of awareness, and we need to explain how thoughts can lead to a change in the physical structure.

The Behaviourists, by disregarding the question of self-awareness, ignored such issues, although some Behaviourists, such as Tolman, Mowrer and Osgood, have proposed a variety of mediational mechanisms for explaining expectancies and thoughts. But on the whole the states of the organism or processes intervening between input and output were outside their domain of enquiry. Therefore subjective phenomena which characterize the mind were considered to play no role in the operation of stimulus–response relationships. A refusal to take account of awareness, our most effective indicator of personal existence, must be considered a significant factor in the lack of popularity of this school of psychology.

By denying that our experience of life could be usefully studied scientifically, the Behaviourists were left with nothing to say about areas of behaviour involving personal knowledge, and the psychology of behaviour has been supplemented with the psychology of cognition. The success of this new approach in describing the processes of perceiving, remembering, communicating and thinking has been considerable, but it too is at risk. Doubts have been voiced about the power of cognitive psychology to account for the existence and variety of mental life, so this school is also in danger of ignoring personal experience. When the laboratory subject responds to artificial stimuli in artificial circumstances we may be able to discover the structural constraints upon experience, but the richness of behaviour provided by individual strategy and intention will require investigations with more ingenuity than has sometimes been shown in the past. Cognitive psychology has, on occasions, given the impression that its description of the mind will consist of the much-parodied structural flow-chart. Among other faults, this description would not account for the variability of behaviour associated with the strategical choice available to the interactive subject, and it would give no account of the quality of consciousness. It is perhaps appropriate for us to extend the model and attempt to describe the experiences of the observer in relation to what we have previously described as the cognitive processes leading to, corresponding with, and resulting from those experiences.

The present discussions argue in favour of the investigation of the personal experience of awareness. They recommend that we take account of subjective experience and correlate it with objective measures. By such a process of converging operations it is possible to overcome the historical objections to introspection and gain a more complete understanding of awareness. The methods of contemporary cognitive psychology will be used in these investigations and may, as some of the contributors argue, be used to correlate evidence collected by the methods of physiological and clinical psychology.

The problems of the generation of awareness by a physical organism, and the effect upon the organism of its awareness, are discussed here without solutions being offered. Suggestions are made which might lead towards solutions, but other discussants are content to attempt to define the relationships between consciousness and behaviour, and to describe the characteristics of awareness which an explanation must take into account. Although the discussions are presented in more than one volume, the relationships between them are profuse. The correlation of evidence from all sources will be necessary for a complete description of consciousness.

In addition to thanking the contributors for the enthusiasm which is in evidence in their chapters, we are pleased to thank a number of colleagues for their comments on earlier drafts of the chapters. For these reviews we acknowledge the help given by Michael Apter, Graham Beaumont, Donald Broadbent, Thomas Carr, Alan Gauld, R. B. Joynson, Donald Norman, Tim Shallice and John Shotter. Thanks also go to Jean Underwood for a mammoth effort towards the co-ordination and organization of the manuscript during its final preparation.

Nottingham *Geoffrey Underwood*
September 1979 *Robin Stevens*

Contents

Contents

Contents of Volume 2

1 The Development of Consciousness

E. A. LUNZER

*School of Education,
University of Nottingham*

1 What is Consciousness?

"When I use a word," said Humpty Dumpty, "it means precisely what I intend it to mean", and in logic he was surely right. In practice, he might have added: "within the limits of what will be acceptable to others". There are at least three ways of defining a word. Dictionary definitions provide synonyms. They are chiefly useful to foreigners and to those who wish to extend their vocabulary. They work best when a word is more or less rare. Rigorous definitions have their place in science: the characteristic of such definitions is circularity within a system, since every technical term within a set is defined with reference to one or more others in the same set. But such definitions pre-suppose that the domain under discussion can be studied in terms of a model which involves a high level of abstraction, like Newtonian mechanics. The word "consciousness" does not belong to such a domain. Nor is it unfamiliar. But it is certainly a "fuzzy concept", and it follows that contributors to this volume will likely have somewhat dissimilar, albeit overlapping, frames of reference for it. Following Humpty Dumpty, I would begin by saying something about how I intend to use the word in this chapter: that is to provide an informal descriptive definition.

One might say that an organism is conscious of an aspect of its environment if it reacts differentially with respect to variation within that aspect. Such a definition extends well beyond acceptable usage since it covers phototropism in plants. But because of the absence of clear boundaries, it cannot be ignored. I will call this "Consciousness I". To the extent that the study of consciousness includes all differential reactions, its domain is co-extensive with that of cognitive psychology. At the other extreme, one might reserve the term consciousness for those aspects of the environment or of the subject's own experience upon which he is in a position to make verbal report. This usage has the weight of precedent from Freud, for in psycho-analytical theory the Unconscious is made up of just those thoughts and feelings which cannot be made available for verbal report in normal life settings, whence the need for hypnosis or the analyst's technique. I hope to show that this definition of consciousness can at the present time serve a valuable explanatory purpose for the developmental psychologist, and I will term it "Consciousness III". But Consciousness III is too restrictive for certain purposes and, like Consciousness I, it fails to correspond with everyday usage. In particular, it is a definition which denies consciousness to any animal which does not possess speech. Common usage would require that we allow consciousness to an animal when it anticipates a treat, or a display of affection, or chastisement—while denying consciousness to a bean plant which grows towards the window. This would point to an intermediate concept, with rather fuzzy boundaries. By way of approximation, I would suggest that if an organism is capable of responding differentially to the same elements (perceptual cues derived from the environment or, alternatively, verbal or quasi-imaginal determinants in its own mentation) in different contexts and hence with different behaviours, that organism is "conscious" of something. Again, if different complexes of cues, often corresponding to the same definable object, elicit similar differential behaviours, we will say the organism is conscious of the relevant object. The first is exemplified by the diverse ways in which a dog will respond to its master, the second when similar warning behaviours are elicited by the sight of an approaching stranger and by the sound of his footsteps. We will call this intermediate awareness "Consciousness II" and this also is relevant to the study of cognitive development.

Thus, for the purpose of this discussion, we can identify three successive levels of consciousness. Consciousness I implies differential reactivity and no more. Consciousness II would seem to imply some sort of internal organization mediating an equivalence class: an organization which might be thought of as a concept, a recognizer or a scheme, depending on the reader's preference. Consciousness III implies that the object of cognition can be attended to by the subject and can therefore become an object for voluntary representation or for verbal communication.

It would be tedious to insist on these terms and I will use them only now and then, to resolve an ambiguity or to make a particular point. Nevertheless, it will be argued that, in the present state of our knowledge, the distinctions which they embody are useful both for exposition and as a heuristic device. Specifically, most of the cognitive development that occurs in the first 12–15 months of life (Piaget's "sensori-motor level") may be thought of as mediating transitions from Consciousness I to Consciousness II. The next phase of development comprising the pre-school years is marked by the growing power of language and representation, i.e. by a transition from Consciousness II to Consciousness III. However, at least one way of describing the limitations of children's reasoning below about 6 years old is by reference to the limited scope of their Consciousness III. The child can readily represent the environment, whether real or imagined—as in dreams or make-believe. But he has difficulty in focussing on the determinants of his own response: he cannot "turn round on the schema" (Bartlett's phrase, cf. Oldfield and Zangwill, 1942). A further extension of Consciousness III is needed to compass the critical features which determine the subject's own decision making, and it is one which appears to intervene in nearly all the achievements which were found by Piaget and others to appear during the years of elementary schooling.

What has been said implies that the quality of thinking is a function of the scope of consciousness. The word "thinking", like "consciousness", is one which is used in many ways. Yet one notes that, increasingly, psychologists who study thinking do so by reference to a model wherein elements which are retrieved from memory are manipulated by substitution or re-arrangement in accordance with some overall plan. The elements may be represented by words or by images and they may serve as precise effective devices for the retrieval of other elements—as when the title of a poem is sufficient to elicit its recall in full, if required. Such a model is explicit in computer simulation programs (cf. Newell and Simon, 1972; Farnham-Diggory, 1972; Klahr and Wallace, 1976) as well as in the neo-Piagetian thinking of Pascual-Leone (1970, 1976) and of Case (1972, 1974, 1978), but it is implicit in such diverse approaches as those of Clark and Chase (1972, 1974), of Kintsch (1974) and of Piaget himself.

Some plans are acquired much later than others. In such cases later acquisition may argue no more than lack of experience. But there are also cases of failure to capitalize on experience, and this may be either because of a limitation on the maximum number of elements that children can handle (Pascual-Leone and Case), or because certain kinds of elements are simply not accessible for such manipulation. The remainder of this chapter will be concerned with a consideration of some evidence for these interpretations.

Specifically, the next section is a brief summary of some recent studies by Piaget and his associates illustrating the lag between accurate execution and correct report (Consciousness III) as defined. This is followed by a résumé of recent and current work on the development of meta-memory, i.e. the ability to make an accurate assessment both of one's own skills as a memorizer, and of what one can do to improve one's own recall. This section draws heavily on the work of Flavell-and his associates. The final section presents an interpretation of development in logical thinking which relies heavily on the notion of consciousness in the sense of reflection (Consciousness III).

2 The Grasp of Consciousness

Skilled motor performance is not always contingent on the prior elaboration of a conscious plan of the relevant sequence of actions. Since animal behaviour is often skilled and animals almost never reach Consciousness III, the statement is self-evident. But it might be supposed that once a human child has reached that level of competence, and especially when he is able to produce fluent verbal reports of his experience, he should have no problem in reporting the plans that direct any well-rehearsed sequence of actions. For there is ample evidence that skilled performance does require the existence of a motor-plan which is self-sufficient in that its execution is largely uninfluenced by visual and kinaesthetic feedback. Thus Posner and Keele (1973) note that when each movement in a sequence is independent, the skill is under "*closed loop* control because the feedback from each movement becomes the input for the elicitation of the next". Such would be the case for the learner driver when changing gears. They note that the effect of practice in the execution of a skill is that the timing and sequencing shift from external feedback to internalized control, when performance is said to be "open-loop", allowing greater overlap between constituents of the sequence, and hence a greater smoothness in the whole.

Since performance is now directed by an internalized plan which was constructed bit by bit, using feedback, one might infer that the skilled subject knows the plan well and can therefore articulate the sequence. Yet a moment's reflection will doubtless be sufficient to convince some readers that they cannot always say just how they do a thing, although that thing is done quite automatically whenever there is need.

Nevertheless, it appears that the adult can often discover the plan which he himself is following, even though he may not know it to begin with. In other words, he can reflect on his own performance—Consciousness III. A recent study by Piaget (1977a) shows that children of 4 or 5 years are unable to reflect on their own performance. Children of various ages were asked to say how they walked on all fours, i.e. which limb was moved first, which went next, and so on. S was first invited to try it and report on what he did. If the report was incorrect, he was told to try it again and think hard about what he was doing, or to stop and then begin again. The most startling finding was that younger children (4, 5 and 6 years old) almost invariably began by describing a Z pattern (e.g. left hand, right hand, left foot, right foot). This was despite the fact that at all ages performance is best described as an X (each hand accompanies the contralateral foot). At 4 or 5 years most children could not be shifted from the Z reply. At 5 or 6 years many were persuaded by a second experience to modify their answer, but they now gave an N pattern or its inverse (e.g. right foot, right hand, left foot, left hand). Many of the Ss now began to crawl this way even though they had first crawled like anyone else (an X). At 7 or 8 years, 50% of the subjects gave X solutions either immediately or after the guided practice, and at 9 or 10 years 66% gave this reply, for the most part spontaneously.

Piaget notes that "cognizance proceeds from the periphery (goals and results) to the centre, i.e. recognition of means employed, reasons for their modification, etc." (1977a, p.334). And later "The subject looks at his actions and these are assimilated . . . by his consciousness as if they were ordinary material links situated in the objects—whence the necessity for a new conceptual construction" (p.339).

When a child begins crawling he enjoys visual and proprioceptive feedback, but there is no reflection. When, much later, he is asked to reflect on what he does, it is clear that he is still unable to "read off" the several moments in the muscular programme which, we may suppose, is now a well rehearsed "open-loop" skill (i.e. one in which the initiation of any activity segment does not wait upon the completion of its predecessor). Instead what he does is to invent a scheme by putting the external elements together following some simple arrangement, which in this case seems to be classificatory: first the two hands, then the two feet (Z). It is very difficult to progress in this fashion and none of the Ss did so in practice. Yet few of the 4-year-olds reported any conflict between what they did and what they said. At 5 years, they were aware of such a conflict, and the evidence is that they changed what they did as well as what they said. An N is still a classificatory scheme. But we may guess that "first one side then the other" is less immediately appealing since the two sides are not as contrasting as are hands and feet. Yet one can crawl in this fashion without inconvenience. So the verbal scheme changes in the light of the action. But what is striking is that the action itself is often distorted to match the scheme: Ss actually begin crawling in the way they describe. It appears as though these youngsters are unable to attend to what they are doing and still do it. From 7 years on, most of them are able to find out what they are actually doing, and increasingly they do so without having to be told—since only a minority of people can answer the question from memory at any age.

Why cannot the 5-year-old revise an incorrect model by observing his behaviour while the 7-year-old can? Perhaps because of a difference in concreteness or determinacy of the schemes that are brought to bear on the observations. The initial Z scheme would be fully determined and independent of observation. The N scheme is usually given after observation as a correction to an initial Z. Perhaps this means that following the Z scheme there is a more open scheme which directs the observation, viz. "limb 1, limb 2, limb 3, limb 4", i.e. a recognition that there is a succession of four elements and what must be established is which comes first and which comes next, etc. Such a scheme would force the child to look for four distinct successive movements and if necessary make them. Finally the X scheme, if not present at the outset can only be compassed by a fully open scheme, one which admits of the possibility of near-simultaneity as well as succession within the same sequence. For the present, however, such an interpretation is somewhat speculative, since the intermediate schemes are inferred and not directly observed, nor are they themselves conscious even though they may direct the consciousness of the action.

The problem and its solution would appear to be analogous to the acquisition of certain important transformations in language, negation being a useful example (Klima and Bellugi, 1966). Forms like "No the sun shining" and "No a boy bed" suggest that the child seeks to link the negation to the frame that he wants to negate but can only do so by juxtaposition while forms like "I didn't did it" and "He not taking the walls down" represent attempts to find a bridge between an intended meaning and a tranformational form where both are familiar, but the latter only as a perceptual object, i.e. in comprehension.

It should be noted that there is not always interference between proprioceptive cognition and action. Crawling may be thought of as a "closed skill" in the sense that the performer is in more or less full control over the situation and is not required to respond to a shifting pattern of environmental cues (Poulton, 1957). Unlike the children observed by Piaget, adult learners are often helped in such skills by increased "knowledge of performance", although open skills benefit more from knowledge of results (Nixon and Locke, 1973).

This experiment is one of several reported in two recent volumes (Piaget, 1977a, 1978). Altogether, there are 27 enquiries with 15 in the first and 12 in the second. Walking on all fours is the first of these enquiries and in many ways the most interesting. It should be said in fairness that these volumes are open to criticism on many counts. The mode of investigation is the loose clinical method favoured by Piaget in his earlier writings, and reporting is inadequate. One suspects that, since there were no rigorous controls in execution, it became impossible to lay down hard and fast criteria for the categorization of results. In any case, no tables are given, and there is some confusion between results and interpretation. Finally, the several inquiries are only loosely related by their relevance to a common theme and were carried out more or less independently by separate individuals. Thus they do not form a sequence in which each experiment is an attempt to resolve some of the issues raised by its predecessors.

Nevertheless, taken as a whole, they do seem to highlight some of the issues. The division into two volumes is supposed to be based on the relative importance of learning for success in a task. In fact, the experiment just cited is perhaps the only one in the 1977 volume where one can feel certain that there is no improvement in execution over successive trials. In other experiments, there is usually improvement, but one is frequently uncertain whether these improvements flow from Consciousness III or whether they can be accounted for by Consciousness II, or even Consciousness I. The same volume includes observation of children's attempts to solve the "Towers of Hanoi" puzzle, in which learning is clearly important, as well as launching an object from a sling, when it is less obvious but nonetheless present.

This last provides a second illustration of the way in which the child's report of his own directive scheme begins as an artificial construction that is remote from the true (sensori-motor) scheme. The apparatus is a stone on the end of a string and a set of wide "goals" situated at each of the four compass points, with the child in the centre of the ring. His job is to turn in a circle, holding the string at arm's length, then let go at the right point to make the stone go into a pre-selected goal. Provided the goals are wide enough, even the 4-year-olds are successful. But they are convinced that the release point is in line between their body and the target and at the point farthest from the target (6 o'clock) as it would be if they were throwing it. Seven-year-olds still site the point of a release in this alignment, but they choose 12 o'clock. This we may suppose to be a compromise between ordinary throwing which is in the direction of the target and the recognition that here there is no distinct throwing movement of the arm but only a release in a rotary movement. At 9 or 10 years there appears to be a gradual improvement in the ability to identify the point of release by observation, and at 11 years most children realize that the true point of release must be between 2 o'clock and 3 or between 9 and 10 o'clock, depending on the sense of rotation and target-distance. Not surprisingly, most of these children imagine the path of the stone after release to curve in the horizontal plane (as well as the vertical), and it is only the more sophisticated (identified by

Piaget as at IIIB) who know, presumably having been told, that the horizontal path is tangential to the circle.

The main thrust of these observations may be much the same as that given above: we are not born with a special analysing device that enables us to observe and interpret our own movements or the schemes that direct them. The things that we do, the order in which we do them, and the cues that elicit them must all be inferred from observation, and this in turn is more an observation of overt aspects of behaviour and their external results than a privileged access to decision processes. But observation implies a selection and categorization (cf. Broadbent, 1971), and these require a cognitive scheme. The latter is evidently a gradual construction, being liable to more than one modification before it reaches its final form. Moreover, despite Piaget's own somewhat arbitrary use of stages (IA, IB, IIA, IIB, IIIA and IIIB) to designate the levels that one observes, it is clear there is no one age or stage that is critical for all tasks: if success is achieving a match between what one does and what one says, then success with walking on all fours may be found at 6 or 7 years, while success with launching from a sling does not occur until a good deal later.

These two tasks are among the best examples involving problems where success is largely a function of sensori-motor co-ordination while preliminary planning plays no more than a minimal role. The "Towers of Hanoi" is at the other extreme. This is a well known puzzle or "game for one", played with a simple piece of apparatus consisting of three sticks on a base and a set of rings in graded sizes. Any number of rings (usually two–six are used) can be arranged in a pyramid on one of the sticks and the puzzle is then to transfer the entire pyramid to one of the other sticks in as few "moves" as possible, with the following constraints: (1) a "move" consists in the transfer of just one ring from one stick to another; (2) a move is not allowed if it means placing a larger ring on top of one which is smaller; (3) the game must consist entirely of moves.

This type of situation has been quite extensively studied and one is not surprised to learn that children under 6 years old had considerable difficulty in mastering the problem even with a pyramid of two and failed altogether when the number of rings was increased to three. At 7 or 8 years, most children were immediately successful with two rings, while three rings was solved by trial and error. Apparently many of the Ss eventually succeeded in solving three-ring problems in the minimum of seven moves, but they were still unable to give a proper account of how the thing was done, nor could they say which piece was moved most often and which one least. At 10 or 11 years, Ss were better able to give a rationale, e.g. "You always take the smaller one, then the middle one: then you put the smaller one on the middle one; so you can get at the big one. That makes a small pyramid there and the way is clear so I can start all over again". Also at this level, there is far greater success with pyramids of four rings.

Previous work by Gagne and Smith (1962) has shown that there are further degrees of learning with the same problem and that success with a tower of four does not generalize immediately to one of five or six. Above all, what remains to be discovered is (a) the rule for the minimum number of moves (m) for any given n, viz. $m = 2^n - 1$ and (b) the rules for deciding which piece must be moved and in which direction (the direction of movement for each ring in the tower is constant; alternate rings move in opposite directions; never move the same ring in successive moves). The instruction to verbalize aloud produced better results than the instruction to think about the goal.

In problems of this kind too, overt trial and feedback are usually an essential pre-requisite for success. What is more, errorless performance without insight is not uncommon. Yet it is interesting to note that both the problem and its solution hinge on the succession of moves, and neither their mode of execution nor their timing is relevant. The problem is therefore not a "skill" in the ordinary sense of the term. Nevertheless, it is not at all clear that this difference in the character of the original task entails a parallel difference in the process whereby S gradually constructs a cognitive scheme to describe his own behaviour.

What is apparent, however, is that the attempt to reflect on the execution may improve performance in the end and it seems reasonable to conclude that this is because such reflection prompts the subject to isolate whatever elements in a task may be critical to its solution. The nature of these elements evidently differs from one task to another. In the "Towers of Hanoi", it is the recursive patterning of successive moves together with the continuing oscillation in their direction. In the mechanical puzzles studied by Ruger more than 60 years ago (interlocking rings or twisted nails to be separated by appropriate rotation without applying force), certain parts of the puzzle itself become critical in that the solution hinges on their being brought into the correct "attitude" relative to each other (Ruger, 1910).

When the solution of a task takes the form of a sequence of physical movements, often including manipulation of concrete apparatus, the adequacy of consciousness seems to depend on the ability of the subject to break down his view of the behaviour as a whole into a series of steps or phases, to organize into a model, and to test this model against the reality of his own practice. Sometimes, but not always, the increased adequacy of the model leads to an improvement in the performance of the task, but it looks as if the younger child is often incapable of constructing models that are flexible enough to permit of adequate consciousness.

3 Meta-memory

It is interesting to look at a very different order of phenomena, where the task is representational rather than practical, and generally verbal. I would therefore turn to a consideration of the development of consciousness in regard to memory. The present discussion is necessarily very limited, since the development of memory is a thriving area of research at the present time (cf. the excellent reviews by Hagen *et al.* and by Ann Brown which appeared in 1975).

Much of the initial impetus for the work on the relation of consciousness to memory derived from the studies of Flavell, beginning with the observation that 5-year-olds rarely rehearsed a simple and arbitrary sequence when required to retain it over a brief interval. (Flavell, Beach and Chinsky, 1966). Each child was shown an array of seven objects. The experimenter pointed to two or three of these, and the task was to point to the same objects in the same order after an interval of some seconds. Only two of the 20 fives rehearsed during a 15 sec. interval but 15 of the sevens did so, and all of the elevens. Subsequent work showed that the failure of the fives was a "production deficit" and not a "mediation deficit": when instructed to rehearse the names of the objects, children of this age were well able to do so and moreover this enabled them to perform the task itself correctly after the interval, while non-rehearsers generally failed. Flavell (1970) takes this as evidence that in this task at least, language can mediate a higher level of response even in younger children, contrary to an earlier view put forward by Kendler (1963).

Perhaps the most striking finding from our present standpoint is the failure of most 5-year-olds to realize the value of rehearsal after demonstration. Although they used the method successfully when told to do so, 50% of the Ss dropped it later when no longer made to use it. Presumably, they were unable to reflect on the successive parts of their own behaviour or, specifically, to relate their own rehearsal to their subsequent task performance (Keeney *et al.* 1967). The case would certainly have been stronger had there been adequate feedback in the form of knowledge of results, as Flavell himself recognized (1970). However, in the light of other findings such as those described in the last section, one would expect such feedback to accelerate understanding only when the child's own information processing has reached a certain threshold. This is because knowledge of results must be set against knowledge of performance if it is to produce a spontaneous new strategy predicated on the recognition of its greater efficacy. Clearly, there is need for further experimentation.

Subsequent studies have thrown little light on this point, although they indicate that rehearsal is the most primitive among memorial aids and that others such as sorting, clustering and image formation and elaboration are all later acquisitions (cf. Brown 1973, 1974, Rohwer, 1973). It is clear there are wide individual differences, from those who feign to despise mere memory (surely this is an area where the popularization of experimental psychology might provide a useful corrective) to the feats of Lesley Welch. The ancient art of memory once practised to mastery by the orators of Greece and Rome has fallen into disuse, doubtless for good reasons (Yates, 1966). However, although the failure to capitalize on the variety of memorial techniques at our disposal is due in part to their irrelevance in an age of print, electronic information processing and CEEFAX, there is also widespread ignorance and contempt by the educationist and the public at large, coupled with neglect of the subject by psychologists until very recent times.

But our immediate concern is with the development of consciousness, and in that context some of the most interesting observations were those that were made of changes in the child's awareness in his own activity as a memorizer—often labelled meta-memory (following Flavell, 1970). Consider first an experiment by Flavell *et al.* (1970) in which children in four age groups were first of all required to predict how many items they could name in sequence after a single presentation (of a word-series accompanied by a picture strip), and than tested to see how good was their recall in practice. Both prediction and performance were tested with series of increasing size, from $n = 1$ to $n = 10$. The actual span increased from 3·5 at 5 years to 5·5 at 10 years, while the predicted span decreased from 7·2 to 6·1. No less that eight of the 14 fives thought they could repeat the maximum series of 10! Similar results were obtained under a variety of conditions by Yussen and Levy (1975).

By contrast, a more extensive—albeit less rigorous—study by Kreutzer *et al.* (1975) indicated that even at kindergarten age children were aware that the more time that is spent studying a display the better one can expect to recall it. They knew, too, that things once remembered are apt to be forgotten later. However, they were unable to predict that a list of associates (e.g. walk–shoe, nice–picture, etc.) would be harder to recall than a list of opposites (e.g. walk–run, nice–nasty, etc.) Or again, they were less able than children aged 7, 9, and 11 years to anticipate the value of categorization in memorizing a display, and more often than not they failed to realize that remembering the gist of a spoken story is easier than verbatim recall. In all these aspects, Kreutzer *et al*. found a continuous improvement in the % of correct replies.

The principal weakness of this study was its reliance on children's spoken replies to questioning. Inevitably one recalls the criticisms of Piaget's work made over the years from Isaacs (1930) to Donaldson (1978). Nevertheless such work does illustrate the fact that we are not born with some sort of inward eye that informs us about our own mental processes. We learn about these gradually just as we gradually attain a better knowledge of the behaviour of things outside us.

Flavell himself points out that the study of meta-recall is still in its infancy: we do not know what sorts of experiences or observations produce improvements in a child's insight about his own remembering, and we do not know whether improvement in execution precedes improvement in meta-memory, or whether it follows from it (Flavell, 1977, 214–15; cf. Flavell and Wellman, 1976). It would be unwise to predict the answer to this last question by analogy with others forms of behaviour, since memorizing is in some respects different: it includes techniques which are easy and effective yet remain for a time in abeyance unless the child is instructed to implement them—production deficiency. There is no obvious parallel here either with physical skills (Section 2) or with most other aspects of cognition, to one of which we now turn.

4 Cognitive Organization

Piaget's studies of cognitive development highlight a spate of achievements that tend to be realized about the same time in a child's life—somewhere between 5 and 8 years old.

One might begin by considering developments in classificatory behaviour. The principal technique for investigating this domain consists in presenting a child with an array of objects which vary in one or more dimensions, and asking him to sort it. Such sorting tests have been widely used since the pioneering studies of Goldstein and Scheerer (1941). Variants of this task include the request for hierarchical arrangement, cross-classification to produce a matrix arrangement, classification in one dimension followed by re-classification in another, and requesting answers to verbal questions such as "Are all the blue counters square?" and "Are all the square counters blue?", questions which take separate answers when the focus array consists of five blue squares, two red circles and two blue circles (Inhelder and Piaget,

1964). While the simpler sorting tasks can be managed by children at 4 years, it is only at 5 years that the majority sort all the objects (younger ones are apt to overlook one or more elements, Kofsky, 1966). But what is especially revealing is that re-classification (e.g. sorting by shape regardless of colour and then sorting by colour regardless of shape) is a late achievement, which is realized by fewer than 50% of children at 6 years, although the majority are successful at 7 and up to 75% at 8 years (Inhelder and Piaget, 1964; Lovell *et al.* 1962; Lunzer, 1970a). The 5- or 6-year-old will often agree quite readily to sort the objects "another way", after he has sorted them correctly by one criterion and then been told to jumble them up again. But typically such a child will promptly sort them by the same criterion. Why?

One possible interpretation is that under 7 years old most children are unable to reflect on the criteria that direct their own decisions. The initial sorting requires the maintenance of a criterion as a guide to action and inhibition of irrelevant features. In order to comply with the request to shift to another criterion, a child must recall the first criterion together with the fact that he has used this, since he requires this evidence to direct him to the second criterion (Lunzer, 1970b). In other words, he must be conscious of his own decision process.

Another illustration is the appearance of insight into the oddity problem at about 7 years. The Terman–Merrill test includes a relevant item at 4–6 years old. The child is asked to select "the one that is different" in an array consisting of several identical elements with only one contrasted. Harlow established that monkeys could learn to respond in similar fashion to novel arrays without verbal instruction, following repeated exposure to discrimination problems of the same form, provided that the pattern of reward over successive trials in each problem was such as to reinforce the desired strategy and to inhibit alternatives.*

A series of studies carred out in the 1950s and 60s indicated that children could form such learning sets from an early age. In these experiments children, like monkeys, must discover the correct strategy without being told. In addition, several studies showed that after a modal age of 6 or 7 years, the rate of improvement over successive problems in children is much more rapid than it is either in younger children or in monkeys and apes. Thus, older children often achieve

---

* For an oddity problem the correct strategy may be presented, using an informal computer language, as: Examine (A), Store (A), Compare (A, B), If (A=B) Select C, Exit; Else Compare (A, C), If (A=C) Select B Exit; Else Select A, Exit. Alternative strategies include selecting a constant object, selecting the same location in the array, alternating the object choice, alternating choice of location, etc. Such alternatives are labelled by Harlow "error factors". (Harlow, 1949, 1959).

errorless performance in one or two problems (see e.g. Hayes *et al.*, 1953; Stephenson and Swartz, 1958).

Inhelder and Piaget (1964) report an inquiry in which the behaviour of 5-year-olds in this type of situation is contrasted with that of 7-year-olds. Both groups learned to make the right selection quite rapidly. However, when asked to explain how they managed to make the correct selection for each problem, younger children gave predominantly invented reasons (e.g. first the leftmost, then the middle, etc., although such a strategy had not been used and would have failed if it had, since the position of the odd item was deliberately randomized), while older subjects replied correctly that they had looked for the one that was not the same as the others. In general, too, these children were also able to reverse the situation by constructing an oddity problem for the experimenter to solve. These findings were replicated in a more controlled study by Lunzer and Astin who tested six children at each of four ages (4, 7, 8 and 10 years). Their findings may be summarized thus: at higher ages (8 years old and above) all 18 subjects gave correct accounts of their solution method and all bar one successfully reversed the situation. In the two younger groups, only two were able to give spontaneously correct accounts and only three produced correct reversals (Lunzer, 1968, 292–3).

Such data suggest rather strongly that the 8-year-old child* is better able to recall the moments of his selection behaviour, i.e. what he noticed and what he decided to do. Given this access to his own decision process a subject is in a position to isolate the critical features of the situation (in this case: what successive problems have in common), and this in turn may enable him to solve a different but related task. In other words, the extension of consciousness is a necessary condition for an extension of the generalizing power of learning.

It seems probable that consciousness of one's own decision process is a factor in most of the acquisitions about this period of development. For instance, in the case of the conservations, the child is required to set aside a perceptually salient criterion, such as the height of the lemonade in a glass or the length of a row of counters, in favour of a criterion which is taken to be critical, e.g. nothing added or removed following a demonstrated equivalence. Without prejudice to the teachability of such behaviour† it is difficult to see how the child would spontaneously alter his perspective without going through a phase of oscillation, marked by a tentative and erroneous judgement, followed by its rejection when the criterion comes to be recognized—and seen to be misleading (Piaget, 1952, 1977b).

*The number of subjects was too small to give more than a rough indication of norms.

In an analysis of one of these experiments (conservation of substance) Pascual-Leone (1976) demonstrates that a subject who is correctly convinced of conservation will have reasoned (i) that the original object b was shown to be equivalent to the comparison object a — say $a = b$; (ii) that the transformed object b' was a change in b — say $b' =$ change (b); (iii) that because the two dimensions longer/thinner compensated each other — $b' = b$; (iv) by transitivity — $(a = b)$ and $(b' = b) \rightarrow b' = a$.†

According to this view, rejection of the misleading cue of perceptual inequality does not enter as a step in the argument. Rather, he sees this as a "silent operator" which helps to determine the reasoning process as a whole, but only in non-conservers. Conservers overcome this silent operator because their reasoning is subject to the force of other learnt silent operators, especially the general rule that when nothing is added or removed a thing is the same.

The conflict with the view presented earlier may be more apparent than real. It is entirely proper to say that the recognition of a red herring does not figure as a step in a valid argument. Nevertheless, the herring needed to be seen for what it was before the valid argument could be sustained. In other words, the reflection on the inadequacy of the perceptually salient cue of length—which conflicts with the identity of the object and is also compensated—does occur in the history of the reasoner, but not at the moment of correct solution. Whether in identical situations encountered in the past, or in comparable encounters met with in daily life or in school lessons, it is such reflection which contributes to the change in strength of the two silent operators.

One of the most significant features of Pascual-Leone's analysis is the consideration of the number of "schemes" or ideas which the reasoner needs to have in mind at any step in his argument. These must always include the task itself or the goal—termed the "executive scheme" e. Additional schemes vary in number, the maximum demand in the present argument occuring at the last step $a = b$ and $b' = b \rightarrow b' = a$. Although only two schemes appear in the left hand side of this description, Pascual-Leone would add a third corresponding to the recognition that $b' = b$ is an identity transformation (despite the fact that this has already appeared at step 2). Thus the load on processing capacity, which he terms M-power, is $e + 3$.

Pascual Leone (1970) produces convincing evidence that the number of schemes a child can attend to increases with age in linear fashion, from $e + 1$ at 3–4 years old to a maximum of around $e + 7$ in the adult. An M-power of 3 is characteristic of the 7-year-old and this

† For a fuller discussion of this from opposing viewpoints, see Inhelder *et al.* (1974) and Brainerd (1978).

would explain why the younger child fails to recognize conservation without very special training.

The facts about age-related limitations in attentional capacity are not in dispute. (McLaughlin, 1963; Pascual-Leone and Smith, 1969; Case, 1974; Scardamalia, 1977). However, there is presently no agreement about its orgin—Pascual-Leone himself takes it to be a quasi-structural limitation corresponding to a stage in neuro-physiological growth, while others, and notably Case, prefer to think of it as due to a coding deficiency; unfamiliar concepts take up extra storage capacity. Another problem is how to specify the M-demand of any task. Both Pascual-Leone and Case confine this analysis to the demands made by each step in an argument. Others might prefer to consider the demands of the overall plan which initiates the sequence—and one notes that these will usually be larger. Perhaps the demands of plans are more relevant to unaided solution of new problems than to the guided assimilation of taught routines.

While many questions are as yet unanswered, it should be made clear that an analysis of problem-solution in terms either of attentional demands or of the demands on STM is very widespread and also very productive (cf. Farnham-Diggory, 1972; Klahr and Wallace, 1976). Moreover, Pascual-Leone and Case and their associates have shown how such an analysis can be turned to pedagogic purpose: by a planned teaching programme which uses a set of well thought out pedagogic principles and which takes into account both the misleading cues and strategies, and correct or to-be-learnt strategies (Case, 1978).

5 Summary

A number of meanings of consciousness were first suggested, and all were shown to be legitimate and useful for their purpose. However, for the purpose of the present chapter, consciousness was taken to denote availability of an item for subsequent recall. The rest of the chapter was devoted to the consideration of a number of examples illustrating the progressive extension of the domain of Consciousness III. It was argued that often, if not always, these extensions contributed to an enhancement of performance in relevant tasks. The three areas studied were "grasp of consciousness" or reflection about how one goes about a practical task or skill which one can do; memory strategies and knowledge about memory; and, finally, the development of reasoning with special reference to the transition occurring at about 7 years.

6 References

Brainerd, C. J. (1978). Learning research and Piagetian theory. *In* "Alternatives to Piaget" (Eds L. S. Siegel and C. J. Brainerd) 69–109. Academic Press, New York and London.

Broadbent, D. E. (1971). "Decision and Stress". Academic Press, New York and London.

Brown, A. L. (1973). Judgments of recency for long sequences of pictures: The absence of a developmental trend. *Journal of Experimental Child Psychology* **15**, 473–80.

Brown, A. L. (1974). The role of strategic behaviour in retardate memory. *In* "International Review of Research on Mental Retardation" (Ed. N. R. Ellis), Vol. 7. Academic Press, New York and London.

Brown, A. L. (1975) The development of memory: knowing, knowing about knowing, and knowing how to know. *In* "Advances in Child Development and Behaviour" (Ed. H. W. Reese), Vol. 10, 103–152. Academic Press, New York and London.

Case, R. (1972). Validation of a neo-Piagetian capacity construct. *Journal of Experimental Child Psychology* **14**, 287–302.

Case, R. (1974). Structures and strictures, some functional limitations on the course of cognitive growth. *Cognitive Psychology* **6**, 544–573.

Case, R. (1978). A developmentally based theory and technology of instruction. *Review of Educational Research* **48**, 439–463.

Clark, H. H. and Chase, W. G. (1972). On the process of comparing sentences against pictures. *Cognitive Psychology* **3**, 472–517.

Clark, H. H. and Chase, W. G. (1974). Perceptual coding strategies in the formation and verification of descriptions. *Memory and Cognition* **2**, 101–111.

Donaldson, M. (1978). "Children's Minds." Collins, Glasgow.

Farnham-Diggory, S. (1972) (Ed.). "Information Processing in Children." Academic Press, New York and London.

Flavell, J. H. (1970). Developmental studies of mediated memory. *In* "Advances in Child Development and Behaviour" (Eds H. W. Reese and L. P. Lipsitt), Vol. 5, 181–211. Academic Press, New York and London.

Flavell, J. H. (1977). "Cognitive Development." Prentice Hall, Englewood Cliffs, New Jersey.

Flavell, J. H. and Wellman, H. M. (1976). Metamemory. *In* "Perspectives on the Development of Memory and Cognition" (Eds R. V. Kail and J. W. Hagan), 3–33. Lawrence Erlbaum, Hillsdale, New Jersey.

Flavell, J. H., Beach, D. H. and Chinsky, J. M. (1966). Spontaneous verbal rehearsal in a memory task as a function of age. *Child Development* **37**, 283–299.

Flavell, J. H., Friedrichs, A. G. and Hoyt, J. D. (1970). Developmental changes in memorization processes. *Cognitive Psychology* **1**, 324–340.

Gagné, R. M. and Smith, E. C. (1962). A study of the effects of verbalization on problem-solving. *Journal of Experimental Psychology* **63**, 12–18.

Goldstein, K. and Scheerer, M. (1941). Abstract and concrete behaviour; an experimental study with special tests. Psychological Monograph No. 239.

Hagen, J. W., Jongeward, R. H. and Kail, R. V. (1975). Cognitive perspectives on the development of memory. *In* "Advances in Child Development and Behaviour" (Ed. H. W. Reese), Vol. 10, 57–98. Academic Press, New York and London.

Harlow, H. F. (1949). The formation of learning sets. *Psychological Review* **56**, 51–65.

Harlow, H. F. (1959). Learning set and error factor theory. *In* "Psychology: A Study of a Science" (Ed. S. Koch), Vol. 2, 492–537. McGraw-Hill, New York and London.

Hayes, K. J., Thompson, R. and Hayes, C. (1953). Discrimination learning sets in chimpanzees. *Journal of Comparative Psychology* **46**, 99–104.

Inhelder, B. and Piaget, J. (1964). "The Early Growth of Logic." Routledge and Kegan Paul, London.

Inhelder, B., Sinclair, H. and Bovet, M. (1974). "Learning and the Development of Cognition." Harvard University Press, Cambridge, Mass.

Isaacs, S. (1930). "Intellectual Development in Young Children." Routledge and Kegan Paul, London.

Keeney, T. J., Cannizzo, S. R. and Flavell, J. H. (1967). Spontaneous and induced verbal rehearsal in a recall task. *Child Development* **38**, 953–966.

Kendler, T. S. (1963). Development of mediating responses in children. *Monographs of the Society for Research in Child Development* **28**, No. 2, 33–48.

Kintsch, W. (1974). "The representation of meaning in memory." Erlbaum, Hillsdale, New Jersey.

Klahr, D. and Wallace, J. G. (1976). "Cognitive Development: An Information Processing View." Erlbaum, Hillsdale, New Jersey.

Klima, S. and Bellugi, U. (1966). Syntactic regularities in the speech of children. *In* "Psycholinguistic Papers" (Eds J. Lyons and R. Wales). University of Edinburgh Press, Edinburgh.

Kofsky, E. (1966). A scalogram study of classificatory development. *Child Development* **37**, 192–204.

Kreutzer, M. A., Leonard, C. and Flavell, J. H. (1975). An interview study of children's knowledge about memory. *Monographs of the Society for Research in Child Development* **40**, (1, Serial No. 159).

Lovell, K., Mitchell, B. and Everett, I. (1962). An experimental study of the growth of some logical structures. *British Journal of Psychology* **53**, 175–188.

Lunzer, E. A. (1968). "The Regulation of Behaviour." Staples, London.

Lunzer, E. A. (1970a). Construction of a standardized battery of Piagetian tests to assess the development of effective intelligence. *Research in Education* **3**, 53–72.

Lunzer, E. A. (1970b). "On Children's Thinking." National Foundation for Educational Research. London.

McLaughlin, G. H. (1963). Psycho-logic: a possible alternative to Piaget's formulation. *British Journal of Educational Psychology* **33**, 61–67.

Newell, A. and Simon, H. A. (1972). "Human Problem Solving." Prentice-Hall. Englewood Cliffs, New Jersey.

Nixon, J. E. and Locks, L. F. (1973). Research on teaching physical education. *In* "Second Handbook of Research on Teaching" (Ed. M. W. Travers) 1210–1242. Rand McNally, Chicago.

Oldfield, R. C. and Zangwill, O. L. (1942). Head's concept of the schema and its application in contemporary British psychology. Parts I, II, III. *British Journal of Psychology* **32**, 267–286, **33**, 58–64 and 113–129.

Pascual-Leone, J. (1970). A mathematical model for the transition rule in Piaget's developmental stages. *Acta Psychologica* **32**, 301–345.

Pascual-Leone, J. (1976). On learning and development, Piagetian style: 1. A reply to Lefebvre-Pinard. *Canadian Psychological Reveiw* **17**, 270–288.

Pascual-Leone, J. and Smith, J. (1969). The encoding of symbols by children: A new experimental paradigm and a neo-Piagetian model. *Journal of Experimental Child Psychology* **8**, 328–355.

Piaget, J. (1952). Logique et Equilibre. *In* "Etudes d'épistémologie génétique", Vol. 2. Presses Universitaires de France, Paris.

Piaget, J. (1977a). "The Grasp of Consciousness." Routledge and Kegan Paul, London.

Piaget, J. (1977b). "The Development of Thought: Equilibration of Cognitive Structures." Viking Press, New York.

Piaget, J. (1978). "Success and Understanding." Routledge and Kegan Paul, London.

Posner, M. and Keele, S. W. (1973). Skill learning. *In* "Second Handbook of Research on Teaching" (Ed. M. W. Travers) 805–831. Rand McNally, Chicago.

Poulton, E. C. (1957). On the stimulus and response in pursuit tracking. *Journal of Experimental Psychology* **53**, 189–194.

Rohwer, W. D. (1973). Elaboration and learning in childhood and adolescence. *In* "Advances in Child Development and Behaviour" (Ed. H. W. Reese), Vol. 8. Academic Press, New York and London.

Ruger, H. A. (1910). The psychology of efficiency: An experimental study of the process involved in the solution of mechanical puzzles and in the acquisition of skill in their manipulation. *Archives of Psychology, New York* **2**, 625–6.

Scardamalia, M. (1977). Information processing capacity and the problem of horizontal decalage: A demonstration using combinatorial reasoning tasks. *Child Development* **48**, 28–37.

Stephenson, H. W. and Swartz, J. D. (1958). Learning set in children as a function of intellectual level. *Journal of Comparative Psychology* **51**, 755–757.

Yates, F. A. (1966). "The Art of Memory." Routledge and Kegan Paul, London.

Yussen, S. R. and Levy, V. M. (1975). Developmental changes in predicting one's own span of short-term memory. *Journal of Experimental Child Psychology* **19**, 502–508.

2 Intuitive Thinking

H. R. POLLIO

Department of Psychology,
University of Tennessee

Over the years one observation has continued to tantalize anyone who would write about human thinking and the observation is this: many problems that could not be solved when the person worked on them in the clear light of day were finally solved when the person dreamed about them at night. Although not every important problem was solved in just this way, nor was every great thinker able to use this technique equally well, a large-enough number of the world's best and most creative thinkers have reported using it to make this observation more than just a passing curiosity. Dreamwork of this sort does not seem related to any one class of creative activity alone; rather, chemists, artists, philosophers, statesmen and mathematicians all report that some of their greatest insights occurred when they seemingly were thinking aside rather than straight on.

Take the well-known case of the chemist Frederick von Kekulé who developed the idea that certain organic compounds are best described as closed rings. In talking about the conditions surrounding his discovery, Kekulé reported the following dream-like incident just before he proposed his famous theory of the benzene ring.

> I turned my chair to the fire and dozed. Again the atoms were dancing before my eyes. This time the smaller groups kept modestly in the background. My mental eye, rendered more acute by repeated visions of this kind, could now distinguish larger structures, of manifold conformation; long rows, sometimes more closely fitted together; all twining and twisting in snake-like motion. But look! What was that? One of the snakes had seized hold of its own tail, and the form whirled mockingly before my eyes. As if by a flash of lightning I awoke (and understood what I had to do to solve the problem).
>
> (Koestler, 1964, p. 118)

Arthur Koestler, in his book "The Act of Creation" (1964), describes a number of other quite similar examples:

(1) Coleridge in writing the poem "Kubla Khan" explains that he dozed off after taking some medicine (most likely opium of one sort or another) and that upon awakening "recollected" 200–300 lines of poetry written while asleep. "On waking I constantly and eagerly wrote down the lines (of the poem)."

(2) After deciding that nerve cells were stimulated chemically, Otto Loewi could not figure out any way in which to test the theory experimentally. For the next 17 years he worked on the problem from time to time. In 1920, on the night before Easter Sunday, he reports:

> The night before Easter Sunday of that year I awoke, turned on the light, and jotted down a few notes on a tiny slip of thin paper. Then I fell asleep again. It occurred to me at six o'clock in the morning that during the night I had written down something most important, but I was unable to decipher the scrawl. The next night, at three o'clock, the idea returned. It was the design of an experiment to determine whether or not the hypothesis of chemical transmission that I had uttered seventeen years ago was correct. I got up immediately, went to the laboratory, and performed a simple experiment on a frog heart according to the nocturnal design.
>
> (Koestler, 1964, p. 205)

Thus, Loewi had to solve his problems in dreams, not once, but twice. We can only wonder what would have happened if he hadn't dreamed a second time.

(3) Finally, there is the case of Archimedes and his law. Here the story goes as follows. The year is something or other B.C., the place, Syracuse, Sicily, and Archimedes is physicist to the court of Hiero. As the story opens, Hiero has presented Archimedes with a problem: "Here is a crown," Hiero says, "supposedly of pure gold. Yet, I suspect," he continues, "it has some silver mixed in. How should we find out if it is made of pure gold or if it is mixed with silver?"

Archimedes accepts the task (not that he has any real choice—Hiero, after all, is King). He knows from the work of many different people that different metals have different weights and that if he could melt the crown down and compare its weight with a block of pure gold he could easily solve the King's problem. To do that, however, would be to destroy the crown; thus the problem remains, and remains, and remains.

For long days Archimedes wrestles with the problem; it gives him no rest, and he gives it no rest. One day, tired from his labours, he goes to the baths. There, surrounded by slave girls, perfumes and steamy air Archimedes looks slowly and tiredly around the baths, and giving himself over to bathing, steps into the tub and sits down. When he does, a very ordinary thing happens: his bath-water rises above the level it was at before he stepped in. He absent-mindedly notes this fact and returns to the heat and luxury of the bath.

Suddenly, without benefit of towel, he jumps up and shouts: "Eureka—I've got it!" And what exactly is it he's got? A cold? No, the solution to Hiero's problem, of course. If an object—his body—placed in water displaces a regular amount of water, then the amount by which the water-level rises could be used as a simple measure of volume or weight. If this holds true for his body, it should also be true for other objects—particularly for crowns made of gold. In just this way did Archimedes come to a general theory of the displacement of bodies in water. No wonder he jumped from the tub; not only had he solved the specific problem at hand, he also had made a general discovery which ultimately would bear his name.

These surely are strange histories for such seemingly rational solutions as those proposed by Kekulé, Coleridge, Loewi and Archimedes. Cases such as these (drawn from so many different fields) all support the notion that not all of thinking goes on rationally and that there is a lot more than careful logic in the best of human problem solving. The case of Archimedes does more than simply repeat this fact one more time: it also provides the important truth that creative thinking is as exciting a bit of human behaviour as there is and that such thinking involves the total person, not just some special part known as "mind." It is the person Archimedes who is concerned with the King's problem; it is the person Archimedes who bodily jumps from the tub; and it is the person Archimedes who shouts: "Eureka!" The idea of thinking as being cold, disembodied and unemotional is belied by this case history of one of the more important results of human thinking.

1 Centration in Thinking—or Losing Oneself in a Problem and Finding an Answer

Archimedes is not the only thinker to have experienced being totally consumed by a problem. Doyle (1976), on the basis of interviews with a variety of writers and musicians on the faculty of Sarah Lawrence College and elsewhere, has come to describe this aspect of creative thinking in terms of what she calls the period of "total centration". By this, Doyle means those periods of personal experience in which the organization and nature of the thinker's personal world is determined almost exclusively by the object or task presently being worked on. "During this time," Doyle notes:

> the person's actions and thoughts interact directly with (the problem) . . .
> without being distracted or narrowed by other concerns. Total centration

is not limited to the making of a work of art—the spectator completely lost in a film; the ball player (lost in a game), the attentive student reaching to grasp what a teacher is explaining may also be totally centered. . . . These are wonderful times; they have been described as moments of full spontaneity and freedom. But freedom and spontaneity do not come from an absence of structure or direction to the flow of thought . . . but from such total concentration on a task . . . that all resources are directed toward it. The person is freed of self-consciousness . . . and can respond fully and freely . . . to whatever he is centered on . . . .

During the period of total centration, all the patterns of the mind are potentially active. There is a center toward which all activity flows, and I believe that center is . . . those ideas-in-flesh developing in relation to that initial intuition which started the creative episode. . . . This is the magnet that attracts and patterns all those resources which become available.

These periods are recalled as periods of incredible joy, even ecstasy. Thought and action . . . (become) . . . as smooth and flowing as a dance, and ideas seem to emerge out of nowhere. The work seems to create itself, because the creator's picture of himself as working does not obstruct the flow between himself and his work.

(Doyle, 1976, pp. 15–17)

Although common to many different types of artistic and scientific activities, the experience of centration always takes place within a medium of one sort or another. For many of us, the medium is words; for the skilled scientist or thinker the medium may be mathematics or other systems of symbolic logic; for the skilled artist it may be paint, metal or even space; while for the skilled actor, dancer or athlete the medium is their own body as it moves within specific settings such as a stage or a playing field. Highly centred activity always takes place within a specific medium and the medium always has to be taken into account in describing the nature of the ongoing episode.

How medium and thinker come together in the case of music was described by the composer Seligman who told Doyle that "the notes you've been working with a long time—they begin to transform themselves . . . (and become a melody)".

The writer, Paley, told Doyle (1976) that she writes "out of pure language".

It was language that started me, made me think . . . I haven't the vaguest idea what the story is, what page three is . . . . Then maybe in a couple months I write the next three pages and then I'm really stuck . . . . Suddenly I get this thing, these three to five pages which I really wrote before and I say 'my God' and that's what the story is about because that's what my head has been forming.

(Doyle, 1976, p. 13)

D. H. Lawrence, the noted writer, described his first experiences in painting in the following terms:

> So for the sheer fun of covering a surface and obliterating that mud-grey, I sat on the floor with the canvas propped against a chair—and with my house-paint brush and colours in little casseroles, I disappeared into that canvas. It is to me the most exciting moment—when you have a blank canvas and a big brush full of wet colour, and you plunge. It is just like diving into a pond—then you start frantically to swim. So far as I am concerned, it is like swimming in a baffling current and being rather frightened and very thrilled, gasping and striking out for all you're worth. The knowing eye watches sharp as a needle; but the picture comes clean out of instinct, intuition and sheer physical action. Once the instinct and intuition gets into the brush-tip, the picture happens, if it is to be a picture at all.
>
> (Lawrence, 1952, p. 63)

Picasso, also talking about painting—his painting—noted:

> The picture is not thought out and determined beforehand, rather while it is being made it follows the mobility of thought. Finished, it changes further, according to the condition of him who looks at it. A picture lives its life like a living creature, undergoing the changes that daily life imposes upon us. That is natural, since a picture lives only through him who looks at it.
>
> (Zervos, 1952, p. 49)

> I behave with my painting as I behave with things. I paint a window, just as I look through a window. If this window when open doesn't look good in my picture, I draw a curtain and close it as in life, directly. Admittedly painting has its conventions, of which it is necessary to take account, since one can't do otherwise. For this reason one must have constantly before one's eyes the very presence of life.
>
> (p. 51)

Mary Wigman, the dancer, described the origin of her dance "Pastorale" in the following way:

> My Pastorale was developed in the following way: I came into my studio one day and sank down with a feeling of complete relaxation. Out of a sense of deepest peace and quietude I began slowly to move my arms and body. Calling to my assistants I said, I do not know if anything will come of this feeling, but I should like a reed instrument that would play over and over again a simple little tune, not at all important, always the same one. Then with the monotonous sound of the little tune, with its gentle lyric suggestion, the whole dance took form. Afterwards we found that it was built on six-eighths time, neither myself nor the musician being conscious of the rhythm until we came to the end.
>
> (Wigman, 1952, pp. 75–76)

What all of these famous and near-famous creative people did was to
live their problem, for a time, within the world of possibilities created
by a specific medium. During this time there was no separation between action and medium, that is, between person, sound, paint,
movement or word; rather, there was only the total involvement of a
skilled person within a medium, within a problem. Lawrence talked
about "swimming in paint", Picasso "behaved with his painting as he
behaves with things", Paley lived with "pure language", while Wigman moved out of a sense of "deepest peace".

Doyle described the relationship of medium to centration in the
following terms and we can do no better than quote her excellent
summary:

> It is the period (for the writer) when the characters take over, when the
> melodies flow without forcing, when the painting seems to paint itself.
> The artist is totally absorbed in the work. All the awkwardness that comes
> from watching yourself at work, from the fear that what you are doing is
> no good, from careful critical selection is no longer a part of the flow of
> thought and action. The artist's head, his hands, his lips are totally
> directed by the forces that have been generated by the sense of direction
> and the ideas-in-flesh as he is working with them. All intellectual and
> emotional resources, all skills and experiences become part of the artist's
> reach and movement toward the eventual goal.
>
> (Doyle, 1976, pp. 14–15)

Although the period of centration is an exciting one, the artist or
thinker must leave it once the creative episode has run its course. When
they look back on it, however, about 50% of a group of artists, writers
and scientists interviewed by Hutchinson (1949) reported that they
experienced a sense of personal detachment from the processes
involved in creative work. For some individuals this detachment took
the form of a "simple feeling of divorce from the process constituting the
(period) of insight". One author quoted by Hutchinson specifically
noted: "Although I feel no one else in the background, I do feel like a
mere vehicle, or lens, too often cloudy, for the insight obtained". As
may be remembered Coleridge noted (p. 22) that he only "recollected"
the poem "Kubla Khan" after having composed it earlier in a dream-
like state.

A second form of detachment from the creative episode concerns a
feeling of what can only be called "delayed impersonality". The novel-
ist Aldous Huxley described it as follows: "When I have finished a
particular piece of work, I feel as though it had nothing more to do with
me, as though I were no longer responsible for it".

In trying to explain why this feeling of separation should occur
Hutchinson points out that:

the period of insight is absorbing (and) the greater the degree of concentration upon the evolving ideas, the greater the extent of separation from normal contact with the surrounding world . . . . Since the system unfolding in the period of insight and that representative of normal awareness may have little immediately in common, forgetfulness (may) arise toward the content of the insight. Perhaps the best analogy is that of a highly motivated dream. While intensely vivid for the moment . . . the dream is with difficulty recaptured in normal waking life. Similarly (the period of) insight tends to slip back into oblivion.

(Hutchinson, 1949, p. 171)

Although the period of centration may bring joy or even ecstasy it is also an uncanny experience quite unlike any other of everyday life. Under this condition is it any wonder that many thinkers and artists are often glad to be done with it once it has run its unsettling course? If we listen to Coleridge and Huxley, the answer seems to be an unequivocal yes, and we can do no better than take their word for it.

2 Being the Problem: The Poetics of Invention

With the exception of Wigman and a few others, creative individuals tend to work alone. Many industrial, government and academic thinkers, however, often come together to do their work in groups, whether such groups are called simulation groups, task-forces or interdisciplinary committees. The theory behind all of these groups is quite simple and assumes that useful ideas are more likely to emerge where talents are pooled rather than where each person works alone.

Although a great many different groups have thought about a great many different problems, perhaps the most far-reaching description of successful group-thinking has been presented by Gordon in his book, "Synectics" (1961). The word "synectics" was coined by Gordon and comes from two Greek words meaning "the fitting together of separate elements". Considered most generally, synectic theory and research is concerned with group creativity and invention, particularly in industrial settings. By definition, synectics applies to the integration of diverse individuals into a problem-setting group and represents "an operational theory for the conscious use of preconscious psychological mechanisms present in all creative activity" (Gordon, 1961, p. 3).

So as to discover the specific nature of these mechanisms, Gordon and co-workers examined the biographies and autobiographies of numerous creative thinkers as well as reports of people in the process of invention. From these data they concluded that the essential process in any and all creative acts, involved trying to make something that was strange or unknown into something familiar or well-known or in trying to make something originally familiar, into something new or strange.

For Gordon, there are four basic techniques people can use in making the familiar, strange or the strange, familiar. Each of these, as Pollio *et al.* (1977) have noted, involves a poetically playful use of language.

(1) Personal analogy—is becoming yourself, one of the objects looked at and then feeling, thinking, and acting like that object. It goes beyond mere role playing in that the person can be an inanimate, as well as an animate object or being. This strategy often involves the poetic category of personification. Gordon points out that John Keats reported using this technique when writing the poem "Endymion":

> "I leaped headlong into the sea, and thereby have become better acquainted with the sounds, the quicksands, and the rocks, than if I had stayed upon the green shore and piped a silly pipe and took tea and comfortable advice"
>
> (Gordon, 1961, p. 24).

(2) Direct analogy—involves a comparison of parallel facts, knowledge or technology. In problem-stating/problem-solving situations, the synectics group headed by Gordon found that analogies from the biological sciences were the most fruitful. A specific historical example is given by the work of Brunel who solved "the problem of underwater construction by watching a shipworm tunnelling into a timber. The worm constructed a tube for itself as it moved forward and the classical notions of caissons" was derived from this observation by direct analogy (Gordon, 1961).

(3) Symbolic analogy—involves a compressed description of the function or elements of a problem as the problem-solver sees it. It is a poetic statement that sums up what has been said in other phases of problem-solving and often takes the form of a direct metaphor or of an oxymoron in which previously opposite ideas are combined. So, for example, Pasteur sometimes spoke of anti-toxins as a form of "safe attack" (Gordon, 1961, p. 270).

(4) Fantasy analogy—is an attempt to solve a problem by wish fulfillment; that is, by wishing the problem solved in any manner whatsoever. This usually occurs at a very early stage of creative problem solving in which the problem has not yet been made strange enough so as to lead to new ways of looking at it.

Although this process may sound like a magical incantation designed to evoke the sleeping goddess of creativity, the use of unorthodox and/or poetic language has been found to be quite helpful in a number of different problem situations. Perhaps the most interesting of these concerns the case of psycho-therapy. Here, the problems to be solved do not usually concern the production of a new invention or work of art but rather have to do with a whole style of life that has become problematic to the person living it.

So as to examine the productive role of poetic language in psychotherapy let us consider the case of a client named Audrey which was first described by Pollio and Barlow in 1975. At the time of this interview, Audrey was 38 years old and in her second marriage, a marriage that was to end 2 years later. She had previously been in individual treatment and although she was now in group therapy, the present session was her first with this particular therapist.

We pick up the conversation somewhere in the first 25 minutes or so. The topic under discussion has to do with Audrey's inability to deal with anger. In order to help her discuss these feelings the therapist has told her to strike a pillow whenever she feels angry. As we look in on the interview, Audrey speaks first.

A: I used to hit my fist against the wall, sometimes I'd just get that mad so that even the walls would have to go over.

T: But when you hit your fist against the wall, wouldn't your fist get hurt too?

A: Yes. When I punch the pillow, I'm not hurt or being hurt, am I?

T: That's right. You can express the feeling of hurting without hurting or having to hurt yourself.

A: Yes. That sure feels good. I love to punch.

T: Uh huh.

A: (sighs) Okay. Now you can shape up (laughs) 'cause I'm already doin' it.

T: Okay. You said, "Now you can shape up"; To whom were you talking?

A: Uh huh, oh, I'm talking to the anger, (pause) So I won't have to hide it anymore, now, do I? I'm not asking you . . . cause it's there. I don't hide it. It's a failure to try and hide it cause it can't be hidden, even from myself. So now what am I going to do with it? Cause I am going to get angry. This isn't going to solve the problem of anger. I am going to get angry. Well, I think I'll just go and punch the pillow. That's the best I can do right now though the kids will think I'm kind of silly . . . but they won't really.

T: All right, so who's going to be thinking you're silly? What part of you is going to be calling you silly when you do this?

A: The adult side.

T: Okay, will you be the adult side of you and pretend you're sitting next to the chair and tell yourself how silly you are for doing something like that? Be your . . .

A: Oh, yes. I'm the moral. I'm the moral Audrey . . . There, she's angry, she's punching the pillow . . . oh, Audrey, you're just silly, you're just acting like the child, and . . . that's how I feel, only much more cold. There's warmth in that and moral Audrey just hasn't any warmth at all, not any.

T: And what does human Audrey say back to that?

A: It's just a . . . melts, it's just lost.

T: Okay. Say that.

A: It just retreats.

T: Okay, be that. Be the moral Audrey, and say that I feel lost when you say that, I try to retreat.

A: You mean be the human Audrey and tell the moral? I can't talk to the moral Audrey, it's me.

T: Say that to the moral Audrey . . . say, I can't talk to you.

A: You're so rigid. You're so unreasoning . . . you're just . . . you're just so cold. There's just no talking to you. I can only fear you . . .

T: Yeah.

A: I've never even looked at you before. I don't even know I was afraid . . . But it is, it's the coldest, coldest . . . oh. (shiver) I'd rather sleep by an iceberg. I'd, I'd rather sleep by an iceberg. I can't even . . . oh . . . all the warmth and feeling I ever had . . . you just . . . just don't change . . . you just . . . ummm . . .

T: Don't melt.

A: Just won't do anything, even an iceberg will melt, but not, not you. And you know, you know my moral side is a very large part of what takes over.

T: Yeah. Will you say that to the moral side, that no matter how angry I get . . . I never have any impact on you.

A: Yeah: oh, I can feel that . . . but I feel like I could tell that moral side from here to eternity; big . . . I could scream it, I could yell it, I could whisper it, I could, I could talk to it nicely. I could give it things could give it my soul and it still wouldn't know I have feelings. And that's what I've done! That's what I've done! That's what I've done exactly. I've sold my soul, my feeling for myself, to that damned moral Audrey, and it hasn't done a thing for me.

T: Tell her . . .

A: You haven't done anything, haven't done a thing for me . . . not anything, You isolate me from people. You make me forget that other people have feelings 'cause I don't . . . you don't let me have my own feelings, and, and I can deal with you from now on. You're just not as big as you think you are. You just aren't. Jesus wouldn't . . . wouldn't back you up even. He didn't he didn't back the righteous, and that's what . . .

T: Tell that to her.

As can be seen from this excerpt, Audrey begins by talking about (and just a bit later, talking to) her anger; a topic that makes her feel decidedly uncomfortable and silly. In questioning her about this, the therapist wants to know "who's going to be thinking you're silly?" This then leads both of them to the idea of "adult (human) side" and a strict moral side they call "moral Audrey". Once Audrey is able to present her problem as one of conflict between the moral and the adult Audrey, the therapist moves in and proposes a face to face confrontation between the two. In so doing, he hopes to allow Audrey to explore her feelings toward herself as both an angry person and an overly demanding person.

This conversation gives some small idea as to how poetic language can be used in psycho-therapy. A careful reading of the complete transcript for this interview revealed that Audrey talked about a number of different problem areas in poetic figures of speech and that it was possible to describe the overall course of the interview in terms of these themes. In the early part of the session, for example, Audrey talked poetically about her hidden desire to love, her harsh will, her strong hostility and her tendency to be a "goody-goody". In the middle part of the interview, she described herself as a cold and hard person and of her inability to face her frail and imperfect human side. By the final segment of the session, she was able to re-evaluate her situation and come to a fuller appreciation of herself as a complex and multifaceted human being.

The flow of topics treated poetically in the session progressed from a general presentation by Audrey of herself as a person with problems, to an even more unfavourable evaluation of the conflict between her moral and human sides. Only once she was able to set up her problems in highly concrete and personal terms was she able to come to a more realistic re-evaluation of herself as a woman who is sometimes angry and sometimes weak. As she finally was able to put it: "That's the way real people are".

An analysis such as this clearly demonstrates some of the major points made by Gordon in his description of synectic theory. In the case of Audrey, figurative language not only helped her to personify conflicting parts of herself, it also helped her to be harsh with just those aspects of herself which were already harsh. In fact, it was this change of perspective which gave her the figurative possibility of "taking the moral Audrey to task" and which permitted her to experience both sides of the problem; something she had not been able to do previously.

Looked at from the perspective of synectic theory, Audrey was only able to move forward when she was able to recast familiar problems into unfamiliar form by building her super-moralist attitudes into the poetic flesh of "moral Audrey". Under these conditions, the therapist's task became one of first allowing Audrey to deal with her problem in this unfamiliar light and of then helping her to move back to a more everyday perspective once she had understood the situation from this new point of view. In a very real sense, the therapist's strategy was to move Audrey from the familiar to the strange and back again.

The case of Audrey adds one more example to the seemingly peculiar nature of innovative human thinking. Each of the phenomena considered—dreaming a solution, creative centration within a medium and synectic thinking and speaking—seems to be cut from the same cloth although exactly what this cloth might be doesn't seem immediately obvious. Yet it should be: what these phenomena all have in common is that they describe the experiences of a person who, for a time, has stepped into a mode of consciousness different from that ordinarily experienced in dealing with a problem. In the case of Kekulé, Coleridge, Loewi and even Archimedes it is quite clear that each of these men experienced insight during, or immediately following, a period in which they abandoned their usual scientific, literary or everyday worlds and for a time entered a much different state of dealing with the world. In some instances, it involved reverie or dreams, in others, a hot bath or even a drug-induced "trip".

In the case of Picasso, Paley and Wigman it seems clear that each of these artists "lost" him or herself within their medium. Not only did they lose themselves within the medium, they seemed to give themselves over totally to this altered state of experiencing and dealing with the work of art already underway. Because the creative experience is so different from that of the person's everyday world, many creative people choose not to deal with this centred world once the creative episode is over; sometimes even talking about it with a sense of personal remoteness or detachment.

Finally there is the case of trying to live or be a problem. Here Audrey was helped into the world of her problem on the basis of poetic language and/or imagery. Synectic-like processes seem to work best to the degree that the person gives up his or her ordinary way(s) of dealing with the world. "Making it strange" is thus an invitation to confront a problem in terms of conscious experience far removed from that usually experienced. It is at this point that the synectic process makes contact with creative centration and thinking in dreams, for in all three cases the person, for a time, comes to deal with his or her problem in a state of consciousness different from that of everyday life.

3 The Hypothesis of Two Modes of Consciousness

Many theorists, from Zen Masters to psycho-analysts, have used these and other similar facts to suggest that there are two primary modes of consciousness and that many of our conscious experiences, creative and otherwise, involve a blending of the two. To give some feeling for what these two modes of consciousness might be like, Ornstein (1972) and Samples (1976) have developed separate lists summarizing a number of different opinions about this issue. Table I presents a combination of parts of both tables as well as some additions not originally listed by either author.

Although differences between columns 1 and 2 seem obvious, they are not easy to describe in words. One of the best descriptions was

TABLE I Some Examples of the Various Modes of Human Consciousness

Who proposed it?	Column 1	Column 2
Bacon	Experience	Causal
Blackburn	Sensuous	Intellectual
Bleuler	Autistic thinking	Realistic thinking
Bruner	Left-hand	Right-hand
Deikman	Receptive	Active
Domhoff	Left (side of body)	Analytic
Freud	Primary process	Secondary process
Husserl	Unreflected	Reflected
I Ching	Dark	Light
I Ching	Space	Time
James	Fringe	Focus
Jung	Acausal	Causal
Kubie	Pre-conscious processing	Conscious processing
Langer	Presentational symbolization	Discursive symbolism
Lee	Nonlineal	Lineal
Levy, Sperry	Gestalt	Analytic
Luria	Simultaneous	Sequential
Many sources	Private knowledge	Public knowledge
Many sources	Metaphorical meaning	Literal meaning
Many sources	The Dreamer	The Doer
Many sources	Intuitive	Intellectual, analytic
Many sources	Spatial	Verbal
Maslow	B-cognition	A-cognition
Neisser	Parallel processing	Sequential processing
Oppenheimer	Eternity, timelessness	Time, history
Polanyi	Tacit	Explicit
Schactel	Trans-schematic experience	Conventionalized experience
Semmes	Diffuse	Focal
Taylor	Divergent thinking	Convergent thinking
Wertheimer	Blind thinking	Productive thinking

offered by Bruner who used the terms "intuitive" and "analytic" to
capture his understanding of the difference separating right- and left-
handed thinking:

> Analytic thinking characteristically proceeds a step at a time. Steps are
> explicit and usually can be adequately reported by the thinker to another
> individual. Such thinking proceeds with relatively full awareness of the
> information and operations involved. It may involve careful and deduc-
> tive reasoning, often using mathematics or logic and an explicit plan of
> attack. Or it may involve a step-by-step process of induction and experi-
> ment . . . .
>
>   Intuitive thinking characteristically does not advance in careful, well-
> planned steps. Indeed, it tends to involve manoeuvres based on an
> implicit perception of the total problem. The thinker arrives at an answer,
> which may be right or wrong, with little if any awareness of the process by
> which he reached it.
>
>   (Bruner, 1960, pp. 57–58)

Although the lists presented by Ornstein and Samples cover a lot of
ground they seem to slight one very essential fact: consciousness is
always *someone's* consciousness and, as such, is always experienced
"from the inside"—that is, by the person involved. To talk about
consciousness always means to talk about it from someone's first-
person point of view (*my* point-of-view) and many of the positions
presented in Table I seem to be talking about the two modes of
consciousness from an impersonal, objective, or third-person point of
view. If we are to capture the nature of human thinking and consciousness, intuitive or otherwise, we need both the first (personal) and third
(public) person points of view.

Of all the theorists represented in Table I only two, William James
and Edmund Husserl, have tried to describe human thinking from both
a first- and third-person point of view. If the truth be told, both ended
up being more concerned with first-person than with third-person
experience. Despite this, both did provide quite reasonable descriptions and any attempt to capture intuitive thinking must begin by
considering their work in some detail. Since Husserl was more a
philosopher than a psychologist, the major psychological implications
of his approach to consciousness were drawn by Schutz, and his colleagues Berger and Luckmann.

4 William James and the Stream of Human Consciousness

When James first set out to describe human consciousness in 1880 he
had no one's insights to lean on but his own. In spite (or perhaps
because) of this, his descriptions still ring true now as then and we can

do no better than start with his "first and fundamental fact of inner experience".

> The first and foremost concrete fact which everyone will affirm to belong to his inner experience is the fact that consciousness of some sort goes on. 'States of mind' succeed each other in him. If we could say in English 'it thinks,' as we say 'it rains' or 'it blows' we should be stating the fact most simply and with the minimum of assumption. As we cannot, we must simply say that thought goes on.
>
> (James, 1880, p. 152)

But how does thought go on? Here, James provides a list of four characteristics which he felt captured the nature of all human consciousness, most expecially, thinking:

(1) Every thought (or conscious state) is always part of some person,

(2) For each person, conscious experience is constantly changing,

(3) For each person, personal consciousness is sensibly continuous, and

(4) Personal consciousness always seems to deal with objects, events and/or experiences outside itself.

In order to combine all of these characteristics into a single representation, James introduced the idea of the stream of personal consciousness. By this image he meant to suggest that each person's subjective life is continuous and overlapping and not anything at all like a series of loosely connected railroad cars or links in a chain. Even though personal consciousness is continuous, ideas and images are more compelling than the transitions between them and it is for this reason that thinking, as consciousness itself, is so often described as a "train" or "chain" of ideas.

The process of thinking, however, is more than just these "solid" islands in the stream; it is the moving stream itself. Only in retrospect is an idea clear, never while we are in the midst of thinking it. For this reason James felt that thinking (like consciousness) must consist of two parts: (1) a main line called the focus which consists of ideas, images, thoughts, words, etc., and (2) a surrounding halo called the fringe which consists of the transitional flow between ideas, images, thoughts, etc.

In addition to focus and fringe, the stream of consciousness has one further defining aspect: it is able to "bend back" on itself. This ability is called reflection, perhaps by analogy with the idea of a mirror. Just as a mirror lets me see me as an object "outside myself," so too reflection (thinking) lets me see me as "something outside me to be thought about." The tendency to reflect on one's participation in the stream of conscious life is so regular an event that it led James to conclude that:

whatever else I may be thinking of, I am always at the same time more or less aware of myself; that is, of my own personal existence.

(James, 1910, p. 176)

There are, however, times during which the experience of self is so overpowering that almost everything else seems secondary. Strong emotional states such as rage or less extreme ones such as embarrassment, shrink the person's world so that it comes to contain only the personal self as angry or embarrassed. "Self-conscious" is the way we usually describe our experience at this time. By the same token, there are other times when the experience of self is so minimal as to seem to disappear entirely. This is most likely to happen in just those cases where the person is totally involved in what it is he or she is doing. Doyle's (1976) description of centration within a medium is one example; being engrossed in a game, film or book, still another.

5 The Constructed World of Everyday Reality

The fact that each of us can become so absorbed in a play, book, or a film has been interpreted by Berger and Luckmann (1966) to suggest that human beings regularly move in and out of many different "realities". Some of these realities are easy to enter and live in because they are so clearly marked as "imaginary". Going to the theatre gives a good example where the change between "real" and "imaginary" is defined by the simple fact of a curtain going up and later coming down. In a theatre we have little or no problem in stepping back and forth between the created world of the play and the "real" world of everyday and this can be seen most clearly in terms of how we carry on a perfectly ordinary life between various acts of the play.

There are two important aspects to Berger and Luckmann's discussion of theatrical plays and of our reactions to them: (1) when we are in the world of the play we experience that world in the same way as we experience our everyday world and (2) the world of everyday (i.e. "ordinary reality") appears larger and somehow more important than the world of the play. In talking about these and other observations Berger and Luckmann note:

> Consciousness, then, is capable of moving through different spheres of reality. As I move from one reality to another, I experience the transition as a kind of shock. This shock is to be understood as caused by the shift in attentiveness that the transition entails. Waking up from a dream illustrates this shift most simply.
>
> Among the multiple realities there is one that presents itself as reality par excellence. This is the reality of everyday life . . . The tension of

consciousness is highest in everyday life; that is, the latter imposes itself upon consciousness in the most massive, urgent and intense manner. It is impossible to ignore, difficult even to weaken in its imperative presence. Consequently, it forces me to be attentive to it in the fullest way. I experience everyday life in the state of being wide-awake. This wide-awake state of existing in and apprehending the reality of everyday life is taken by me to be normal and self-evident; that is, it constitutes my natural attitude.

(Berger and Luckmann, 1966, p. 21)

How do the spheres of multiple reality described by Berger and Luckmann relate to the stream of consciousness described by James? Put most simply, my personal stream of conscious experience always flows within the context of a particular sphere of reality even if I am not explicitly aware of it. This is true whether I am now experiencing the reality of everyday life, that of a play, or even that of a scientific discipline.

These latter two cases, as well as many others, are always temporary for it is the inexplicit world of everyday which provides a continuing framework for my life. This is true for no matter how much I might doubt the importance of my everyday world, I do have to suspend such doubt as I go about my daily activities, thinking and attending plays included. This means that each of my other "realities" is always embedded within the reality of everyday and it is to this world that I always return.

Sometimes switching between realities can cause a bit of difficulty as, for example, when I want to describe my experiences in a reality other than that of everyday. While poetic language can be of some help, I usually end up by feeling I've distorted this other realm when I talk about it to someone else. Berger and Luckmann point out that such difficulties can be seen in a great many different cases particularly if I restrict myself only to ordinary language.

This may be readily seen in terms of dreams, but is also typical of people trying to report about theoretical, aesthetic or religious worlds of meaning. The theoretical physicist tells us that his concept of space cannot be conveyed (in words), just as the artist does with regard to the meaning of his creations and the mystic with regard to his encounters with the divine. Yet all these—dreamer, physicist, artist and mystic—also live in the reality of everyday life. Indeed, one of their important problems is to interpret the coexistence of this reality with the reality . . . into which they have ventured.

(Berger and Luckmann, 1966, p. 26)

What Berger and Luckmann have done is to add another dimension to the nature of human consciousness. Not only must any description of consciousness deal with processes directly concerned with focal and fringe thinking, i.e. with anticipating something new, making transitions between ideas, and so on, it must also deal with social aspects as well. Exactly what these social aspects might be in any specific situation will always depend on the particular sphere of reality I am now in, i.e., poetic, artistic, mystic, scientific, etc. If the present sphere is not that of everyday, consciousness will always also contain the world of everyday as a further backdrop lying behind those presently involved in experiencing.

6 Tacit Knowing

James is not the only theorist to be concerned with non-focal awareness. More recently, the British scientist–philosopher Polanyi (1959, 1965) has offered a somewhat different, but related, view of human experience. In agreement with James, Polanyi feels that there is a lot more that we know than we can talk about. Such knowledge is called "tacit" knowledge so as to distinguish it from "explicit" knowledge where we know what we know and can talk about it. Because explicit knowledge seems so much easier to deal with and so much less subjective than tacit knowledge, Western society has come to value it more highly than tacit knowledge. Despite this, Polanyi feels that tacit knowledge is the more important of the two.

> This exalted valuation of strictly formalized thought (i.e., explicit knowledge) is self-contradictory. It is true that a traveler, equipped with a detailed map of a region across which he plans his itinerary enjoys a striking intellectual superiority over the explorer who first enters a new region—yet the explorer's fumbling progress is a much finer achievement than the well-briefed traveler's journey. Even if we admit that an exact knowledge of the universe is our supreme mental possession it would still follow that man's most distinguished act of thought consists in producing such knowledge; the human mind is at its greatest when it brings unchartered domains under its control. Such operations renew the existing framework. Hence they cannot be performed within this framework but have to rely on tacit powers.
>
> (Polanyi, 1959, p. 18)

The major psychological principles used by Polanyi in developing his ideas concern those of focal and subsidiary awareness. Although Polanyi uses a great many different situations to distinguish between the two, consider the case where a person points his finger at an object and then says to someone else: "Look at that!" What is likely to happen in this situation is that the second person will look at the object noted and pay little or no attention to the pointing finger. According to Polanyi, the person will be focally aware of the object intended and only subsidiarily aware of the finger as pointer. In knowing something, we usually attend to a specific focus directed by one or more subsidiaries.

Words, and other symbols such as maps, work in just this way. We do not usually pay focal attention to the word or map; rather they direct us to a content that is much more important and interesting to us. If we do, in fact, pay continuing focal attention to a symbol such as a word by repeating it over and over again, we find that it will soon lose its meaning. Words are meaningful only as they point to a focal content different from themselves.

The same is true for many other kinds of skilful knowing and doing: as we all know, the skilful use of a tennis racket can be totally destroyed by watching the racket instead of the ball. The difference between focal and subsidiary awareness has also been described as a contrast between "knowledge by attending to" and "knowledge by relying on". For Polanyi, no doing or thinking can ever be wholly focal.

To come now specifically to the case of original or innovative thinking. Here Plato, speaking for Meno and Socrates, set the following question on behalf of anyone who has ever tried to deal with a problem:

> On what lines will you look, Socrates, for a thing whose nature you know not at all? Pray, what sort of think among those that you do not know, will you treat as the object of your search? Or even supposing, at the best, that you hit upon it by accident, how will you know it is the thing you did not know?

From Polanyi's point of view, the solution to Meno's problem is quite simple: because we do not know, in a focal sense, what we are looking for does not mean that we cannot look for (and find) it in terms of clues that are only known tacitly (Green, 1969). Meno's paradox is easily resolved if and when we recognize that not all knowing is focal.

At the same time that tacit clues guide the person in dealing with a problem, they also tell something of the person working on the problem. The specific problem being dealt with in focal attention is always nourished by what the person knows, and is, tacitly. Each of us always lives in the tension between what is explicit and what is tacit both in terms of how we deal with a problem as well as in terms of how we express and deal with ourselves, dealing with that problem. In the final analysis, all knowledge is "personal knowledge" and the idea of an impersonal problem or of an impersonal solution is neither an accurate nor a reasonable one.

There is much to Polanyi's use of subsidiary awareness to suggest the Jamesian fringe. Polanyi explicitly denies this.

It is a mistake to identify subsidiary awareness with the fringe of consciousness described by William James. The relation of clues to that which they indicate is a logical relation similar to that which a premise has to the inferences drawn from it, but with the important difference that tacit inferences drawn from clues are not explicit. They are informal.

(Polanyi, 1965, p. 212)

Although Polanyi rejects this interpretation, it does seem quite reasonable to talk about fringe consciousness in terms of subsidiary awareness. What Polanyi has done for the Jamesian fringe, however, is to give it a bit of sense and a bit of direction by describing how focal and subsidiary awareness relate to one another. Unlike James, who kept fringe and focus fairly static, Polanyi's approach suggests movement between the polarities of subsidiary and focal awareness and it is this movement which directs the continuing flow of consciousness.

What is more important than these differences between James and Polanyi is that both call attention to the fact that not all of thinking goes on in the clear light of focal awareness. Focal and fringe awareness are both part of, and determiners of, the stream of human consciousness and if fringe directs us to focus, the incompleteness of any focus always moves us further in the ongoing flux that is human consciousness. The rule of conscious life is that of change, and James and Polanyi have tried to describe such change in terms of a set of constantly shifting relations between what one is now focally aware of and what one was subsidiarily aware of a moment ago. Focal and subsidiary awareness are but two moments in a single process, and that process is a living, moving one properly called the stream of consciousness by William James.

7 A Bit of Summary and a Small Conclusion or Two

The history of productive human thinking seems to suggest that creative people often do their best work when they leave the world of everyday reality. This is the case whether such leave-taking is accomplished by falling asleep and dreaming, by taking a bath and thinking aside, by becoming totally immersed in one's medium or by the rather eccentric procedure of speaking poetically of some problem presently at hand. In each of these cases the creative problem-solver leaves the security of everyday for the excitement of an uncertain, but continually evolving world.

It would be nice to report that such excursions always end in success. As a matter of fact most of the time they do not. When they do, however, we all know it for although not every creative thinker jumps from the tub screaming "Eureka!" almost all do report an experience of personal excitement following the attainment of a long sought solution. Such a profound reaction suggests that it is the whole person who thinks and that creative problem-solving is never done by clear-sighted "mental" work alone.

Unfortunately, there is a tendency in Western philosophical tradition to deal only with the clear focus of thinking as worthy of the name thinking. Although Plato surely grasped the difficulty of this view, it remained for James and then Polanyi some 2000 years later to offer a resolution to Meno's paradox of creative thinking. James' answer to this problem depends on the rather straightforward fact that human consciousness always has both a clear focal portion and a less distinct, inarticulate fringe. Polanyi's more detailed answer relies on the fact that what we know explicitly is always less than what we know tacitly.

Since, as both of these positions suggest, much of what is important for productive thinking is unspoken (or even unspeakable), it seems perfectly reasonable to wonder how tacit and explicit knowing relate to one another. Although a great many different theorists have talked about global differences between left and right handed thinking, it remained for Polanyi to suggest that the basic relationship is one of "from—to"; that is, *from* what I know tacitly *to* what I know explicitly. Every problem situation thus sets up a tension between "what I now know and am" and "what I seek to become and know better" and it is this tension which moves the problem-solver forward in his or her attempt to solve one or another problem.

Berger and Luckmann add the further suggestion that personal consciousness always flows through a largely unspoken world of social reality and constraint. This is true whether the social context is that of everyday or of a specific sub-world such as provided by disciplines such as physics, psychology, literature, art and so on. Even though the constraints which operate in these latter few cases may be more explicit than in some others, we should not miss the fact that there is always constraint on how we will be able to go about dealing with a given problem.

What this means is that each of the realities we live in and move through has its own set of possibilities and its own set of limitations, and what might not be do-able or even thinkable in one reality might be quite do-able and quite thinkable in a different one. To solve a problem or to create a new work of art often requires the person to change realities so as to push aside certain limitations for the time being. Such pushing-aside, however, can only be temporary for every innovative thinker, artist or inventor must always bring his or her insight back to the world of everyday for others to understand and use.

Thus, human thinking always involves a series of constantly

changing perspectives. Sometimes the problems we construct (or are set for us by others) can be solved with only a small shift of attention from one aspect of the situation to another; sometimes they require side-trips in and through fringe, focus and fringe, and back; while sometimes nothing less than a complete change in social or personal perspective will do. To solve a problem is to make use of all that a person is and all that a person knows, and often it is necessary to step outside of these constraints to deal effectively with a given problem.

Because the pull of any problem truly confronted is so compelling, creative artists and thinkers often work at their problems by living them from "the inside". When this happens, the person leaves the world of everyday (or of his or her discipline) and enters the formless, but emerging world of the problem. In the case of the artist there is always the medium to appeal to for help; in the case of the scientific, philosophical, or personal problem-solver, there is always the imagery and symbolic possibilities of poetic language or mathematics to appeal to: in both cases, however, the person must renounce what is familiar even to the point of his or her ordinary, everyday self. Sometimes, such renunciation is experienced in retrospect as if person and outcome were separate; at least that's the way many artists and thinkers describe their reactions to an episode of creative centration.

There is one final point to any journey of innovative thinking and this concerns the person's re-entry into the world of everyday. In the vast majority of cases, the nature of our ordinary social world is little affected by what we have done even though we personally may be dramatically changed. There are other times, however, when a particular bit of thinking seems to change the everyday world all of us will live and work in from then on. Sometimes it is a highly speculative idea such as Einstein's "Theory of Relativity"; sometimes it is a new medicine such as penicillin or a new technique such as anaesthesia; and sometimes it is a new style such as Impressionism or Jazz. What is true in each of these cases is that we and our everyday world are never again quite the same. In this we are again reminded that innovative thinking often grows out of experiences that are a bit disturbing not only because they are intuitive but because they ask us for a time (and longer) to give up the security of our familiar world of everyday reality.

8 References

Berger, P. L. and Luckmann, T. (1966). "The Social Construction of Reality." Doubleday, New York.

Bruner, J. S. (1960). "The Process of Education." Harvard University Press, Cambridge.

Doyle, C. L. (1976). The Creative Process: A Study In Paradox. *In* "The Creative Process" (Ed. C. B. Windsor). Bank Street College of Education, New York.

Ghiselin, B. (1952). "The Creative Process." University of California, Berkeley.

Gordon, W. J. J. (1961). "Synectics: The Development of Creative Capacity." Harper, New York.

Green, M. (1969). Introduction. *In* "Knowing and Being" (Ed. M. Green), IX–XVII. The University of Chicago Press, Chicago.

Hutchinson, Eliot D. (1949). "How To Think Creatively." Abingdon Press, Nashville.

James, W. (1892). "Psychology." Henry Holt, New York.

James, W. (1950). "The Principles of Psychology." Dover Publications, New York.

Koestler, A. (1964). "The Act of Creation." Pan Books, London.

Lawrence, D. H. (1952). Making Pictures. *In* "The Creative Process" (Ed. B. Ghiselin), 62–67. University of California Press, Berkeley.

Ornstein, R. C. (1972). "The Psychology of Consciousness." W. H. Freeman, San Francisco.

Polanyi, M. (1959). "The Study of Man." University of Chicago Press, Chicago.

Polanyi, M. (1969). The Structure of Consciousness. *In* "Knowing and Being" (Ed. M. Green). University of Chicago Press, Chicago.

Pollio, H. R. and Barlow, J. M. (1975). A behavioural analysis of figurative language in psychotherapy: one session in a single case study. *Language and Speech* **18**, 236–254.

Pollio, H. R., Barlow, J. M., Fine, H. J. and Pollio, M. R. (1977). "Psychology and the Poetics of Growth: Figurative Language in Psychology, Psychotherapy, and Education." John Wiley, New York.

Samples, Bob. (1977). "The Metaphoric Mind: A Celebration of Creative Consciousness." Addison-Wesley, Menlo Park.

Wigman, M. (1952). Composition in Pure Movement. *In* "The Creative Process" (Ed. B. Ghiselin). University of California Press, Berkeley.

Zervos, C. (1952). Conversation With Picasso. *In* "The Creative Process" (Ed. B. Ghiselin), 48–53. University of California Press, Berkeley.

3 Human Action and Theory of Psychological Reversals

M. J. APTER

Department of Psychology,
University College Cardiff

1 Motivation in Experience and Behaviour

There are many reasons why psychology should be concerned with conscious experience as well as behaviour, and there are signs that psychologists are, after many years in which behaviourist orthodoxy of one kind or another has dominated the subject, becoming increasingly aware of this. In this respect the present book is a sign of the times.

One of these reasons is simply that conscious experience is an interesting topic in its own rights—indeed, what topic could possibly be more fascinating? In any case one suspects that in many areas of psychology, psychologists and even behaviourists, have really been primarily concerned with experience all along but have managed to disguise this, to themselves and others, through certain linguistic subterfuges. To take just one example, in clinical psychology the problem which the patient poses is not really a problem of abnormal "behaviour"; typically the problem is really that of the distress which this behaviour evidences, or which is caused by the behaviour in the patient himself or in others. After all, not all behaviour which is odd or unusual—e.g. solving problems in original ways—is considered to be abnormal in the clinical sense and treated therapeutically, even by behaviourists.

But even if we accept that the prime concern of psychology is behaviour, it can still be argued that reference to conscious processes is necessary in order to understand behaviour fully. A number of chapters in this book will be exploring this thesis, explicitly or implicitly, in relation to various psychological topics. The present chapter will be mainly concerned with the argument in relation to motivation. The basis of the argument in this respect is that unless we know what an individual's intentions are, or what his goal is at a given time, we cannot hope to understand his or her behaviour. In other words, we need to know how the individual himself understands his own actions. This is an argument which has been put most forcefully in recent years by those psychologists and especially philosophers who have argued for the utility of concepts like that of "action" in preference to that of "behaviour". These include Macmurray (1957), Peters (1958), Melden (1961), C. Taylor (1964), Hampshire (1965), Shwayder (1965), Anscombe (1966), Louch (1966), R. Taylor (1966), Mischel (1969), Harré and Secord (1972), Shotter (1975) and Gauld and Shotter (1977). (The concept of "action" appears to have been assimilated earlier by sociology than psychology since it dates back in sociology at least as far as Weber, 1922; in particular much use was made of the concept by Talcott Parsons, 1937).

The point about the word "action" here is that its use implies recognition of the fact that there is some conscious intention on the part of the person who is acting, whereas the word "behaviour", and related words like "responses" and "movements" make no such implication, and are indeed deliberately chosen by behaviourists for that very reason as part of their attempt to be objective at all costs. An example should make the distinction clear. Saying that someone is running is to describe a piece of behaviour; saying that he is trying to catch a bus is to describe what he is doing as a meaningful and intended action.

Typical of such "action" theorists are Harré and Secord (1972) who have argued that human beings should be seen as "conscious social actors, capable of controlling their performances and commenting intelligently upon them" (see preface). They contrast the more traditional view in psychology that the person is "an object responding to the push and pull of forces exerted by the environment" (p.8) with their own "ethogenic" view that the person acts "as an agent directing his own behaviour" (p.8). In the former case explanation involves referring to causes, whereas in the latter, reference is made instead to rules and plans which may inform the behaviour but which do not in themselves bring it about. One of the key distinctions which they make is between "movements", "actions" and "acts": "A movement is given meaning as an action by being identified as the performance or part of the performance of an act" (p.158). An example they give is that of the movement of a man's hand towards the extended fourth finger of the hand of a woman and the placing of a gold ring on the woman's finger; in the appropriate circumstances this movement may be seen as an action which is one of a number of actions which together constitute the act of getting married.

Rather than describing in more detail the views of Harré and Secord and the other writers listed above, the present chapter will describe a new theory—"reversal theory"*—which is in some respects strongly influenced by this tradition but which goes beyond it in ways which will become apparent in later sections of the chapter. By focussing on one theory in this way it will be possible to examine in a more sustained manner some of the problems which are involved when the individual's behaviour is looked at in the light of his own understanding of what he is doing, and why he is doing it.

First of all, however, let us consider in a little more detail why it should be necessary to take into account an individual's conscious intentions in understanding his behaviour. The argument which follows is very much in the spirit of "action" theories, but is constructed in such a way that it leads naturally into the specific theory which we shall be concentrating on in this chapter.

Let us start by noting that a given piece of behaviour may be performed to achieve various different goals at different times, and unless one knows which goal it is that the individual "has in mind" in performing the behaviour at a given time, the behaviour will be understood at best only superficially and might even be completely misunderstood. Let us take, for example, the behaviour of eating. One might assume that this behaviour is always directed to the conscious goal of overcoming feelings of hunger, but a moment's consideration of one's own eating behaviour is likely to disclose that there are many alternative goals which may at different times be achieved by means of this behaviour—e.g. to enjoy the taste of the food, to satisfy a feeling of curiosity about a new food, to please someone (one's host for example), to feel part of a group of people who are eating or simply because one is bored and there is nothing better to do. This point can be made even more strongly by reference to some simple piece of instrumental activity like walking down the road: this could be part of the means to satisfying an almost infinite number of goals, related to almost any need which a human being may have. Furthermore, the goal may change even in the course of the same piece of behaviour. Thus eating to overcome hunger may at a certain point change to eating for the pleasure of the taste or out of curiosity; similarly, while walking down the road to catch a bus one may change one's mind and continue on to the tobacconist to buy some cigarettes. This is not to say that the subject's intentions at a given moment are necessarily inaccessible to an observer or experimenter. The argument is simply that, to understand the behaviour, such reference must be made.

A behaviourist would presumably not necessarily disagree with this,

* The theory was proposed originally by Dr K. C. P. Smith and the present writer at a one-day meeting of the South West Inter-Clinic Conference, Bristol (1975), which was devoted to a consideration of the theory and its clinical applications.

although he would no doubt state it rather differently. His own approach would typically be to define the goal operationally through some experimental technique like food deprivation. One problem with this is that it tends to lead to a simplistic interpretation of an organism's behaviour in terms of this single presumed goal which has been imposed externally. As a result certain aspects even of an animal's behaviour may become puzzling within the context defined by the experimenter. To take just one example, what is one to make of an animal's behaviour in a maze when it reaches the entrance to the goal box, verifies that the food is there, and then backs off to run around the maze before returning to the goal box and eating the food?* One suspects that puzzling and awkward behaviour which does not apparently conform to the operational definition of the animal's goal is often lost sight of in the reported results of an experiment, e.g. by an averaging of results over many animals. The effect of this is that the relationship between behaviour and goals is made to look simpler than it really is.

However, the situation becomes even more problematic for behaviourists if one looks at the relationship between goals and behaviour from the opposite point of view. If it is true that a given piece of behaviour may be performed to achieve various different goals at different times, then the converse is also true: the same goal may be achieved at different times by means of many different behaviours. For example, there are many different ways of making money, achieving status, becoming powerful or satisfying curiosity. Or, to take a more specific goal, a particular meal may be prepared with different sequences of steps and different utensils. There are even different ways of boiling an egg. It is exactly this flexibility, and even novelty, of behaviour in arriving at a goal which has given behaviourists so much trouble over the years; to give a classic experimental example, a rat, having learned to run a maze successfully will swim it correctly when the maze is flooded (Macfarlane, 1930). Even Thorndike, as long ago as 1898, worried about the lack of stereotypy in cats as they learned over trials to escape from puzzle boxes. What all this implies is that although the goal may remain the same, the trajectory may differ—a principle which has come to be known in cybernetics and general systems theory as that of equifinality (Bertalanffy, 1968). (That is, systems which display equifinality can arrive at a given end state by a number of different routes and from different starting conditions).

Returning specifically to human beings, the argument so far may be

* I am indebted to Dr S. Sara of the University of Louvain for this example of a kind of behaviour which she has observed on a number of occasions in a laboratory setting. Not dissimilar behaviour was noted by Liddell (1966) in his classic work with sheep.

summarized by saying that there is not a simple one-to-one correspondence between behaviours produced by an individual and goals perceived by that individual. The relationship between the levels of behaviour and experience is in this respect a complex one: different conscious intentions may underlie the same behaviour and different behaviour may be generated from the same conscious intentions. We have here an analogy to the situation in linguistics as suggested by Chomsky (1965) and others in which a given surface structure may be derived from different deep structures, as happens in ambiguous sentences like "Barmen do not stop drinking"; and conversely, the same deep structure may underlie different surface structures as in "Samantha threw the ball to Sarah" and "The ball was thrown to Sarah by Samantha". Without wishing to make too much of this analogy, it can nevertheless be seen that the meaning of behaviour, according to the argument given above, is not necessarily given unequivocally in the behaviour itself; any more than the meaning of a sentence is necessarily given unequivocally in the surface structure of the utterance. In the case of behaviour, the meaning of the behaviour cannot be understood without reference to the intentions of the individual performing it and these intentions are part of the experience of the individual concerned: we may suppose that he normally knows what he is trying to do, just as he normally knows what he is trying to say. Both have meaning to him and the meaning underlies the generation of the utterance or the behaviour; in each case this meaning must be arrived at by an outside observer through suitable interpretation.

2 The Concept of Meta-motivational States

However, it is possible to carry this whole argument one step further and demonstrate the need for at least one further level of analysis beyond this. At this point we enter the realm of reversal theory proper.

The argument is this. Even if one knows what the goal is which an individual sees himself to be pursuing, one still does not necessarily understand that individual's experience in relation to his motivation. One also needs to know something about the way in which the subject interprets his own goal at a given time together with his behaviour towards that goal. This can be made clear most easily by means of an illustration. Consider a person who is riding a bicycle in order to get to a particular place. The behaviour is the cycling, the goal is arrival at the place in question. Now there are two different ways in which the subject may interpret this combination of his goal and his behaviour. In one case the goal may be felt to have priority and the behaviour be chosen in order to achieve this goal. Thus the individual may have to get to the place concerned because he works there: he therefore has no choice over the goal, he feels it essential that he achieves it, and everything is directed to this end. He may however vary his behaviour in getting there. In the other case, the behaviour may have priority and the goal be simply an excuse for the expression of the behaviour. Thus the individual may enjoy cycling and the focus of his attention be on the cycling itself for its attendant pleasures. In this case the goal chosen, which may be to visit a village church, is merely an excuse to give the performance of the behaviour some *raison d'être*; in any case, the goal is freely chosen and is not felt as imposed or essential. And it can be changed. In terms of the organization of the individual's phenomenal field* we could say that in the first case the goal is the figure and the behaviour the ground; in the second case the behaviour is the figure and the goal the ground. In both cases the figure remains invariant, but the content of the ground may change: where the goal has priority the behaviour towards it may be flexible, where the behaviour has priority the goal may change (thus the cyclist may decide to visit somewhere else instead). Here is one further example. Consider someone doing woodwork. If he is a professional carpenter and someone has ordered a specific object from him, then his behaviour relates to this particular essential goal; if on the other hand his woodworking is a leisure activity carried out for its own enjoyment, and he therefore makes whatever he chooses to make, then his goal at any particular time stems from his behaviour and is of secondary importance. In the first case the orientation of the phenomenal field is around the goal, in the second around the behaviour.

Note that I am now asking how the individual sees his own goals and behaviour and therefore this discussion is taking place at this point entirely at a phenomenological level. But I am also distinguishing two levels within the phenomenological level in respect of motivation: firstly goals and behaviours as they present themselves as part of the content of consciousness and secondly the way in which these goals and behaviours are interpreted and given meaning within consciousness.

It will now be appreciated that the relationship between these two phenomenological levels is something like that between the level of behaviour and that of the intended goal of the behaviour. That is, the more "superficial" level does not in itself unequivocally express the "deeper" level. The same goal-and-behaviour in the individual's phenomenal field may be related by him to one or other of two different mutually-exclusive interpretations of the kind I have described.

* "Phenomenal field" may be defined as "the entire universe including himself, as it is experienced by the individual at the instant of action" (Snygg and Combs, 1959).

Just as behaviour may be ambiguous to an outside observer without knowledge of the goal which is being pursued, so an individual's experience of his own behaviour and goals and other aspects of his motivation may be ambiguous to an outside observer without knowledge of the states which underlie the interpretation of this experience by the individual. It is these states which are of prime interest in reversal theory. Since these phenomenological states are not themselves motivational but are *about* motivation they are referred to in the theory as "meta-motivational states".

Although the concept of meta-motivational state has been introduced here in the context of a rather abstract argument, it should not be thought that the identification of such states by the experiencing individual requires lengthy intellectual analysis or that the distinctions involved are merely conceptual. On the contrary, such states are directly amenable to introspection and, once one has become sufficiently sensitive to their existence, the different states are recognizable without much difficulty in everyday experience. In other words, the distinctions which will be made in the next two sections of this chapter are based on phenomenological rather than logical considerations.

3 Telic and Paratelic States

We come now to two of the basic hypotheses of reversal theory. The first is that certain meta-motivational states go in pairs of opposites; at any one time, one member of each pair of meta-motivational states is presumed to be operative and therefore to provide some aspect of the meaning of the experience. So far in the development of the theory three such pairs have been identified, each concerned with one dimension of the interpretation of motivation. The first of these pairs, which consists of what have been called the telic and paratelic states, will be the subject of this section of the chapter, although the pair of states has already been exemplified in the previous section. The second pair, which concerns the interpretation of arousal, will be discussed in the next section. The third pair of states, which have been called the negativistic and conformist states, will not be discussed in this chapter for reasons of space; but the (albeit still brief) discussion of the first two should give a good idea of the lines along which the theory is developing.

The second hypothesis is that each pair of states exhibits bi-stability. That is to say, each state is relatively stable but a switch is always possible into the opposite relatively stable state. When such a switch occurs, since it is a switch between opposites it may be referred to as a "reversal". Hence the name of the theory.

A few words are probably needed on the notion of "bi-stability" which essentially comes from cybernetics. If a homeostatic system is one which maintains a certain variable (e.g. the temperature of a thermostatically controlled room) within specifiable limits, then a bi-stable system is a more complex form of homeostatic system in which there are two alternative stable states, each specifiable in terms of limits of the variable. A simple example of a bi-stable system would be a light switch, the two stable states consisting of the on position and the off position; intermediate positions are operated on by the system in such a way that the switch returns after disturbance to one or the other of the stable states and rests there until there is further disturbance. Bi-stability is also apparent in a number of psychological processes—the perception of reversible figures like the Necker cube is an example. There are two stable mutually exclusive ways of perceiving such reversible figures and the whole time the figure is inspected one or other of these configurations is perceived. However, from time to time a rapid transition occurs from one to the other—the figure reverses. A similar thing happens with figure–ground reversals. These perceptual reversals are in fact good analogies for what is suggested by reversal theory to happen in relation to bi-stable pairs of meta-motivational states, except that there may be a number of factors which induce reversals between members of a given pair of meta-motivational states.

The example given earlier of riding a bicycle illustrated one pair of meta-motivational states. One of the members of this pair has been labelled the "telic" state (from the ancient Greek "telos" meaning an end), and the other member of the pair has been labelled the "paratelic" state. The telic state is defined as a state in which the individual's phenomenal field is oriented towards some goal which he sees to be essential; the paratelic state is defined as a state in which the individual's phenomenal field does not have this characteristic. In the latter case, as we have seen, the goal, if there is one, is an excuse for the ongoing behaviour and is not seen as essential by the person performing the behaviour. An example of someone in a telic state of mind would be someone filling in his tax return form, where he saw completing the form as an essential and unavoidable goal and the behaviour in itself was not at all enjoyed, although acheiving the goal eventually provided some satisfaction. An example of someone in a paratelic state of mind by contrast would be someone reading a novel, where the goal of completing the novel was not seen by him as an essential one, but the behaviour itself and the stimulation related to that behaviour, was felt as enjoyable and in need of no further justification. Behaviour performed in a paratelic state of mind in which there is no goal at all in the individual's phenomenal field might be exemplified by the individual chatting to a friend on a street corner, or sitting in an armchair smoking a pipe. (As can be seen from these examples, the difference between having a non-essential goal and no goal at all can be very slight.)

Although some activities are much more likely to be performed in a paratelic state of mind than others—e.g. those activities which are conventionally designated as "play" are often (but not necessarily) performed in the paratelic state of mind, while those designated "work" are often (but again not necessarily) performed in the telic state of mind—there are a whole range of activities which are much more ambiguous and are frequently performed in different states of mind at different times. In any case, one can never be sure from the behaviour itself, or even from knowledge of the goal underlying the behaviour, what the meta-motivational state is at a given time without supplementary information. As in interpreting ambiguous sentences, context is often important in disambiguation. If someone takes a bath before going for an interview one may suppose that the bath is taken in a telic state of mind in that the subject sees it as part of the route to the essential goal of succeeding in the interview; if the same person takes the bath after the interview, and if it is a long, lingering, soaking bath with little washing, it is reasonable to suppose that it is being enjoyed in itself and that the state of mind is paratelic.

We saw earlier that in Harré and Secord's terms, an action is a piece of behaviour which is seen by the individual performing it as a means to an end, the end itself being embodied in or achieved by some act which the actions make up: for example the act of getting married involves a number of constituent actions which each derive their meaning from the act of which they are part. In these terms, in the telic state the act is seen as one which embodies essential goals which cannot, for one reason or another, be altered; in the paratelic state the act, although it gives meaning to the actions, does so in terms of an arbitrary rather than essential goal, if a goal is involved at all. The act of getting married is presumably seen by most people, by the time they are confronted with it, as an essential and unavoidable one and is therefore undertaken by most people in a telic state. By contrast, playing a game of tennis is an act which gives meaning to the actions which make it up (serving, running to the net, etc.) but the goal which it embodies (that of winning) is not necessarily seen as essential—e.g. if one loses this does not necessarily mean that playing was not worth while. If winning the game is not seen as essential by a given individual at a given time, then at that time he may be said to be in a paratelic state. It should not be supposed therefore that the difference between telic and paratelic is that of whether the individual sees himself as performing an act or not; rather, as should now be clear, the difference concerns the nature of the act which he sees himself to be performing.

The reader may feel a little confused at this point, since, in adopting Harré and Secord's terminology, I have accepted that acts give meaning to the actions which make them up. And yet I have also argued, in terms of reversal theory, that at least some acts, those performed in a paratelic state of mind, derive their meaning from their constituent actions. This is however not a contradiction since two different aspects of meaning are being referred to. The meaning to which Harré and Secord refer is essentially the way in which parts derive their meaning from wholes to which they belong. The meaning which reversal theory is referring to is that of the *raison d'être* of a piece of behaviour. Thus hitting a tennis ball has a meaning in the first sense in terms of the game of tennis of which it is part; in the second sense the game of tennis derives its meaning from the enjoyment of various aspects of the situation which will include that of hitting a tennis ball. In the telic state both these meanings work in the same direction since the whole embodies the goal which is also the *raison d'être* of the actions; in the paratelic state these two meanings may work in opposite directions.

There are a number of different factors which may induce a reversal from one meta-motivational state to its opposite. One kind of factor which may bring about a reversal in the telic direction is obviously that of essential biological need; when it reaches a certain strength in a person, it will become recognized by him as constituting an essential goal at that time and pursuit of the goal will normally be initiated; that is, if the individual was previously in the paratelic state, a reversal will occur to the telic. The same may be true of various social needs which may impose themselves on the individual. Context may also help to bring about a reversal in one direction or the other. Certain contexts, like the living room, the theatre or the swimming pool, may, other things being equal, induce the paratelic state; other contexts, like the office, a law court or a hospital waiting room, may similarly induce the telic state. People may also induce reversals in each other, perhaps through subtle social cues, at what Bateson has called the meta-communicative level (Bateson, 1973), which helped to define the situation. Apart from all this, it is also possible that sufficiently strong frustration may cause a reversal, be it frustration in reaching a goal in the telic state, or frustration in expressing certain behaviour in the paratelic state. Finally, it may be supposed that each state may also be subject to satiation and that satiation may lead to reversal. These factors presumably combine, or work against each other, in some way, to determine whether a reversal will or will not take place at a given moment. One thing to note about all this is that reversals back-and-forth may occur even in the course of a single sequence of actions. For example, in starting to play tennis one may be in a paratelic state of mind, enjoying the behaviour in itself; but if one starts to lose badly a point may be reached at which the goal of saving-face imposes itself and the mood changes to a telic one; the mood may change back to paratelic if one starts to play better, so removing the threat of humiliation, or if one's opponent helps to re-define the situation as paratelic with a joke or in some other way; at this point one may start to enjoy the playing in itself once more.

Although it is reasonable to suppose that everybody experiences both of these states at different times and reverses reasonably frequently from one to the other during everyday life, nevertheless it would also appear that people are predisposed to be in one rather than the other and, if given the opportunity, spend more time in one state than the other. In other words, in a given individual one meta-motivational state may dominate the opposite state to some degree. In fact a psychometric scale, the Telic Dominance Scale, has now been developed to measure such individual differences along a dimension of telic/paratelic dominance (Murgatroyd *et al.*, 1978). Dominance of this kind cannot be equated with a personality trait, since a trait in the normal sense of the term is meant to represent some characteristic which remains reasonably constant; e.g. if someone is extroverted to a given degree he is assumed to be always extroverted to something like this degree, and certainly not to be introverted for regular periods. A telic dominant person, however, would nevertheless be expected to be in a paratelic state for substantial periods of time, and a paratelic dominant person to spend substantial periods of time in a telic state of mind. One point which the whole reversal theory analysis underlines therefore is that individuals are inherently inconsistent.

4 The Interpretation of Arousal

So far we have been looking at one aspect of motivation— the relationship of means and ends. Another aspect of motivation is that of arousal. The interpretation of this arousal by the individual is therefore, in the terms I have introduced here, meta-motivational. According to reversal theory, not only does the individual interpret "means–ends" relationships in the two different ways involved in the telic and paratelic states, but he also interprets the arousal he feels in two opposite ways at different times. These two opposite types of interpretation, as we shall see, result in different types of affect rather than different ways of structuring the phenomenal field—although affect is also of course part of the phenomenal field. It is also suggested by reversal theory that this pair of meta-motivational states makes up a bi-stable system. There is of course good experimental evidence from the classic work of Schachter and Singer (1962) that the individual does interpret his arousal in different ways depending on various circumstances; the reversal theory view of this is, however, rather different from Schachter's in that it suggests a definite structure underlying the different possible interpretations.

The two ways of interpreting arousal suggested by reversal theory may be represented by the two hypothetical curves in Fig. 1 which

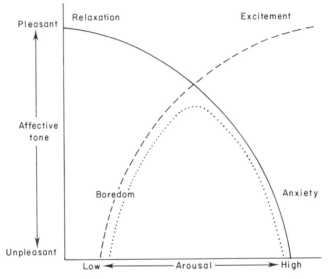

Fig. 1 The two hypothetical curves relating "felt arousal" to affective tone suggested by reversal theory.

relate arousal level to affective tone. In one meta-motivational state the higher the level of arousal the more pleasant it is felt to be; in this state the individual may be said to seek high arousal which is then felt as "excitement" and to avoid low arousal which is felt as "boredom". In the other state, the higher the level of arousal the more unpleasant it is felt to be; in this state the individual may be said to seek low arousal which is then felt as "relaxation" and to avoid high arousal which is felt as "anxiety". We may describe one meta-motivational state therefore as an "excitement-seeking" state and the other as an "anxiety-avoiding" state.

This view of the relationship between arousal and affective tone stands in sharp contrast to the view of the relationship suggested by optimal arousal theory, pioneered by Hebb and Thompson (1954) and Leuba (1955) but adopted and developed by many others since including Berlyne (1960), Fiske and Maddi (1961) and Schultz (1965). The relationship typically suggested by optimal arousal theorists is one which may be described by means of a single inverted U-curve, as shown dotted in Fig. 1. In optimal arousal terms an intermediate level of arousal is generally supposed to be optimum and to provide maximum pleasure to the individual, whereas in reversal theory the two extremes of arousal are supposed to maximize pleasure depending on which of two states the individual is in. Where optimal arousal theory assumes homeostasis—the intermediate position is supposed to be stable—reversal theory assumes bi-stability. It should be noted though that if the shape of the two curves is of the form suggested in Fig. 1, then intermediate levels of arousal will also be fairly pleasant in both states and the reversal theory interpretation therefore to this extent subsumes the optimal arousal theory interpretation.

Describing the relationship between arousal and affective tone in this way by means of two curves, allows the four distinguishable states signified by the words "excitement", "anxiety", "boredom" and "relaxation" to be accounted for—something which would not appear to be possible in terms of the single curve of optimal arousal theory. To put it another way, reversal theory is more consistent with everyday experience in that it takes into account those situations in which very high arousal is pleasant (e.g. in sexual behaviour, in playing in an exciting football match, in watching a tense film) and those situations in which very low arousal is pleasant (e.g. just after eating a good meal, just before going to sleep, lying in the shade on a hot day). Both of these kinds of situation are difficult to explain in terms of optimal arousal theory. That high and low arousal situations can indeed be pleasant has been demonstrated, if such demonstration is needed, in an experiment in which 67 subjects (psychology students) were asked individually to rate the items in a list of a variety of situations firstly for felt arousal and secondly for affective tone in relation to the felt arousal itself. Two seven-point rating scales were used for this purpose. Averaging over all the subjects, some of the situations which were agreed to be among the most pleasurable in felt arousal also turned out to be among the highest on estimated arousal, whereas others turned out to be among the lowest on estimated arousal (Apter, 1976).

Just as with telic–paratelic reversals, reversals may occur between the anxiety-avoiding and excitement-seeking states during the course of the same activity. For example, the excitement of being in an aeroplane may turn to sudden anxiety at the moment of take-off, and then when the take-off is safely accomplished revert back to excitement before the arousal diminishes. In this case there is a switch from one way of interpreting high arousal to the other and then back again while the arousal is still high*. Similarly, arousal during sexual behaviour may be felt as pleasurable excitement; however, if anything sufficiently threatening occurs—for example one of the partners does something which suddenly reminds the other of some previous sexual failure—then the excitement may switch to anxiety which in turn inhibits the performance of the behaviour and leads to temporary impotence or frigidity in the partner. In this case, the greater the original sexual excitement then, paradoxically, the greater the anxiety if a switch occurs and the greater the degree of resulting dysfunction. Similarly, at the low arousal end of the scale, relaxation may well, after a certain period, satiate and switch to boredom and a consequent need for excitement. Thus sunbathing on holiday may lead after a while to a feeling that one wants to do something exciting—e.g. like plunging into the sea and swimming vigorously.

The factors which may provoke a reversal between these two states fall into the same categories as those which may provoke a reversal between the telic and paratelic states. Indeed, it may have occurred to the reader that there is a relationship between these two pairs of states such that a particular factor which induces one member of one pair will also tend to induce a related member of the other pair. This does indeed seem to be the case over a range of circumstances. Thus some factor which induces a reversal into the telic state, some form of threat for example or some serious problem, is also likely to bring about a reversal into the anxiety-avoiding state. In the same way, a factor which brings about a reversal into the paratelic state, for example the achievement of some goal which is seen as essential, or a context like the cinema in which the emphasis is on the ongoing behaviour of watching the film, is likely to induce a reversal into the excitement-seeking state. (Of course, excitement itself could be said to be a goal, but it is not usually seen to be an essential goal as it would need to be associated with the telic state; it is generally seen more as an enjoyable aspect of the activity itself). So although these two pairs of meta-motivational states do not necessarily go together, nevertheless they do appear to be linked over a wide range of activities, the telic state tending to be associated with anxiety-avoidance and the paratelic state with excitement-seeking. Therefore for many purposes these two pairs of states are treated in the theory as different aspects of the same bi-stable system.

* This ties in neatly with Zillmann's theory (1972) of excitation-transfer for which he has now accumulated much evidence (e.g. Cantor and Zillmann, 1973, Cantor et al., 1975).

If we turn back to the kind of analysis with which we set out in this chapter, but relate it now to arousal, we can see that the same behaviour can be carried out with different underlying degrees of felt arousal which are not necessarily evident from the behaviour itself. This is fairly obvious. For example, it is possible for a person to watch television over a period of time with various levels of arousal, without it being apparent to someone observing him that his arousal levels are changing. Conversely, a given arousal level may express itself in quite different ways at different times in the same individual—a low level of arousal may for example result in very little behaviour at one time, but at another time be expressed through various agitated movements, or through yawning. In turn, at the next level of analysis, knowledge to an outside observer of the arousal which an individual is experiencing is, as we have seen, not in itself sufficient to disclose how the individual is interpreting this arousal. So a given degree of arousal may be interpreted by the subject in different ways depending on whether his underlying interpretative state is the excitement-seeking state or the anxiety-avoiding state. Conversely, one or other of these states may underlie any degree of felt arousal at a given time.

What this kind of analysis does is to bring out something of the complexity of the relationship between behaviour and experience, and between different aspects of experience, in relation to motivation. It should not, however, be taken to imply that knowledge of the meaning which behaviour has for an individual must necessarily remain inaccessible to an outside observer—unless of course he restricts the methods he uses to those which are allowed by one or another variety of behaviourism.

There are several other things to notice about this analysis. Firstly, not only does the theory of reversals, with its idea of opposite optimal motivational states, represent a departure from optimal arousal theory; it also represents a break with most other major theories of motivation in psychology, since most of these theories assume some single optimal level of whatever they identify as being their major motivational variable; the optimal level is usually assumed to be low. For example, the central idea in Freud's theory of motivation in both its earlier and later forms, was that of tension-reduction (for an excellent recent summary and critique of this aspect of Freud's theory see Fromm, 1977). Similarly, Hull based his influential learning theory on the notion of drive-reduction (e.g. Hull, 1943). Lorenz's more recent "hydraulic theory" (Lorenz, 1950) would appear to be yet another formulation of essentially the same idea.

Secondly, discussion of arousal from the reversal theory point of view brings out even more clearly than was possible in the previous section

the emphasis which the theory places on the inconsistencies which it
believes underlie human behaviour.

5 Experience and Mechanism

It is generally the case that where experience is taken seriously by
psychologists the tone of the resulting theorization and research is
anti-mechanistic. Thus phenomenological psychology questions many
of the assumptions of mechanistic behaviourist psychology and merges
into existential psychology in which the notion of free-will— "existence
precedes essence" in Sartre's celebrated phrase (Sartre, 1946)—is, in
one form or another, a central feature. Mechanistic approaches to man,
on the other hand, tend not only to be deterministic in the sense that
free-will is discounted, but they also tend to disregard consciousness—both because it cannot be observed objectively, and also because
it is felt to be difficult to incorporate in a view of organisms, including
man, as machines. Where the real world was put "in brackets" by
Husserl (1913) in establishing phenomenology, Watson (1913) in
establishing behaviourism at about the same period took the opposite
step and put consciousness "in brackets"; in both cases the bracketing
was carried out for methodological reasons, removing certain topics
from consideration in order to deal more satisfactorily with those which
remained.

The more sophisticated mechanistic conceptions of man which one
associates with cybernetics also tend to avoid reference to conscious
experience. Although to exclude such reference is no part of the programme of cybernetics, as of behaviourism, and although cybernetics
tends to be highly centralist and cognitive in orientation with respect of
psychology, human psychological processes still tend to be defined and
studied by cyberneticians from outside rather than through the perspective of the experiencing individual himself. (I have discussed consciousness from the cybernetic perspective in more detail elsewhere, in
the context of computer simulation: Apter, 1970, Ch. 9.)

Reversal theory therefore finds itself in some respects in an unusual
position. On the one hand it is very much concerned with experience;
and the experiental states which it postulates are defined in terms of the
way in which the subject himself sees his actions. Thus an "essential"
goal in reversal theory is a goal which is seen by the subject himself to be
essential, not a goal which is judged to be essential for the individual by
some outside observer like a biologist, a physiologist or psychologist. In
this sense reversal theory is clearly phenomenological, at least in the
modern sense of phenomenological psychology in English language

psychology and psychiatry which has developed from the approach of such workers as MacLeod (1947, 1964) and Rogers (1951, 1964) and which may be described as an approach which treats personal experience as a central part of psychology.* On the other hand, it is also clearly strongly influenced by cybernetic, and hence mechanistic, ways of conceiving psychological processes. These two contrasted approaches are, as we have seen, brought together in particular through the suggestion that certain ways in which an individual interprets his own experience are themselves governed by the principle of bi-stability, which is a cybernetic concept. The assumption underlying reversal theory is that it is more fruitful scientifically to assume determinism than free-will, but that at the same time it is necessary to make reference to conscious experience and the dynamics of this experience in trying to understand behaviour. If, as I believe to be the case, one must take into account the way the individual himself interprets his own experience, this does not mean that this interpretation by the individual is itself not determined in various ways and that one cannot deal with it from the perspective of a sophisticated mechanistic view of man such as that of cybernetics. (In arguing in this way, therefore, reversal theory might be characterized as a form of "cybernetic phenomenology".)

If phenomenological psychology is anti-mechanistic, then so is the kind of psychology which derives from the use of the concept "action", such as the ethogenic approach of Harré and Secord, in which as we saw at the outset of this chapter the individual is viewed as initiating his own actions, in accordance with various rules, rather than emitting causally determined sequences of behavioural responses. Indeed, in its concern with understanding how the individual sees his own behaviour, the ethogenic tradition may be said to merge with the phenomenological tradition. So just as reversal theory finds itself in an odd position in relation to phenomenological psychology because of its determinist assumptions, it also finds itself in an odd position in relation to the ethogenic approach for the very same reason. For while it shares with the ethogenic approach the assumption that behaviour cannot be fully understood unless one takes into account the intentions of the person concerned and the meaning which the behaviour has for him or her, it does not make the further assumption that the subjective

*This contrasts with the more traditional and philosophically based type of phenomenological psychology developed from the original work of Husserl by continental philosophers and psychologists like Merleau-Ponty (1945) in which, among other things, the attempt is made to arrive at the "essence" of various psychological terms and concepts by means of certain techniques of phenomenological reflection. This is a complex area and the interested reader wishing to find out more is advised to turn initially to an introduction such as that of Spiegelberg (1972).

meanings and intentions assigned to the behaviour by the individual are not determined in some casual way.

In the space of this single chapter I have not been able to do more than sketch some of the main ideas of reversal theory. Furthermore the ideas which I have presented here have, of necessity, had to be introduced without much argument or illustration, and it has not been possible to deal with many of the conceptual problems which are raised by this analysis. Hopefully, however, I have been able to impart some of the flavour of the theory and make clear the general lines of the approach. The reader may, in any case, be interested to know that the theory has already been used to throw light on various kinds of behaviour and experience, including that which is associated with humour (Apter and Smith, 1977a), religion (Apter and Smith, 1977b), sexual behaviour (Apter and Smith, 1978, 1979) and negativistic behaviour in adolescence (Apter and Smith, 1976a). Research is currently in progress to test various hypotheses derived from the theory. Finally, in case the theory is thought to be too academic in tone and orientation, it can be added that it has also been used extensively in therapy, especially in family therapy in the setting of a child guidance clinic (Apter and Smith, 1976b; Smith and Apter, 1978a, in press).

6 References

Anscombe, G. E. M. (1966). "Intentions." Cornell University Press, Ithaca.

Apter, M. J. (1970). "The Computer Simulation of Behaviour." Hutchinson, London. (Also, Harper and Row, New York, 1971.)

Apter, M. J. (1976). Some data inconsistent with the optimal arousal theory of motivation. *Perceptual and Motor Skills* **43**, 1209–1210.

Apter, M. J. and Smith, K. C. P. (1976a). Negativism in adolescence. *The Counsellor* **23/24**, 25–30.

Apter, M. J. and Smith, K. C. P. (1976b). "Psychological Reversals: Some New Perspectives on the Family and Family Communication." Paper presented at the First International Family Encounter, Mexico City, November, 1976.

Apter, M. J. and Smith, K. C. P. (1977a). Humour and the theory of psychological reversals. *In* "It's a Funny Thing, Humour" (Eds A. J. Chapman and H. C. Foot), 95–100. Pergamon Press, Oxford.

Apter, M. J. and Smith, K. C. P. (1977b). "Religion and the Theory of Psychological Reversals." Paper presented at the Second Lancaster Symposium on the Psychology of Religion, Oxford, January, 1977.

Apter, M. J. and Smith, K. C. P. (1978). Excitement–anxiety reversals in sexual behaviour. *British Journal of Sexual Medicine* **5**, No. 38, 23–24; No. 39, 25–26.

Apter, M. J. and Smith, K. C. P. (1979). Sexual behaviour and the theory of psychological reversals. *In* Love and Attraction—An International Conference" (Eds G. Wilson and M. Cook), 405–408. Pergamon Press, Oxford.

Bateson, G. (1973). "Steps to an Ecology of Mind." Paladin, St. Albans, Herts.

Berlyne, D. E. (1960). "Conflict, Arousal and Curiosity." McGraw-Hill, New York.

Bertalanffy, L. (1968). "General System Theory." G. Braziller, New York.

Cantor, J. R. and Zillmann, D. (1973). The effect of affective state and emotional arousal on music appreciation. *Journal of General Psychology* **89**, 97–108.

Cantor, J. R., Zillmann, D. and Bryant, J. (1975). Enhancement of experienced sexual arousal in response to erotic stimuli through misattribution of unrelated residual excitation. *Journal of Personality and Social Psychology* **32**, 69–75.

Chomsky, N. (1965). "Aspects of the Theory of Syntax." MIT Press, Cambridge, Mass.

Fiske, D. W. and Maddi, S. R. (1961). A conceptual framework. *In* "Functions of Varied Experience" (Eds D. W. Fiske and S. R. Maddi), 11–56. Dorsey Press, Illinois.

Fromm, E. (1977). *In* "The Anatomy of Human Destructiveness", 581–631. Penguin, London. (Originally published, 1974.)

Gauld, A. and Shotter, J. (1977). "Human Action and its Psychological Investigation." Routledge and Kegan Paul, London.

Hampshire, S. (1965). "Thought and Action." Chatto and Windus, London.

Harré, R. and Secord, P. F. (1972). "The Explanation of Social Behaviour." Blackwell, Oxford.

Hebb, D. O. and Thompson, W. R. (1954). The social significance of animal studies. *In* "Handbook of Social Psychology" (Ed. G. Lindzey), 532–561. Addison-Wesley, Cambridge, Mass.

Hull, C. L. (1943). "Principles of Behaviour." Appleton-Century Crofts.

Husserl, E. (1913). "Ideen." Niemeyer, Halle. (Translation by W. R. Boyce Gibson. "Ideas: General Introduction to Pure Phenomenology." Collier, New York, 1962.)

Leuba, C. (1955). Toward some integration of learning theories: the concept of optimal stimulation. *Psychological Reports* **1**, 27–33.

Liddell, H. (1966). Conditioning and emotions. *In* "Frontiers of Psychological Research". (Ed. S. Coopersmith), 130–138. Freeman, San Francisco. (Originally published in 1954.)

Lorenz, K. (1950). The comparative method in studying innate behaviour patterns. *Symposia of the Society for Experimental Biology* **4**, 221–268.

Louch, A. R. (1966). "Explanation and Human Action." Blackwell, Oxford.

Macfarlane, D. A. (1930). The role of kinesthesis in maze learning. *University of California Publications on Psychology* **4**, 277–305.

MacLeod, R. B. (1947). The phenomenological approach to social psychology. *Psychological Review* **54**, 193–210.

MacLeod, R. B. (1964). Phenomenology: A challenge to experimental psychology. *In* "Behaviorism and Phenomenology" (Ed. T. W. Wann), 47–78. University of Chicago Press, Chicago.

MacMurray, J. (1957). "The Self as Agent." Faber and Faber, London.

Melden, A. I. (1961). "Free Action." Routledge and Kegan Paul, London.

Merleau-Ponty, M. (1954). "Phénoménologie de la Perception." Gallimard, Paris. (English translation by C. Smith, Humanities Press, New York, 1962.)

Mischel, T. (1969) (Ed.). "Human Action." Academic Press, New York.

Murgatroyd, S. J. Rushton, C., Apter, M. J. and Ray, C. (1978). The development of the telic dominance scale. *Journal of Personality Assessment* **42**, 519–528.

Parsons, T. (1937). "The Structure of Social Action." McGraw-Hill, New York.

Peters, R. S. (1958). "The Concept of Motivation." Routledge and Kegan Paul, London.

Rogers, C. R. (1951). "Client-centered Therapy." Houghton Mifflin, Boston.

Rogers, C. R. (1964). Toward a science of the person. *In* "Behaviorism and Phenomenology" (Ed. T. W. Wann), 109–140. University of Chicago Press, Chicago.

Sartre, J. P. (1946). "L'Existentialisme est un Humanisme." Nagel, Paris.

Schachter, S. and Singer, J. (1962). Cognitive, social and physiological determinants of emotional state. *Psychological Review* **69**, 378–399.

Schultz, D. D. (1965). "Sensory Restriction: Effects on Behaviour." Academic Press, New York.

Shotter, J. (1975). "Images of Man in Psychological Research." Methuen, London.

Shwayder, D. S. (1965). "The Stratification of Behaviour." Routledge and Kegan Paul, London.

Smith, K. C. P. and Apter, M. J. (1978). Clare—a nervous child. *The Counsellor* **4**, 15–21.

Smith, K. C. P. and Apter, M. J. (In press). Jonathan—a demanding child. *The Counsellor* **3**.

Snygg, D. and Combs, A. W. (1959). "Individual Behavior: A Perceptual Approach to Behavior." 2nd edn. Harper, New York.

Spiegelberg, H. (1972). "Phenomenology in Psychology and Psychiatry: A Historical Introduction." Northwestern University Press, Evanston.

Taylor, C. (1964). "The Explanation of Behaviour." Routledge and Kegan Paul, London.

Taylor, R. (1966). "Action and Purpose." Prentice-Hall, New Jersey.

Thorndike, E. L. (1898). Animal intelligence: an experimental study of the associative processes in animals. *Psychological Review Monograph Supplement* No. 8.

Watson, J. B. (1913). Psychology as the behaviorist views it. *Psychological Review* **20**, 158–77.

Weber, M. (1922). Translation (1968) as "Economy and Society." Bedminster Press, New York.

Zillmann, D. (1972). The role of excitation in aggressive behavior. *In* "Proceedings of the Seventeenth International Congress of Applied Psychology, 1971", 925–936. Editest, Brussels.

4 Actions Not as Planned: The Price of Automatization

J. REASON

Department of Psychology,
University of Manchester

1 Introduction

Apart from the recent revival of interest in "slips of the tongue" and other verbal mistakes (Fromkin, 1973, Shaffer, 1976), the everyday lapses that we commonly attribute to absent-mindedness have, with some notable exceptions (James, 1890, Freud, 1901, 1922, Jastrow, 1905), received scant attention from psychologists. One could suggest that they were understandably reluctant to contemplate the absence of mind while its presence continued to prove so troublesome. But a more likely factor is that the essential feature of these errors, namely the deviation of action from intention, has little or no credibility within two of the major psychological traditions. Behaviourists would not willingly admit of the intention, at least not as something having any theoretical utility; and the psycho-analysts would deny the deviation, in keeping with Freud's view that erroneous actions are expressive of some unconscious need or purpose. Not only has Freud's own interest in these 'parapraxes' been enormously influential, but also curiously double-edged in its consequences. It was his genius for noting the minutiae of life that first revealed the rich pickings to be found among what he called "the refuse of the phenomenal world". And yet it was his talent for fashioning simple, powerful but largely unassailable explanations that effectively closed the lid again on this fascinating psychological dustbin. The aim of this paper is to re-open it so that we can take a fresh look.

Freud believed that through the study of these trivial and usually inconsequential blunders ". . . one may find a road to the study of the great problems" (Freud, 1922, p. 21). Two such "great problems", the one of theoretical and the other of practical significance, suggest themselves.

As psycho-linguists like Fromkin (1973) have shown with regard to language, a systematic study of minor slips and lapses can tell us something more about the underlying structure and organization of skilled behaviour in general, and particularly about the way in which we monitor—or occasionally fail to monitor—our largely automatic actions. In the same way that an adequate theory of language production must draw upon and account for slips of the tongue, so also must a theory of motor skills consider the apparently non-random lapses of attention and memory that appear so frequently among our daily actions. And it is with these "slips of action" rather than verbal errors that this paper is mainly concerned.

The second problem, and the one that initially prompted this enquiry, is that of accidents. Progress in this most pressing area of human factors research has encountered many impediments, as Suchman (1961) and Kay (1971) have pointed out. Aside from the obvious methodological difficulty that accidents are rare and, by definition, largely unpredictable events, there is also the conceptual confusion that exists between the act and its consequences. As Cherns (1962) succinctly put it, an accident is "an error with sad consequences". But unless we adopt the strict Freudian line that errors (and therefore their consequences) are unconsciously motivated, we have no reason to suppose any *psychological* connection between the erroneous action and its outcome. An "absent-minded" error in the kitchen can be merely comical, but the same mistake on the flight deck of a large passenger aircraft can be catastrophic (Reason, 1976). The difference lies not in the nature of the error but in the extent to which the circumstances of its occurrence will penalize it. If, as is maintained here, errors "with sad consequences" are simply a subset of the total error population, and one that is distinguished by environmental rather than by psychological considerations, then the accident researcher would be well advised to extend the scope of his investigations to include the full gamut of human error, irrespective of its consequences. Whatever further contribution the psychologist may make towards the prevention of accidents, it must surely be predicated upon a better understanding of error-producing mechanisms in general, and of the factors which promote their activity.

1.1 Redefining the Problem: Actions Not as Planned

Clearly, the term "absent-mindedness" leaves much to be desired, referring as it does to the absence of something that itself defies adequate definition. But before we can arrive at a satisfactory label, we need to establish how these particular lapses fit within the broader spectrum of human error. And to do this, we must consider what exactly is meant by the term "error".

Central to the notion of error is the failure of "planned actions" to achieve a desired outcome. We must emphasize "planned actions" since not all failures to attain a goal can be classed as errors. If the failure was due solely to the intervention of some chance or unforeseeable agency, it could not legitimately be described as an error. By the same token, not all actions that bring about the intended consequences can be regarded as "non-errors", as in the case of the golfer whose mis-directed ball is deflected into the hole by a passing bird. In establishing the status of an error, therefore, we need to distinguish it from both the "unlucky" and the "lucky" accident.

Logically, we can fail to achieve a desired outcome in at least two ways: when the actions go as planned, but the plan is inadequate; or when the plan is satisfactory, but the actions do not go as planned. It is this last category of error—"actions not as planned" (ANAPs)—that is the focus of the present chapter. Excluded from it are the "errors of judgement" and the wide variety of "planning failures" that comprise the former category.

The term "actions not as planned" can only be claimed as an improvement over "absent-minded behaviour" so long as there is some general agreement as to what constitutes a "plan". Notions such as "intention" and "plan" have a long and vexed history within psychology (Ryan, 1970); but in recent years, due largely to the increasing use of computer programming analogies in cognitive theorizing, there has been a revival of interest in the relationship between mental plans and the actions they control (Miller *et al*, 1960, Shallice, 1972, Luria, 1973, Mandler, 1975). For our present purposes, we can draw extensively upon the formulations of G. Miller, E. Galanter and K. Pribram and state that a plan is a hierarchically organized set of stored instructions, analogies in certain respects to a computer program (we will consider in what ways this analogy breaks down subsequently): it governs the nature, order and time-scale of a sequence of actions, either overt or covert, leading to a particular outcome or goal. In essence, therefore, a plan consists of a mental representation of both a goal (together with its intermediate sub-goals) and the possible actions required to achieve it; where both are related to some time period which may be stated either very precisely or only in the vaguest terms, but which must be specified in some degree.

2 The Diary Study

Thirty-five volunteer subjects, 23 women and 12 men with an average age of 29 (range 15–46 years), kept diaries of their "actions not as planned" over a continuous 2-week period. The main purpose of this study was to generate a corpus of "actions not as planned" akin to those assembled by Fromkin (1973) and others for "slips of the tongue".

The diarists were instructed as follows:

> The purpose of this diary is to provide a daily record over a continuous period of two weeks of your various unintended or absent-minded actions, and of your 'accidental behaviour' in general. In other words I am interested in all those occasions on which you became aware that you had done something you did not intend to do. Since this is a preliminary investigation, I would prefer to keep the definition of such actions fairly vague at this point. In the first place, I want to cast the net as widely as possible with regard to the types of incident; and secondly, only you are in a position to judge whether or not your actions deviated from your intentions, and what kind of actions they were.

The diarists were asked to record the date and time of the occurrence, what they intended to do, what they actually did, and the circumstances prevailing at the time of the slip.

The study yielded a total of 433 recorded slips, an average of just over 12 per person (SD = 7·54) over the 2 weeks, with a range from 0 to 36 incidents. There were no significant effects due to age or sex. Women, on average, recorded slightly more errors—12·5 as opposed to 10·9 for men—but this may simply have reflected their greater conscientiousness in reporting rather than actual proneness. There was a tendency which fell just short of statistical significance (Chi-squared = 15·1; d.f. = 9) for errors to occur more frequently at three periods of the day: between 08.00 and 12.00 hours, between 16.00 and 18.00 hours and a smaller "peak" between 20.00 and 22.00 hours. Over 20% of all the men's errors occurred between 08.00 and 10.00 hours; whereas for women the morning peak was somewhat later, falling between 10.00 and 12.00 hours. It should be noted that only three of the women were full-time housewives, the remainder having jobs or regular commitments away from home in the daytime.

2.1 Error Classification

The errors were classified according to the scheme set out below, showing the defining characteristics of each category, the relative frequency of its occurrence and illustrative examples. Since reporting styles varied widely, these examples have all been converted to first-person statements. The classification scheme incorporates only 94% of the recorded errors, the remainder were excluded either because they did not involve any overt action, or because no unambiguous classification was possible.

2.1.1. *Discrimination failures (11% of total errors)*

Where inputs are misclassified, usually due to a confusion between the perceptual, functional, spatial or temporal attributes of stimulus objects.

(1) Perceptual confusions (where the objects confused are physically similar)

> "I put shaving cream on my toothbrush."
> "I found myself pushing someone else's trolley at the supermarket."
> "I have two mirrors on my dressing table. One I use for making up and brushing my hair, the other for inserting and removing my contact lenses. On this occasion I intended to brush my hair, but sat down in front of the wrong mirror, and removed my contact lenses instead."

(2) Functional confusions (where the objects confused are functionally similar)

> "I decided to do some sunbathing in the afternoon, so I changed into my bikini and fetched my sunglasses and suntan lotion. I meant to leave the suntan lotion indoors as it tends to go funny when it gets hot, but when I got outside I found I'd left my sunglasses indoors and still had the lotion with me."
> "There were two objects before me on the draining board: a cloth and a container of cleaning fluid which I normally keep in the bathroom but had brought to the kitchen to use. I decided to return the cleaning fluid to its place in the bathroom, but set off with the cloth in my hand instead."

(3) Spatial confusions (where the objects confused are in close proximity)

> "I turned on my electric fire instead of my transistor radio which was on the floor near it."
> "I decided to fill a vase with flowers. I went to the drawer in the kitchen (where I keep the garden scissors) and took out a tin opener. Then I set off down the garden with it."

(4) Temporal confusions (where time is misperceived and inappropriate actions initiated)

> "When I got up on Monday morning, I found myself putting on Sunday's sweater and jeans instead of my working clothes."
> "I woke up, got dressed, but when I reached the bedroom door I realized it was my morning off and I could have stayed in bed."

2.1.2 *Program assembly failures (5%)*

Where the errors seem to result from the transposition of program elements, either within the same program, or between two currently active programs, or between an ongoing program and one in store.

(1) Behavioural spoonerisms (where program elements are reversed)

"I unwrapped a sweet, put the paper in my mouth and threw the sweet into the waste bucket."

"I put the butter on the draining board and two dirty plates in the fridge, instead of the other way round."

"When I leave for work in the morning I am in the habit of throwing two dog biscuits to my pet corgi and then putting on my earrings at the hall mirror. One morning I threw the earrings to the dog and found myself trying to attach a dog biscuit to my ear."

(2) Confusions between currently active programs

"My office phone rang. I picked up the receiver and bellowed 'Come in' at it."

"I intended to wash up after cooking a meal. I also wanted to put the ingredients back into the cupboard. I ended up by putting a tube of tomato paste in the washing-up bowl."

(3) Confusions between ongoing and stored program

"I intended to pick up a knife to cut the potatoes, but actually picked up the tea-towel. I wanted to cut the potatoes I had just peeled for boiling. Normally when I prepare chips, I dry the potatoes with a tea-towel before chipping them. Today I was doing boiled mashed potatoes."

"I fetched a box of matches to light the electric fire."

"I was at a party looking after my friend's cigarettes in my shoulder bag. She asked me to get out a cigarette for her, but instead I got out my purse, opened it up and offered it to her."

"We now have two fridges in our kitchen and yesterday we moved our food from one to the other. This morning I repeatedly opened the fridge that used to have our food in."

2.1.3 *Test failures (20%)*

Where the errors stem primarily from a failure to verify the progress of an action sequence at key "checkpoints". The result is that the actions proceed toward a goal other than that specified by the current program.

(1) Stop-rule overshoots (where the actions proceed beyond their intended end-point)

"I went up to my bedroom to change into something comfortable for the evening. I stood beside my bed and started to take off my jacket and tie. The next thing I knew I was getting into my pyjama trousers." (c.f. James, 1890).

"I brought the milk in from the front step to make myself a cup of tea. I had put the cup out previously. But instead of putting the milk into the cup, I put the bottle in the fridge."

(2) Stop-rule undershoots (where the actions are terminated prior to their intended end-point)

> "I was just about to step into the bath when I discovered that I still had my underclothes on."

(3) Branching errors (where an initial sequence of actions is common to two different outcomes, and the wrong 'route' is taken)

> "I meant to get my car out, but as I passed through the back porch on my way to the garage I stopped to put on my wellington boots and gardening jacket as if to work in the garden."
>
> "I intended to drive to Place X, but then I 'woke up' to find that I was on the road to Place Y."

(4) Multiple side-tracking (where the actor is seemingly diverted from his original intention by a series of minor side-steps)

> "I meant to go from the kitchen to the larder to get potatoes and carrots. I started toward the larder but then veered off into the living room and began talking to my husband about our holidays. Then I looked at the calendar to consider holiday dates, glanced at an atlas, and then wandered back to the kitchen where the larder door reminded me of my original intention."
>
> "I went upstairs to sort out and fetch down the dirty washing. I came down without the washing having tidied the bathroom instead. I went upstairs again to collect the washing, but somehow got side-tracked into cleaning the bathroom. I forgot all about the washing until I returned to the kitchen where the washing machine was pulled out in readiness."

2.1.4 *Sub-routine failures (18 %)*

Where the errors occur at the level of the component actions within a sub-routine.

(1) Insertions (where unwanted actions are added to a sequence)

> "I came out of the sitting room in the daytime and flicked on the light as I left the room."
>
> "I sat down to do some work and before starting to write I put my hand up to my face to take my glasses off, but my fingers snapped together rather abruptly because I hadn't been wearing them in the first place."

(2) Omissions (where necessary actions are left out of the sequence)

> "I filled my electric kettle with water, plugged the lead into the back of the kettle and switched on the wall socket. When the kettle failed to boil I discovered I had not inserted the plug into the wall socket."
>
> "The kettle was just about to boil when I noticed the tea caddy was empty. I fetched a fresh pack of tea from the cupboard and refilled the

caddy. Then I poured the water into the teapot and only when I came to pour it into the cup did I realise that I had omitted to put any tea into the pot."

"I picked up my coat to go out when the phone rang. I answered it and then went out of the front door without my coat."

(3) Misordering (where the correct actions are carried out but in the wrong order)

"Sitting in the car about to leave work, I realised I had put the car into gear and released the handbrake without first starting the engine."

"While running water into a bucket from the kitchen tap, I put the lid back on the bucket before turning off the tap."

2.1.5 *Storage failures (40 %)*

These are characterized by the forgetting or misrecalling of plans and actions.

(1) Forgetting previous actions (where preceding actions are forgotten or misrecalled. This can result in losing one's place in an action sequence, or in the mislaying of previously used items)

"I started to pour a second kettle of boiling water into a teapot full of freshly made tea. I had no recollection of having just made it."

"As I was leaving the bathroom this morning, it suddenly struck me that I couldn't remember whether or not I had shaved. I had to feel my chin to establish that I had."

"I started to walk home and had covered most of the distance when I remembered I had set out by car."

"I was spooning tea into the pot when I realised that I couldn't remember how many teaspoonfuls I had already put in."

"I put a cigarette in my mouth, got my matches out, then instead of lighting the cigarette I took another one out of the packet."

"My boyfriend asked for a cigarette. I took two out of the packet, put them both in my mouth intending to light them together. Then I struck a match and held it out to him, forgetting that I had both cigarettes in my mouth."

(2) Forgetting discrete items in the plan.

"Buying groceries for the weekend, I forgot to buy some orange squash, although I had noticed in the morning that we needed some."

"I had intended to post a letter while I was out shopping but when I got home I found I still had the letter in my pocket."

"I walked down the garden to put some rubbish in the dustbin. I intended to bring in the washing from the line on my way back, but I walked right past it and came back to the house empty-handed."

(3) Reverting to earlier plans

"I was making shortbread and intended to double the amounts shown in the recipe. I could not understand why the mixture seemed so soft, but blamed it on the hot weather. It was only when I looked in the oven and saw it melting that I realised I had doubled the first ingredient—butter—but had forgotten to double everything else."

"I decided to make some pancakes for tea. Then I remembered we didn't have any lemons so I decided not to bother. Five minutes later I started getting together the ingredients for pancakes, having completely forgotten my change of mind."

(4) Forgetting the substance of the plan

"I queued up to get a train ticket, but by the time I reached the window I had forgotten which station it was I wanted. My mind had gone a complete blank."

"I went upstairs to the bedroom, but when I got there I couldn't remember what I came for."

3 Explanatory Notions

An explanation of these "actions not as planned" must address itself to two questions. Under what circumstances do they occur? And, given an adequate knowledge of these circumstances, can we predict the form that the error will take? The next section presents three notions—mode of control, critical decision points and "strength" of the motor program—which together form the basis of the hypotheses given later to account for particular kinds of error.

3.1 Modes of Control

A plausible explanation for the reduced demand upon the skilled as opposed to the unskilled performer is that motor learning is accompanied by a gradual shift from a predominantly "closed-loop" (CL) or feedback mode of control to a predominantly "open-loop" (OL) or feedforward mode (Keele, 1973, Keele and Summers, 1976, Kelso and Stelmach, 1976). In the former, control resides primarily in the limited capacity central processor and relies heavily upon visual and proprioceptive feedback, and hence conscious attention, for the moment to moment control of motor output. In the OL mode, motor output is governed by "motor programs" or pre-arranged instruction sequences, that run off independently of feedback information, thus leaving the central processor free to concentrate upon future aspects of the task, or indeed to devote itself to matters quite unrelated to the current activity. One of the basic assumptions relating to the arguments that follow is that when control is delegated to some subordinate motor program, as in the OL mode, the central processor *will* engage in some activity that is *not immediately* related to the ongoing motor behaviour. For convenience of exposition, the object of central processor attention during OL control will be termed "parallel mental activity (PMA)".

It is clear that neither mode of control can be mutually exclusive of the other. Elements of both are likely to be present at all phases of motor learning. Even in the very early stages of skill acquisition, the novice will have within his response repertoire some preformed motor programs that are relevant and necessary for the task he seeks to master. And at the end of the training period, the highly skilled operator will still need to resort to the CL mode of control to cope with critical decision points and with unexpected occurrences. The essential point to be made here, therefore, is that skilled performance involves continual switching between the CL and OL control modes.

3.2 Critical Decision Points

It is proposed that during the execution of any sequence of planned actions, no matter how familiar or well-practised they may be, there are critical decision points in which the CL mode of control is necessary to ensure the intended outcome. The matter is neither as simple nor as obvious as it might first appear since there are clearly moments during the performance of a well-practised task when close attention to the component actions, far from being essential, has a profoundly disruptive effect. As Freud (1922) remarked, ". . . many acts are most successfully carried out when they are not the objects of particularly concentrated attention, and that mistakes may occur just on (those) occasions when one is most eager to be accurate . . ." (p.23). In view of the adverse consequences of an untimely switch from the OL to the CL control mode, the question of when such a switch is necessary becomes central to our understanding of skilled performance.

Some of the errors described earlier seem to provide a clue as to the spatio-temporal location of these critical decision points. For example, in the case of the man who started to put on his gardening clothes when he intended to take his car out of the garage, it seems reasonable to assume that the kitchen porch, a place that gave access to both the garden and the garage, constituted a critical decision point which, on this occasion, was evidently missed.

On the basis of this and similar mistakes, let us hypothesize that critical decision points occur when actions or situations are common to two or more motor programmes. In other words, they are associated with branch points in the instructional sequence beyond which the actions governed can proceed to different outcomes. Other factors such as the level of skill attained and the predictability of the environment will also influence the frequency with which these attentional switches need to occur. For the moment, however, let us simply assume that such critical checkpoints exist, and that they occur as relatively high level "if-statements" within the hierarchy of motor program organization.

3.3 "Strength" of the Motor Program

One of the most consistent findings of the diary study was that when actions deviate from current intentions they tend not to take the form of isolated and novel fragments of behaviour, but of well-practised and functionally intact behavioural sequences. Indeed, these "slips of action" quite often proceed with such coherence that the deviation from the current plan can remain undetected for quite some time. The form of these errors, therefore, would seem to provide strong evidence for the existence of motor programs that operate independently of centrally processed feedback information (Pew, 1974, Schmidt, 1976).

It seems that motor programs can acquire the "strength" to wrest control from the executive program at certain critical points in the plan. Like the Sirens' call, some motor programs possess the power to lure us into unwitting action, particularly when the central processor is occupied with some parallel mental activity. This power to divert action from intention seems to be derived in part from how often and how recently the motor program is activated. The more frequently (and recently) a particular sequence of movements is set in train and achieves its desired outcome, the more likely it is to recur uninvited as a "slip of action".

Suggestions such as these are clearly reminiscent of the Hullian concept of "habit strength" (Hull, 1952). In Hull's theory, habit strength $(_sH_R)$ reflects the degree of association between the component elements which grows with the number of reinforced repetitions of that response. Although these "habits" are firmly rooted in the S–R tradition while motor programs belong more properly to the TOTE counter-reformation (Miller *et al.*, 1960), both are more readily translated into action the more frequently (and recently) they are used. In its simplest form, Hull expressed the relationship between habit strength and reaction potential $(_sE_R)$, the strength of the tendency to respond, as follows:

$$_sE_R = D \times {_sH_R}$$

where D is drive, "a nonspecific state . . . of the nervous system to which all specific needs contribute" (Spence, 1951). The role of drive in human affairs is clearly more complex than this, but it seems highly probable, as Lashley (1951) suggested, that motivational factors can "prime" particular motor programs to render them more likely to gain control of action. We will return to this possibility when we come to speculate about the mechanics of the "Freudian slip". For the present, it is sufficient to postulate that the likelihood of a motor program being activated, and against the dictates of the current plan, will increase with the frequency and recency of its previously successful employment.

4 Some Hypotheses

4.1 Test failures

An examination of the erroneous actions that occur when activity proceeds beyond its intended end-point (stop-rule overshoots), or takes the wrong "turn" (branching errors), serves to reaffirm that we are indeed "creatures of habit". Such errors are almost invariably drawn from the individual's own repertoire of highly skilled or habitual action sequences, and reveal the existence of a systematic bias toward the activation of long-established motor programs. Furthermore, the erroneous action sequence usually possesses elements in common with the intended one, be it particular movements, objects or spatio-temporal locations.

These general observations suggest that the underlying motor programs interconnect with one another at nodal points representing elements common to different outcomes. In considering the possible mechanics of these errors, it is difficult to escape the image of a railway system, albeit a rather curious one. Let us imagine that the progress of the train along the track relates to running off a sequence of actions where each position of the train corresponds to a particular movement of the human actor. The tracks themselves are analogous to motor programs. The peculiar feature of this metaphorical railway system is the semi-automatic way in which the train's route is controlled. As in a conventional system, the points are preset by means external to the train; but in this case they are adjusted so that they always direct the train toward the most frequently and recently travelled route associated with that particular juncture. Also contrary to normal railway practice is the fact that the driver (equivalent to the closed-loop mode of control) has within his cab the means to over-ride the automatic settings so that, provided he exercises this direct control at the right time, he can take whatever route he chooses. But if he fails to take positive action, the train will be directed automatically along the most "popular" route. Furthermore, if none of the existing routes are satisfactory, the driver also has the unusual capability of laying down new tracks. This is normally accomplished by relocating existing lengths of track along the desired route, but in exceptional circumstances it can even be achieved by forging and laying entirely new sets of rails. But such resources are limited and the preliminary surveys are often inadequately carried out, so that progress by this means is always slow and more often than not needs further adjustment before a suitable route is found.

Translating this metaphor back into psychological terms, we can attempt to make specific predictions as to when a test failure will occur and what form it will take. In answer to the "when?" question, it is hypothesized that *test failures will occur when the open-loop mode of control coincides with a critical decision point where the strengths of the motor programs beyond that point are markedly different.* It is also predicted that when an error does occur, *it will involve the unintended activation of the strongest motor program beyond the node.*

4.2 Discrimination Failures

In addition to the precise nature of the confusion—perceptual, functional, spatial or temporal—discrimination failures also differ with respect to their immediate consequences. On some occasions, the misclassified item is merely incorporated erroneously into an otherwise intended action sequence; but in other instances the misclassification appears to be instrumental in causing the subsequent behaviour to switch to a wholly unintended path. Two examples will help to make this distinction clearer.

In its simplest form, discrimination failure involves the confusion of two similar items, as in the case of the man who squeezed shaving cream instead of toothpaste on to his toothbrush. Here it seems likely that the error was due to the interaction of two factors. First, that the tubes of toothpaste and shaving cream were superficially alike in appearance and, in this instance, located in close proximity to one another. And, second, that the OL mode was predominant during the "strong" tooth-brushing program. Although such misclassifications are unlikely to be the exclusive province of the OL mode, it is probable that one of the penalties we pay for being able to run off preformed action sequences in a largely automatic fashion is that the *discriminative criteria or "templates" for anticipated inputs become degraded so that they are likely to accept crude approximations to the desired stimulus configuration, particularly when the two items are close together.*

In the example cited above, the shaving cream was wrongly incorporated into the tooth-brushing routine, but until the perpetrator of this error started foaming at the mouth, it did not substantially alter the course of the subsequent actions. Sometimes, however, a discrimination failure appears to trigger the "strong" motor program normally associated with the mis-selected input so that later actions deviate radically from intention. This occurred in the case of the girl with two mirrors on her dressing table, one used for brushing her hair and the other for inserting and removing her contact lenses. On the occasion in question, she intended to brush her hair, but looked into the "wrong" mirror and removed her contact lenses instead. In many respects, this type of error is akin to the test failures discussed previously where an initially common sequence of actions—approaching the dressing table and sitting down in front of it—can lead to two different outcomes, and where the route leading to the unintended outcome is selected. It also illustrates a feature of "strong" motor programs that is explicit in the original "Hullian" formulation, namely that they are readily transformed into action.

If, instead of removing her contact lenses, the girl had used the "wrong" mirror to brush her hair, this example would have been indistinguishable from the earlier case in which shaving cream was substituted for toothpaste. The important difference lies in the immediate consequences of the error and requires the formulation of an additional hypothesis: *when the erroneous item is associated with a "strong" motor program, then subsequent actions will be dictated by that program so long as the OL mode of control is maintained.*

4.3 Forgetting Previous Actions

When focal attention is engaged with some parallel mental activity, and the practised task in hand is being run off in a predominantly OL mode, it seems highly probable that only a very short-lived record of the immediately preceding actions is retained in the memory store. As William James (1890) put it: ". . . an object once attended to will remain in memory, whereas one inattentively allowed to pass will leave no traces", and subsequent research (Underwood, 1976) has caused us to modify this statement only slightly to indicate that the unattended input is preserved for a brief period in some pre-storage buffer. An enduring record of the reafference generated by these pre-programmed motor acts would, in any case, have little or no functional value so long as they proceed as intended.

While actions remain under OL control, all that is required to maintain the intended sequence is some mechanism akin to a program counter that checks off the actions as they are executed. Errors can occur, however, when for some reason control reverts to the CL mode and focal attention is directed at the ongoing activity. On most occasions, the point reached within the sequence is immediately obvious from visual inspection. But this assessment of the current position can be incorrect as in the case of the diarist who found himself pouring a second kettle of boiling water into a teapot already full. At other times, the switch from the OL to CL mode may occur during a critical "counting" phase of the sequence. Such a thing happened to me whilst making tea. I "woke up" to find myself spooning tea into the pot with no recollection of how many teaspoonfuls I had already put in. Since a visual check of the inside of the teapot was of little help, the only information available was that provided by the faint kinaesthetic "echo" of my immediately preceding actions. In other words, the only check that seemed in any way reliable was to ask myself "how many teaspoonfuls do I *feel* that I have put in?"

4.4 Omissions

A number of observations recorded by the diarists suggest a possible explanation for the occurrence of certain errors involving the omission of necessary steps from a planned sequence of actions. The observations in question appear to have at least two features in common. First, the omissions occur during the execution of a "strong" motor program under predominantly OL control. Second, they follow immediately upon the resumption of the program after a brief interruption to deal with an unexpected event. Yet another personal tea-making example will serve to illustrate these "interruption-contingent" omissions.

Having filled the kettle and set it to boil, I automatically reached for the tea-caddy to spoon tea into the pot. Then I became aware that the caddy was empty, so I retrieved a fresh packet of tea from the cupboard, and emptied it into the caddy. But instead of resuming the tea-making sequence at the correct point, I shut the lid of the caddy and poured the now boiling water into an empty teapot.

These and similar sequences of events raise the possibility that *the program counter*, alluded to earlier, *is, on occasions, unable to distinguish between planned events and unexpected ones that occupy approximately the same time-period and involve a comparable degree of activity during the running of a largely automated series of actions.* Consequently, when the interruption is dealt with, the program resumes not at the next action in the sequence, but at one or two actions further on. Given that some kind of program counter is implicit in the notion of a motor program, the idea is not altogether implausible though difficult to test empirically.

Keele and Summers (1976) carried out an ingenious series of studies that bears tangentially on the present discussion. They were concerned with the question of how the motor program is stored centrally. Are the movement instructions linked to one another by a chain of associations or are they associated with their expected position in the sequence? The hypothesis outlined earlier would presume the latter rather than the former mode of association.

To investigate these possibilities they measured how quickly and accurately subjects dealt with the first event back in sequence after an unexpected interruption. The task involved responding sequentially to an array of lights with the corresponding keys. Where the sequence was unstructured except for the linear ordering of events, the findings indicated that the central representation of the motor program is likely to be a chain of associations. But sequences that possess some inherent structure appear to be stored as hierarchical structures or movement generating rules. In everyday skills, both forms are likely to exist. When more complex organizations are not available, the motor program is likely to be sequentially associated on event-to-event basis; but where there is some form of repetition or patterning present in the sequence, its running off is likely to be governed by rules rather than by associative chaining.

5 Wider Implications

Error and correct performance are two sides of the same coin, and an adequate theory of the former necessarily entails a more complete understanding of the latter than we currently possess. It would seem inappropriate at our present state of knowledge to strive too earnestly for an all-embracing theory of "actions-not-as-planned", assuming that such a goal was feasible or even desirable. For the moment, at least, we must acknowledge that the apparent diversity of these errors and the wide range of psychological processes implicated in their production force us to resort to an untidy patchwork of hypotheses of the kind presented in the foregoing section. Nevertheless, the formidable variety of potential error-inducing mechanisms should not deter us from pursuing the encouraging consistencies revealed by the present investigation in both the conditions that promote these errors and the nature of the erroneous actions themselves. These consistencies are summarized below.

(1) The "slips of action" considered here seem to have occurred almost exclusively during the largely automatic execution of highly practised

and "routinized" activities. In other words, these lapses are characteristic of skilled rather than unskilled activity. This is an interesting
departure from the normal expectation that errors decrease with the
acquisition of skill. The probability of these particular lapses occurring
appears to increase as the individual's actions come more and more
under the OL mode of control.

(2) A large proportion of these slips appear to have resulted from the
misdirection of focal attention, either by maintaining an unsuitable
control mode or by making an untimely switch. Most commonly, these
were apparently due to a failure to select the CL mode at a critical
branch point in the running of the motor program. But the suggestion
was also made that "place-losing" errors could be triggered by an
inappropriate shift from OL to CL control during the execution of a
"strong" motor program. Related to this, of course, is the disruption of
automatized activity that is produced by over-attention to the details of
the task, presumably because the sub-routines thus closely observed
come to claim more than their customary share of the central processor's limited capacity. In view of the potential that exists for both forms
of attentional misdirection in complex skilled performance, it is
remarkable not so much that we make these errors but that we make
them so comparatively seldom.

(3) Far from exhibiting novelty, these departures from intended action
usually took the form of some frequently and recently performed
behavioural sequence. Not only are these slips of action a feature of
well-practised activities, they are themselves coherent and familiar
segments of skilled or habitual behaviour, albeit unsuited for the task in
hand. Like the slips of the tongue, therefore, they give every indication
of being systematic rather than random in origin.

Taking this last point further, it seems highly probable that a large
proportion of these slips can be ascribed to the operation of a well-
established bias in verbal and motor performance that has been
described variously as the appearance of "inert stereotypes" (Luria,
1973). "strong associate substitution" (Chapman and Chapman,
1973), or "banalization" (Timpanaro, 1976). A response bias has been
defined by Underwood (1952) as a pre-disposition to select one of a
number of possible responses that might be made in a given situation,
and the essential feature of this particular bias is the replacement of a
correct or intended response by a more familiar associate. It would thus
seem relevant at this juncture to consider what is known of the circumstances that promote this tendency, and of the conditions under which
it is unusually accentuated.

Luria (1973) described the disturbances of planning and the inadequate maintenance of intention that result from massive lesions of the

frontal lobes. For example: "One such patient . . . when asked to light a candle, struck a match correctly but instead of putting it to the candle which he held in his hand, he put the candle in his mouth and started to "smoke" it like a cigarette. The new and relatively unstabilized action was thus replaced by the more firmly established inert stereotype. I have observed such disturbances of a complex action program and its replacement by elementary, basic behaviour in many patients with a clearly defined 'frontal syndrome'" (Luria, 1973, 199–200). With such extensive damage, it is difficult to isolate any one cognitive factor as being responsible for the unwanted intrusion of these "inert stereotypes" or "strong" motor programs; but the problem seems to lie mainly in the inability of the damaged frontal lobes to formulate or sustain an organized plan of action. The goal-directed linkages between one sub-routine and the next seem to be weakened, or perhaps never established, so that the course of action is readily diverted along well-trodden, associated paths. It is possible that such a condition may be approached in everyday life when our plan of action is ill-defined, or when we struggle toward a remote or unappealing goal. When we have no clear idea of what we intend to do next, or when the next step is too difficult or unpleasant, we are likely to "free-wheel" along these familiar paths of action.

Also working in a clinical context, but this time with schizophrenics, Chapman and Chapman (1973) have suggested that many of their apparently bizarre utterances reflect an excessive yielding to normal biases, and in particular to the tendency to substitute strong associates for appropriate responses. As an illustration they cite the case of a patient who, when asked to describe the members of her family, began by listing "father, son," but then concluded with, ". . . and the Holy Ghost". And indeed there is an impressive body of experimental evidence to support this idea (Chapman and Chapman, 1973, 119–136). These authors have also demonstrated that such tendencies are present to a lesser degree among normal controls, and show up most clearly when the subject is given insufficient information to make a correct response selection, or when the task is too difficult. For example, normal subjects were found to choose associative alternatives on multiple-choice vocabulary items when they did not know the correct answer (Boland and Chapman, 1971, Willner, 1965).

Of particular interest to the present discussion were the various attentional deficiencies offered as possible explanations for this accentuated response bias in schizophrenia. These included Jung's (1906) proposal that schizophrenics suffer "diminished" or "relaxed" attention which leads them to produce familiar rather than appropriate associates. Similarly. Broen and Storms (1966) and Venables (1964) have argued that schizophrenics are characterized by narrowed attention, which in turn may be due to heightened drive (Easterbrook, 1959). There is clearly a close correspondence between these ideas and the notion of attentional misdirection advanced here to account for slips of action. In this case, however, the misdirections are transitory and relatively infrequent. The performance of a highly practised and largely automatized job liberates the central processor from moment-to-moment control; but since, like Nature, focal attention abhors a vacuum it tends to be "captured" by some pressing but parallel mental activity so that, on occasion, it fails to switch back to the task in hand at a "critical decision point" and thus permits the guidance of action to fall by default under the control of "strong" motor programs.

Most of the slips of action netted in the diary study occurred during the routine domestic undertakings of daily life, and the diarists' comments suggest that, in these familiar and largely predictable surroundings, the "capture" of the closed-loop mode is usually achieved by preoccupation with some engaging line of thought or future planning. But in more demanding situations, such as piloting an aircraft, the same result may be achieved by the onset of an emergency or the need to make an unusual manoeuvre; circumstances that demand close attention while still maintaining control of the aircraft. A recent examination of British civil aircraft accidents (Reason, 1976) revealed a number of instances of pilot error that closely resembled absent-minded behaviour in that they involved slips of action rather than errors of judgement. It is interesting to note that a significant proportion of these errors were committed while the crew were dealing with genuine emergencies such as the failure of one engine (in multi-engined aircraft), or when the same asymmetric condition was deliberately induced during a training exercise. By themselves, these events were not sufficient to precipitate the ensuing crashes, the critical factor would appear to have been the degree to which they "captured" the attention of the pilots thus creating the conditions necessary for the erroneous response substitution to take place. For example, in two separate accidents involving twin-engined Dove aircraft, a fault developed in one engine, but instead of shutting down the ailing engine, both pilots switched off the healthy one by mistake, an action that resulted in total power failure. A year later, in 1956, a Viscount aircraft crashed shortly after take-off from Blackbushe Airport. In the opinion of the investigators, this accident was due to an error by the Training Captain who operated No. 3 high pressure cock lever instead of No. 4 when simulating a failure of No. 4 engine during take-off. In 1963, a Varsity aircraft crashed while practising asymmetric (single-engine) approaches and overshoots, the likely cause being the selection of starboard engine "idle-cutoff" switch to "cut-off" instead of the port engine's switch to "run" when attempting to re-start port engine. In another training flight, this time involving a Piper Apache aircraft in 1967, the port engine failed to respond when overshooting from a simulated single-engine approach. The probable cause: the instructor omitted to return the mixture control lever of the port engine to "full-rich-on" when the propeller was unfeathered during the approach. Although we can only speculate about the precise causes, accidents such as these lend some credence to the notion of attentional "capture" leading to an inappropriate and possibly strongly associated response being made. And if the present line of investigation has any practical value, it is to highlight the ease with which this response substitution can occur and to specify more precisely the circumstances under which such errors are made.

Although the concept of drive was touched upon briefly in an earlier reference to Hullian formulation of habit strength, we have so far taken no account of the role played by motivation and arousal in the production of slips of action. The present data do not permit any direct assessment of these factors, and whatever speculative inferences we can make conform with the expectation that these errors may be associated with both low and high states of arousal (Kahneman, 1973). Thus, it has been suggested that essentially similar error mechanisms are at work in the relative calm of familiar domestic settings and also in the far from tranquil conditions present on the flight deck of an aircraft during a real or simulated state of emergency. There is, however, another tentative line of theorizing we could follow that takes us away from our primary concern with slips of action and back to Freud's original analysis of slips of the tongue.

Timpanaro (1976) subjected the "slips of the tongue" cited by Freud in "The Psychopathology of Everyday Life" to the analytical devices of the textual critic, and concluded that they can often be more simply if less ingeniously explained by the process of banalization. That is, the tendency to substitute one word for another whose meaning is more familiar, or to change the form of a quotation so that irregularities in the syntactic structure are minimized. As indicated earlier, this process is clearly similar to that of "strong associate substitution", and would fit closely with the thesis presented here. But there is another way of regarding "Freudian slips" that would still conform with this general thesis, yet would also acknowledge the value of Freud's insight that we occasionally say the very words we seek to avoid.

Basic to Freud's thinking concerning the origin of verbal mistakes was the assertion that "a suppression of a previous intention to say something is the indispensable condition for the occurrence of a slip of the tongue" (Freud, 1922, p. 52). How can we accommodate this principle within the present theoretical framework? Consider the following story. A dinner guest is expected who has a nose of Cyrano-like proportions. The host, anxious not to cause him hurt, briefs himself to avoid any reference to noses in the conversation, to avoid staring at his guest's nose, and, in fact, to steer the course of the evening as far as possible from any consideration of noses whatsoever. Yet when the guest arrives and they sit down to dinner, the host, intending to ask for the salt, leans toward his guest and asks "Pass the nose, please."

Two possible explanations for this gaffe suggest themselves, the one involving drive and the other "strength". The first is that the host's concern to suppress any mention of noses served to invest this otherwise emotionally neutral sub-routine with additional drive, thus increasing its probability of being uttered. In other words, it is proposed that emotional factors can exert a "priming effect" upon particular verbal sub-routines, a view not unlike Freud's own. The second possibility is that the host's repeated resolutions to censor the "nose sub-routine" brought about an increase in its "strength". By seeking to suppress a particular word, it is argued, we can achieve the same effect as if we had actually practised uttering it. What matters for "strength" is not the context, nor the mode of rehearsal, but the number of times the particular verbal sub-routine was activated, and how recently that activation occurred.

These suggestions should not be interpreted as an attempt to replace the Freudian explanation of these slips of the tongue with what many would regard as an equally moribund Hullian account. Rather, they were offered to indicate, if only very sketchily, how the computer metaphor employed here could be extended to encompass certain forms of "motivated error". Without this facility, a largely mechanistic theory of these slips and lapses would clearly be inadequate.

Let me conclude with a brief comment on the method of investigation described in this chapter. Natural history observations of this kind, for all their obvious limitations, would appear to provide a valuable adjunct to carefully controlled laboratory studies that, of necessity, can only deal with isolated aspects of cognition under artificial conditions. In the accounts of "actions-not-as-planned" presented here, we can catch recognizable glimpses of real people going about the routine tasks of everyday life. It has been argued that these glimpses provide valuable insights into the underlying organizations of skilled behaviour, but perhaps more importantly they help to bridge the formidable gap that still exists in contemporary psychology between cognitive theorizing and our subjective experience of daily life. The sustained empirical attack of the past two decades upon such problems as attention,

memory and motor control is beginning to yield the bare conceptual
bones. It is hoped that natural history studies of this kind, and others
like it (Morton and Byrne, 1975, Broadbent, 1977), will help to give
them flesh.

6 References

Boland, T. B. and Chapman, L. J. (1971). Conflicting predictions from
    Broen's and Chapman's theories of schizophrenic thought disorder.
    Journal of Abnormal Psychology **78**, 52–58.
Broadbent, D. E. (1977). Levels, hierarchies and the locus of control. *Quarterly
    Journal of Experimental Psychology* **29**, 181–201.
Broen, Jr, W. E. and Storms, L. H. (1966). Lawful disorganization: the
    process underlying a schizophrenic syndrome. *Psychological Review* **73**,
    265–279.
Chapman, L. B. and Chapman, J. P. (1973). "Disordered Thought in
    Schizophrenia." Prentice-Hall, Englewood Cliffs, New Jersey.
Cherns, A. B. (1962). *In* "Society: Problems and Methods of Study" (Eds A.
    T. Welford *et al.*). Routledge and Kegan Paul, London.
Easterbrook, J. A. (1959). The effect of emotion on cue utilization and the
    organization of behaviour. *Psychological Review* **66**, 183–200.
Freud, S. (1901). "The Psychopathology of Everyday Life." Penguin, Har-
    mondsworth.
Freud, S. (1922). "Introductory Lectures on Psychoanalysis." George Allen
    and Unwin, London.
Fromkin; V. A. (1973). "Speech Errors as Linguistic Evidence." Mouton, The
    Hague.
Hull, C. L. (1952). "A Behaviour System: An Introduction to Behaviour
    Theory concerning the Individual Organism." Yale University Press,
    New Haven.
James, W. (1890). "The Principles of Psychology", Vol. 1. Dover, New York.
Jastrow, J. (1905). The lapses of consciousness. *The Popular Science Monthly* **67**,
    481–502.
Jung, C. G. (1936). The psychology of dementia praecox. *Nervous and Mental
    Diseases. Monograph Series No. 3.* (Originally published, 1906.)
Kay, H. (1971). Accidents: some facts and theories. *In* "Psychology at Work"
    (Ed. P. B. Warr). Penguin, Harmondsworth.
Kahneman, D. (1973). "Attention and Effort." Prentice-Hall, Englewood
    Cliffs, New Jersey.
Keele, S. W. (1973). "Attention and Human Performance." Goodyear, Pacific
    Palisades.
Keele, S. W. and Summers, J. J. (1976). The structure of motor programs. *In*
    "Motor Control: Issues and Trends" (Ed. G. E. Stelmach). Academic
    Press, New York.
Kelso, J. A. S. and Stelmach, G. E. (1976). Central and peripheral mechan-

isms in motor control. *In* "Motor Control: Issues and Trends" (Ed. G. E. Stelmach). Academic Press, New York.

Lashley, K. S. (1951). The problem of serial order in behaviour. *In* "Cerebral Mechanisms in Behaviour" (Ed. L. A. Jeffries). John Wiley, New York.

Luria, A. R. (1973). "The Working Brian." Penguin, Harmondsworth.

Mandler, G. (1975). "Mind and Emotion." John Wiley, New York.

Miller, G. A., Galanter, E. and Pribram, K. H. (1960). "Plans and the Structure of Behaviour." Holt, Rinehart and Winston, New York.

Morton, J. and Byrne, R. (1975). Organization in the kitchen. *In* "Attention and Performance" (Eds P. M. A. Rabbitt and S. Dornic), Vol. 5. Academic Press, London.

Pew, R. W. (1974). Human perceptual-motor performance. *In* "Human Information Processing" (Ed. B. H. Kantowitz). Erlbaum, Hillsdale, New Jersey.

Reason, J. T. (1976). Absent minds. *New Society*, 4 November.

Ryan, T. A. (1970). "Intentional Behaviour." Ronald, New York.

Schmidt, R. A. (1976). The schema as a solution to some persistent problems in motor learning theory. *In* "Motor Control: Issues and Trends" (Ed. G. E. Stelmach) Academic Press, New York.

Shaffer, L. H. (1976). Intention and performance. *Psychological Review* **83**, 375–393.

Shallice, T. (1972). Dual functions of consciousness. *Psychological Review* **79**, 383–393.

Spence, K. W. (1951). Theoretical interpretations of learning. *In* "Comparative Psychology" (3rd edn.) (Ed. C. P. Stone). Prentice-Hall, New York.

Suchman, E. A. (1961). A conceptual analysis of the accident. *In* "Accident Research: Methods and Approaches" (Eds W. Haddon, E. A. Suchman and D. Klein). Harper and Row, New York.

Timpanaro, S. (1976). "The Freudian Slip." NLB, London.

Underwood, B. J. (1952). An orientation for research on thinking. *Psychological Review* **59**, 209–220.

Underwood, G. (1976). "Attention and Memory." Pergamon, Oxford.

Venables, P. H. (1964). Performance and the level of activation in schizophrenics and normals. *British Journal of Psychology* **55**, 207–218.

Willner, A. (1965). Impairment of knowledge of unusual meanings of familiar words in brain damage and schizophrenia. *Journal of Abnormal Psychology* **70**, 405–411.

5 Memory Systems and Conscious Processes

G. UNDERWOOD

*Department of Psychology,
University of Nottingham*

1 Conscious and Unconscious Memories

Whatever else we may be able to say about our memories and their psychological investigation, we should start by saying that they are particularly well impregnated with the correlates of awareness. We are sometimes aware of a memory, and at other times unaware but capable of bringing it into awareness. It is this change of state of memories which is the subject of the present discussion, and the purpose of this chapter is to relate the psychological phenomena of memory to the experience of awareness— to insert this variable of awareness into the psychological description of memory performance. With the notable exception of William James, there have been few workers prepared to relate the introspective, experiential aspects of memory to the overt indicators of processing. Accordingly, much of this chapter will be speculative. The blind eye of behaviourism has denied the usefulness of looking at any aspect of behaviour as covert as consciousness, but the appearance of a cognitive psychology in recent years has demanded that we take account of all of the phenomena of "knowing ". A vital variable here is that we are sometimes aware of knowing at the same time as not being aware of *what* we know— we may be confident about our chances of retrieving a piece of information from memory without actually proceeding to retrieve it. When we do retrieve it, then it has changed its state from being an unconscious memory to being a conscious memory. It is this dichotomy which is the subject of the first section of the chapter.

The study of memory seems heavily burdened with dichotomies— short-term v. long-term memories (or working v. long-term memories), episodic v. semantic memories, immediate v. permanent memories and primary v. secondary memories. With what justification can an additional dichotomy, between conscious and unconscious memories, be established? An immediate objection to this new dichotomy (or more accurately, revised dichotomy) is that it is encompassed within existing distinctions. Whereas it is undoubtedly mentioned in earlier descriptions of memory, the points to be made here are firstly that the existing dichotomies fail to account satisfactorily for the phenomena of conscious and unconscious memories, and secondly that such dichotomies can all be subsumed under this one valid distinction. The present discussion will argue that the phenomena upon which other distinctions have been based are all aspects of this one universally held distinction between what we are currently aware of, and what we have been aware of in the past. This is, in effect, a homage to William James who, in his "Principles of Psychology" (1980), distinguished between primary memory and secondary memory but could have called them conscious and unconscious memory respectively. James's descriptive terms were resurrected by Waugh and Norman (1965) and a new interpretation applied to them. To distinguish between the Waugh and Norman view and the present view it is necessary to create new labels, and the most appropriate terms from the point of view of the phenomenology of memory are "conscious" and "unconscious" memory. In the following discussions there terms will be used to describe different states of activation of memories, and they are similar in meaning to the terms as orginally used by James.

According to James, the distinctions between primary memories and secondary memories derive from whether the item or object has just been perceived and is still the subject of conscious scrutiny, or whether it has passed from consciousness. The view of Waugh and Norman also depends upon primary memory as holding the current contents of consciousness, and secondary memory representing the store of events passed from consciousness. The essential difference between these two views is with the coding of information in the two systems. Whereas James does not distinguish between the categorical processing applied to primary and secondary memory events, Waugh and Norman refer to the predominantly acoustic nature of primary memory. It resembles, in short, the "Precategorical Acoustic Storage" of Crowder and Morton (1969), in which the physical properties are employed to retain information, and in which the semantic properties have not been appreciated. It should be added, however, that Waugh and Norman were not clear on the matter of the categorization of items held in primary memory and they may have intended to mean that the acoustic attribute was present *in addition* to the semantic attribute gained upon categorization.

Events stored in primary memory, for James, are events just *perceived*, that is, events just comprehended by conscious processing:

> An object which is recollected, in the proper sense of that term, is one which has been absent from consciousness altogether, and now revives anew. It is brought back, recalled, fished up, so to speak, from a reservoir in which, with countless other objects, it lay buried and lost from view. But an object of primary memory is not thus brought back; it was never lost; its date was never cut off in consciousness from that of the immediately present moment.
>
> (James, 1890, 646–647)

Whereas James is also not as explicit as he might have been in the matter of the level of coding of primary memory processes, he certainly makes no attempt to distinguish them from secondary memory processes except in the one quality of existence as part of the current contents of consciousness:

> Memory proper, or secondary memory as it might be styled, is the knowledge of a former state of mind after it has already dropped from consciousness; or rather *it is the knowledge of an event, or fact*, of which meantime we have not been thinking, *with the additional consciousness that we have thought or experienced it before.*
>
> (*op. cit.*, p. 648, original italics)

For Waugh and Norman, however, the contents of primary memory can be seen in the early readout of the final two or three items in the free recall of a series of words (i.e. the "recency" effect). This read-out is said to be based upon acoustic features, for primary memory . . . . .

> . . . as we have defined it here, is best illustrated by a person's ability to recall verbatim the most recent few words in a sentence that he is hearing or speaking, even when he is barely paying attention to what is being said, or to what he is saying . . . The most recent items in a verbal series reside temporarily in a kind of 'echo box', from which they can be effortlessly parroted back.
>
> (Waugh and Norman, 1965, 101–102)

Waugh and Norman go on to suggest that primary memory is probably not a peripheral sensory mechanism, and that the unit of storage in primary memory is verbal, but the extent of meaningful analysis of these verbal units seems to be decidedly impoverished. A more recent view suggested by Norman (personal communication, 1978) is that primary memory should not be identified with consciousness or awareness, and that a person is not necessarily continuously aware of items in primary memory. This is a considerable departure from the view of primary memory suggested by William James (although it is quite consistent with Waugh and Norman's view of the passive, unattended, entry of events into primary memory), and gives us all the more reason for keeping separate the two descriptions of memory. For James and for the present discussion the dichotomy is straightforward: primary memory stores the events currently in consciousness, those events of which the individual is aware. Secondary memory may store events once in consciousness, but of which the individual is no longer aware. To keep the distinctions reasonably clear the terms "conscious" and "unconscious" memories will be used here.

1.1 The Unitary Memory Trace

In accepting the distinction between memories of which we are aware, and those of which we are not, we can still accept the arguments of Melton (1963), Gruneberg (1970) and Wickelgren (1973, 1975) supporting the view of the unitary nature of the memory trace. This rejection of the notion of separate "short-term" memory stores requires brief explanations of how the dichotomy might be supported, and of how a unitary memory trace can exist in a state of conscious or unconscious memory.

Evidence in favour of two separate memory stores has suggested differences in the coding of information and in the forgetting processes. Evidence of capacity differences, differential serial position effects, differential amnesic effects and differential association effects can all be viewed as special cases of coding and forgetting differences, and the interaction of these differences. The "short-term" store has been said to retain information which is coded according to acoustic or phonemic characteristics, whereas semantic coding is said to correspond to storage in "long-term memory". Information is said to be lost from the "short-term" store through decay or through displacement, whereas the loss of items in "long-term memory" proceeds through interference, and these forgetting processes have different time-bases. Details of the empirical support for these suggestions, and of the consequent critical experiments, are reviewed by Baddeley (1976) and by Underwood (1976a), and will not be presented here.

The alternative to the dual-trace view suggests a single memory trace with a variety of attributes. These attributes are the components of the memory, and define it. The modality of input may be encoded as an attribute, the phonemic recoding applied during input may also be encoded, the semantic associations generated by strategical processing and by structural features of the network will also be encoded, as will any visual images, and any episodic associates dependent upon the general context of encoding. The memory trace is the composite of any of these attributes which the individual chooses to use or which are an unavoidable part of the encoding situation. Different attributes will be observable during recall depending upon the strategy of input processing and the context of retrieval. Now, each of these attributes will have different coding characteristics (acoustic, phonemic, semantic, etc.), and the codes will have different forgetting characteristics (decay of acoustic characteristics, interference between similar semantic characteristics). There is nothing in this description to imply that the development of different attributes is restricted by the time in storage except in so much as the different forgetting functions may reduce the ability to retrieve an item on the basis of its acoustic features after the onset of decay. To postpone decay we can attend to or rehearse items, but this in itself restricts the number of items maintained, and hence the appearance of capacity limits, and of displacement processes. If an individual is unable to use a modality of encoding then *specific* amnesic effects will be observed. If an individual is aware of the transient state of the acoustic and phonemic attributes, and uses these attributes early in his recall of a list of items, then a recency effect will appear in the serial position curve for recall. The combination of attributes with different properties can be applied to the effects which have been used to support the dual-trace theory of memory. If an attribute can be viewed as a memory in its own right, then the present proposal is for a memory system with very many traces, but this is unnecessary. The trace *is* the composite of its attributes in this description, and that is sufficient to account for the available data. Instances which contradict the dual-trace view are abundant, and range from the demonstration of acoustic attributes in recall from "long-term memory", to the presence of semantic attributes in "short-term memory", and of forgetting by interference in "short-term memory".

1.2 Levels of Processing and the Dynamics of Memory

Craik and Lockhart (1972) suggested that we may look at a memory in terms of the *level of processing* to which it has been exposed. A shallow level of processing would be the maintenance of the phonemic attributes by repetitive rehearsal, whereas a deep level of processing would be the development of the meaning of a word by the elaboration of its associations with other words in memory. The depth of encoding of words upon presentation was indicated in a set of experiments reported by Craik and Tulving (1975). In these experiments their subjects were asked a variety of questions of individual words displayed tachistoscopically. The questions dictated the level of processing required and ranged from structural ("is the word in capital letters?") and detection ("is there a word present?") to categorical ("is the word a type of fish?") and linguistic/contextual ("would the word fit in the following sentence?"). Questions produced slower answers as their depth of processing increased, and an unexpected recognition test at the end of the experiment indicated that words processed to a deeper level were also remembered better. Furthermore, this effect is not one of *longer* perceptual processing leading to a more resilient memory, for in one of Craik and Tulving's experiments difficult structural questions produced longer processing times, and poorer recognition scores than linguistic/contextual questions. Clearly, it is not the length of time occupied by the processing of a word which dictates its probability of recall, but the *type* of processing. The more a word is integrated with established memories, the more likely it is to be remembered.

This view of memory as a stage of processing, with a variety of processes available for application to the input, is totally compatible with the notion of attributes of memory being developed over time. The development and use of an attribute may indicate that a particular process has been applied to a word, and the extent of the interactions of this attribute with other attributes may indicate what Craik and Lockhart refer to as the level of processing. A memory attribute which relates well to other attributes of the same memory, and to other attributes of other memories will necessarily be processed "deeply". The level of processing applied to a simulus will dictate where attributes are developed, for it would be difficult to integrate with other words a word which has been processed structurally.

1.3 Consciousness and States of the Unitary Memory Trace

It is arguable that the only justifiable dichotomy in the description of the human memory system is that of the state of awareness given to the memory trace. We are sometimes aware of a memory, and sometimes unaware, but the issue is not even as straightforward as this, for on some occasions we may be unable to retrieve a memory and yet have a "feeling of knowing" about it. William James, of course, documented the "tip-of-the-tongue" phenomenon, and Brown and McNeill (1966) were able to produce empirical evidence of the existence of an effect in which we are unable to recall a word but can provide information above its acoustic attributes. Similarly, experiments by Hart (1965) and Gruneberg and Monks (1974) have demonstrated that even when subjects are unable to answer questions like "what is the capital city of Syria?", then a high subjective estimate of a feeling of knowing was associated with success on subsequent recognition and cued-recall tests. If we feel that we know the information, then it appears that we *do* know it, even when we may be unable to retrieve it. What may be producing this feeling is partial activation: if some, but not all, of the attributes of the memory are activated by the retrieval cue, then we may be unable to recall it, and at the same time be aware of an activated memory. Activation of the whole assembly of attributes might produce awareness of the memory, but partial activation may be not always sufficient for generating a state of awareness.

It is the extent of activation of a memory which is said to determine whether the individual will be aware of the memory, in which case it will be a conscious memory in the terms of this discussion, or whether the individual will be unaware of it, in which case it will be an unconscious memory. This description is not totally tautologous, for the extent of activation is not directly correlated with the awareness which we have for an activated memory. Partial activation may produce a "feeling of knowing" or a "tip-of-the-tongue" experience when we are trying to retrieve something, and partial activation may also produce effects without our being aware of them. The activation of some memories can influence the volitional retrieval of other memories. The following experiment demonstrates the effect of an unattended word upon the retrieval of an associate of an attended word.

1.3.1 *The activation of lexical associates: an experiment*

A group of 18 university students first learnt a list of 30 pairs of words. This list of words is presented in Table I, and was learnt to the extent that the subjects could recall the second word of each pair upon presentation of the first word. It will be noticed that each first word is a homographic homophone—an ambiguous word in which the sound and orthographic representations of each interpretation of the word are identical. Thus, the different meanings of the word "ball" are represented by the same written word and the same spoken form of the word. After learning the list of paired-associates, each subject was tested with a tachistoscopic presentation (60 msec) of the first word, and the task was again to respond with its associate. The response latency was measured via a voice switch. At a point 3° from fixation a second word was printed on each card shown in the tachistoscope. The eighteen subjects were allocated to one of three groups, without knowing it, and whereas each group of subjects saw the same 30 test words, they were presented with different words in the parafovea of vision. A latin-square design determined which of three types of unattended, or parafoveal, words would accompany each test word. Ten of the test words were accompanied by a "congruous" word, 10 had an "incongruous" word, and 10 an "unrelated" word. Congruous words had the same semantic context as the test word and the retrieved word (e.g. with "ball", the retrieved word was "gown" and the unattended word

TABLE I *Word-pairs used in the retrieval experiment. Subjects first learnt this list of associates sufficiently well for them to be able to retrieve the second word (e.g. "earl") upon presentation of the first word (e.g. "count"). The order of presentation of pairs was randomized for each subject. In a final test they were presented tachistoscopically with the first word of each pair in turn, and the response was again the recall of the second word. At the side of the first word was a distractor word. The distractor was either* congruous *with the meaning of the first word (e.g. "duke"), or it was* incongruous *(e.g. "number"), or it was* unrelated *to either of these meanings (e.g. "bird"). The dependent measures, retrieval time and % of correct retrievals, are presented in Fig. 1.*

count	—	earl	hide	—	leather
mean	—	petty	cape	—	boots
race	—	white	plot	—	grow
court	—	pursue	boil	—	face
page	—	serve	mint	—	penny
ball	—	gown	fleet	—	glance
feet	—	inches	punch	—	party
case	—	clothes	rake	—	flirt
plant	—	factory	wax	—	moon
ground	—	wheat	duck	—	avoid
lap	—	race	rest	—	left
bill	—	duck	corn	—	foot
port	—	glass	grave	—	words
stern	—	ship	sound	—	estuary
perch	—	swim	fine	—	jail

was "dress"); incongruous words had a different semantic context (e.g. the unattended word was "bat"); and unrelated words corresponded to none of the meanings of the test word (e.g. "chair"). Each subject was exposed to each of these types of unattended words, but for a third of the subjects any particular test word was accompanied by a congruous word, another third of the subjects would have an incongruous word, and the other third had an unrelated word.

The questions were whether the meaning of the unattended word would influence the speed of retrieval of the test word, and in particular whether the incongruous meaning would inhibit retrieval more than the unrelated word. The encoding specificity hypothesis of Thompson and Tulving (1970) would suggest that the incongruous words would interfere with retrieval, because an inappropriate retrieval cue would be available, given that there is to be any effect at all. In the experiment reported by Light and Carter-Sobell (1970) subjects had difficulty in recognizing the word "jam" in the context of "strawberry" after initially encoding "jam" in the context of "traffic". A similar design was used here, except that the retrieval context was presented in the parafovea of vision, and the short exposure duration prevented the viewer from inspecting the context and attending to it.

The results are summarized in Fig. 1. It is clear that the subjects were faster and more accurate in their retrieval responses when given a congruous unattended word, slowest and least accurate with an unrelated word, but, and this is the interesting point, their performance with incongruous words was intermediate to those other two types of unattended words. The retrieval times differed in this ordering ($F = 7.13$, d.f. = 2,34; $P < 0.003$), as did the frequency of errors ($F = 5.72$; d.f. = 2,34; $P < 0.01$).

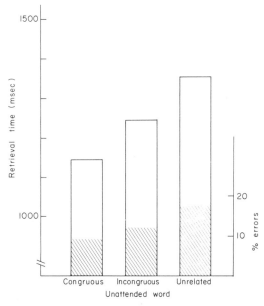

Fig. 1 Response times and errors from the retrieval experiment in which subjects first learnt a series of word-pairs (see Table I), and then responded to a 60 msec presentation of the first word of each pair. The speed and accuracy of these retrievals are indicated here.

Incongruous words inhibited the responses, relative to congruous words, but facilitated the responses relative to unrelated words. It is this latter relationship which is the more puzzling. On the basis of earlier experiments with unattended printed words, facilitation of processing was anticipated when the unattended word was congruous with the attended message (Bradshaw, 1974; Underwood, 1976b). On the basis of the result reported by Light and Carter-Sobell, however, an incongruous word might be expected to offer no facilitation in comparison with an unrelated word. The encoding specificity hypothesis predicts that if the word "ball" is encoded in the context of "gown", then supplying the word "bat" as a retrieval cue should give no facilitation. The encoding specificity hypothesis is therefore disconfirmed by this result.

Facilitation was obtained here with both congruous and incongruous words presented in the parafovea of vision, and presented for a very short interval so as to prevent the viewer looking at them and attending to them. It is unclear just how incongruous words aided the retrieval of the words associated to the fixated words. It may be that incongruous words aid the *perception* of the fixated word rather than affect the retrieval of its associate *after* it has been perceived. Whatever the route of facilitation, it is apparent that a word may activate its lexical representation and aid ongoing, attended activities without the individual directing these processes volitionally.

1.3.2 *Activation and awareness of memories*

The distinction between "conscious" and "unconscious" memory is a distinction between that of which we are aware, and that of which we are no longer aware. There is no distinction here between the encoding processes applied to the two forms, between the levels of processing applied, or between the attributes which are stored. The only distinction is whether or not we are *currently* aware of the event in question. This description does not suggest that two memory systems are necessary, for the same memory trace may be at different times active or dormant. A memory trace which is active may be said to be under conscious attention—it is an event of which we are aware—whereas a dormant memory trace is one which is available for conscious attention but is an event of which we are currently unaware. A memory which Waugh and Norman might describe as "being in primary memory" would be a memory which has reached a critical level of activation.

In a picture-naming experiment in which viewers gave names to simple line-drawings which were accompanied by "unattended" parafoveal words, Underwood (1977) asked the subjects to report the word wherever it was available. Two interesting features from that experiment are worth mentioning here. In the first place a difference was observed between the naming latencies to the pictures accompanied by semantically related or unrelated words, even when the subjects were unable to report those words. However, when they could report the words, the direction of the effect reversed, thus satisfying one of Dixon's (1971) criteria for accepting the presentation as being subliminal.

In the picture-naming experiments and in the paired-associate retrieval experiment mentioned here, there is evidence of a word-memory being activated without the individual being aware of the activation. This leads us to qualify the description of memories which are activated, for there appears to be no one-to-one correspondence between a memory which is activated and one of which we are aware. When we are aware of a memory it is possible to argue that it is activated, but activation alone is not enough to ensure that we will become aware of it. Activation, in other words, is a necessary but not sufficient condition for awareness. In the same way, we can talk of volitional selection as being a sufficient but not necessary condition for awareness—we may become aware of a memory because we have retrieved it intentionally, or because it has become sufficiently activated through other sources for us to be aware of it. This discussion will continue into the possibilities of the spontaneous retrieval of memories in Section 2.2.

When Penfield and Roberts (1959) electrically stimulated the surface of the temporal cortex of conscious subjects, they were able to elicit specific memories, and repeated activation of the same area would elicit the same sequence of memories. It is possible that what Penfield and Roberts were doing was to artificially activate "unconscious" memories, and thereby convert them into "conscious" memories. As the activation was terminated and a different memory evoked then its state would revert to being one of secondary memory. The distinction between "conscious" memory and "unconscious" memory, then, is one of the level of activation at a particular instant, but this is to say nothing of the *function* of the primary memory state. This question will form the basis of the discussion in the next session.

2 Some Consideration of the Use of Conscious Memories

"Selection is the very keel on which our mental ship is built" said James (1890, p. 680), and put his finger on the whole problem of consciousness. If an organism is simultaneously aware of all the information available to its senses at a particular moment, and at the same time aware of all the information stored in memory, that organism would be totally unselective provided that it remained inactive. The instant it started to act upon information available from its senses, and this includes the act of interpreting or perceiving its sensations, then it must select some data at the expense of other data. To react is to select, and a feature of the environment or a memory which gains a reaction is being differentiated from other features and memories. The processing applied in the reaction cannot be applied to all data unless the organism has a processing capacity which not only matches the input characteristics of the sensors and the storage capacity of its memories, but also matches the permutations necessary for the interaction of information. To combine two sets of information the organism will need a certain amount of processing capacity, but to combine all possible permutations of two sets from the data array the organism will require P units of processing capacity, where

$$P = \frac{n!}{2.\,(n-2)!}$$

and where n is the number of sets of information available. With restricted sensory apparatus and memory storage, the processing capacity required by an unselective organism would be reasonably small—in the order of a few thousand units. With refined apparatus and good storage the figure rapidly becomes huge. If the organism requires to combine not two, but three or four sets of information, then the unselective processing capacity required starts to approach an astronomical number of units. As the great man said, ". . . the mind is at every stage a theatre of simultaneous possibilities . . ." (James, 1890, p. 288). The combination of information is necessary in even the simplest of adaptive organisms. Sensory data are most often combined with data from memory to *select* the most appropriate response to a new environmental situation, based upon past experience.

Information is not only selected *for* further processing, for selection implies rejection. That which is not selected is rejected, and must be prevented from interfering with the current activity. If our organism were to be continuously aware of all the memories it had collected in its lifetime, it would certainly have unselective retrieval, but with limited capacity for integrating this information and for organizing a sequence of adaptive responses, the organism would be unable to make use of the available memories. An existence in which an organism is simultaneously aware of all its memories and perceptions would be inconceivably chaotic, and at the instant that the organism chose to analyse any stimulus or any memory in particular it would be exhibiting selectivity. This form of selective and directed processing, corresponding to what we call "consciousness", is a necessary feature for an organism which needs to store large amounts of information and yet remain free to inspect its environment without the requirement of actively maintaining its memories. If the organism needs to respond to its environment in the context of memories selected from store, and to choose between those memories, then it will also need to choose between possible responses. Here we have the essence of the operant conditioning paradigm, and it may be the case that any organism which chooses between its available operants demonstrates some form of consciousness. Or, to put this argument from a different point of view, consciousness may have evolved to serve the selection of memories and responses necessary for the varieties of learning which are indicated by operant conditioning procedures.

A most significant attribute of consciouness is that it is sequential. We are aware of a succession of individual elements in what James referred to as the "stream of thought". These elements merge into each other in our continuous awareness of the world and the perceptual moments become indistinguishable from each other. We are aware of a single stream of thought, or experience, however, and Underwood (1978) has argued that consciousness has this characteristic as a preparation for response. Conscious activity is seen as the anticipation of volitional sequences of responses. Acts which have become automatized through extensive practice (or "pre-wired" through genetic transmission of instinctive patterns of behaviour) will not require the preparation and organization afforded by consciousness. These actions may then be executed without continuous reference and control by consciousness. So, the organism may give the appearance of producing multiple response sequences by controlling a number of automatized response sequences concurrent with a single consciously controlled response sequence.

To organize and produce a single sequence of responses the organism must be selective in the information accepted from the environment, and in the information retrieved from memory. For guided processing selectivity is necessary, and unwanted information must be kept out of the processing sequence. The device for selecting the required information, and for inhibiting the invasion of irrelevant information is that which we experience as consciousness. Conscious memories, those events of which we are currently aware, serve the purposes of making information actively available for integration with the current problem, and of repressing the interference which would be caused if irrelevant memories were to interact with the problem. When I am trying to remember which brand of baked beans I was instructed to buy in the supermarket, it is no use my attention wandering to the memory that my car needs servicing, or that 3 years ago I had a camping vacation in Italy. The vast amount of information stored in memory will be largely irrelevant to whatever problem is in hand at any moment in time. Conscious memories can therefore be viewed both as being available for integration with the current problem, and as excluding other memories from integration or interference. Unconscious memories may be brought into the problem space by way of paths of association from the conscious memories, by the process of spreading activation described by Collins and Loftus (1975). As those unconscious memories become more activated via association (just as those memories artificially stimulated by Penfield and Roberts become activated), the organism becomes aware of them, and their state changes to one of a conscious, or primary, memory.

2.1 Forgetting as a Selective, Adaptive Process

The selective use of memories is a necessary process for any organism which cannot immediately achieve all of its goals. If an organism can choose to delay the gratification of one of its goals, or can work towards that goal at the same time as working to other goals, then the organism has either huge processing capacity or a selective processor such as that of consciouness. As we have seen, only the simplest of organisms can simultaneously process all of the information available to their crude receptors and memories in all possible organizations. Delayed gratification, then, requires the selective "forgetting" of a goal temporarily whilst a second goal receives attention. When the first goal, and any information relevant to it, is out of awareness, it is in this sense "forgotten". This goal and its relevant information remains accessible, but is temporarily unavailable, and so does not interfere with current activity. When we are unable to selectively forget or inhibit this information maladaptive behaviour ensues, and the subject in Luria's (1969) book "The Mind of a Mnemonist" is a case in point here. Luria's subject had, what appeared on the surface, to have a superb memory and was so efficient at remembering unconnected lists of digits, words and nonsense in general that he was able to find employment as a stage performer. Indeed, he was so good at remembering that he found himself recalling information from previous performances at inappropriate moments. Rather than having a very efficient memory it would be just as reasonable to describe this subject as having an inefficient forgetting process. His confusion led him to try a number of different methods of repressing or symbolically destroying old unwanted information, such as writing it out on a piece of paper which wa then screwed up into a ball, or thrown away, or even burnt. His forgetting methods were all based upon strong forms of visual imagery, which was one of his principal methods of remembering. Imagery as a mnemonic is an adaptive tool, but Luria's subject was so practised at this process of intermodal transfer that words would suggest images to him as if of their own accord. Imagery had become automatized, and as such provided a source of interference in the comprehension of metaphor.

Our capacity to forget is an essential selective device, but forgetting is not always an adaptive process. When we "forget" it may be because the information is no longer available, e.g. through trace eradication, or because the information is stored somewhere, but is inaccessible. If the inappropriate retrieval strategy is applied then even the simplest information may appear to be "forgotten". The ease with which the forgetting system may be misdirected is illustrated well in the intentional-forgetting experiments of Epstein and Wilder (1972). When subjects were misinformed as to which of two groups of two memories they should selectively search, correct retrieval occurred on 13% of occasions, whereas if this false search cue was not given over 50% of the searches produced correct responses. With a false "forget" instruction, a set of items would be effectively neglected. If appropriate items are inappropriately neglected, then they appear to be forgotten. When the subjects were informed that the "forget" instruction was misleading, performance went up to 46% correct retrieval. Forgetting is a process of non-search, this experiment suggests, and the neglect of whole search paths results in a performance equivalent to trace-eradication. In one case the memory remains in a state of availablity (but with no accessibility), but when the memory is removed it can be neither accessible nor available. The familiar experience of retrieval failure can be manipulated with the use of inappropriate retrieval cues just as the probability of successful retrieval can be increased by the presentation of appropriate cues.

2.2 The Spontaneous Retrieval of Inactive Memories

Luria's subject provides us with examples of unselective retrieval— facts which were no longer required did nevertheless intrude into his conscious processes and interfere with his current behaviour. Only in perfect retrieval systems is this effect not present. We all have experiences of attempting to retrieve a certain piece of information which just will not present itself to awareness, and at the same time a related piece of information is available. At these times we may have a "feeling of knowing" with regard to the information which we are attempting to retrieve, and we may feel that the memory is on the "tip of our tongue". These infuriating experiences are poorly understood at present, but appear to be connected with the partial activation of attributes or lexical associates of the required memory. Attributes and associates can often be reported at times of a retrieval block (Brown and McNeill, 1963; Gruneberg *et al.*, 1973), though it is not clear whether this helps or hinders in the removal of the block. This unwanted information may well provide a clue as to the required information, or it may serve as a retrieval block, but we are often aware that it is not the correct answer to the question we have set ourselves. Forgetting is a very adaptive process, but it is at its most adaptive when information can be switched voluntarily between its conscious mode to its unconscious mode. Whether categorized events—those which are well perceived—are ever forgotten completely is still an open question. We have no method of distinguishing between an event which is unavailable and one which does not exist in the memory system, although psycho-analysts may wish to dispute the meaning of "unavailable". It is used here to indicate an event which cannot be voluntarily recalled nor retrieved with the most appropriate cues nor recognized as a familiar event when presented in its original form. Forgetting of this variety is adaptive only if either the information is trivial or the storage space occupied by the information is required for new information. It is questionable whether permanent memories can be obliterated in human memory to create new space, and the failure to forget trivial information is all too familiar to us. Why, for example, am I unable to forget completely that in 1975 the deepest gold mine in the world was 3488 m deep? This cannot possibly have any bearing on any of my goals—it is useless information—and yet it is available in my memory system waiting continuously to be called upon. (It is, of course, now arguable that this piece of information has had a use in serving as an example in this argument, but whether or not it now disappears is another question.)

The retention of trivial information becomes maladaptive only when it is activated into its conscious mode, and "enters" primary memory at times when we are directing attention to any of the immediate goals or sub-goals. At these times trivial information becomes a distractor. The involuntary activation of trivial memories raises the question of spontaneous remembering, and of what we must do to ensure remembering something. "Remembering" in this sense is the activation of a memory to its conscious mode. It is sometimes the case that the memory of an event or episode from some months or years ago will appear to present itself to awareness (i.e. become activated) without our attempting to remember it. The first question to be asked whether the memory was activated by some retrieval cue of which we may or may not have been aware, or alternatively whether the memory was spontaneously and randomly activated. The second question concerns the possible adaptive function of a process by which old memories are activated in some random sequence with no intention of retrieval on the part of the individual. Psychologists have been reluctant to discuss these questions on the grounds of empirical difficulty,* and so we are left once again with speculation.

* Since writing this Norman has reported a survey which he conducted to investigate instances of spontaneous retrieval (personal communication, 1978). He found that in

Memories of events which have been inactive for some period of time do not seem to be activated when we are busy, that is, when a rapid succession of information is achieving its conscious state and then returning to its unconscious state. When engaged with a long car drive, or taking a long walk, such memories do become activated more often, and this difference leads to two possibilities. One theory of the incidence of spontaneous retrieval might argue that all memory sequences are activated spontaneously and randomly to a level which is below that required for awareness when the organism is concerned with some problem or other, that is, can successfully divert his attention away from these memories. The other theory might argue that the incidence of old memories being activated is a direct consequence of sensory inactivity. If we have nothing new to engage our minds, as in a state of sensory isolation (see Chapter 7), then the tendency to occupy awareness with old events might be necessary for the same reasons as it is necessary for the subject in sensory isolation to generate experiences which are not based upon his sensory input. Spontaneous memories may, in other words, be a first product of isolation or inactivity. These two theories are not mutually exclusive, and a combination of the two might argue that inactivity not only causes the generation of memories, but also allows us to become aware of them as a result of a lowering of the threshold of conscious activation.

Just as forgetting has its uses, and indeed is necessary in any selective system, so the spontaneous activation of old memories may have its uses. The anomaly of walking across a moor and "suddenly" being aware of remembering oneself in a car collision 3 or 4 years ago may help us to keep in touch with the world, but it may also help us to remember the important events of our experience. Spontaneous retrievals are not necessarily pleasant, but it is sometimes the unpleasant events which teach us best about how we might behave in the future, and in this sense they serve two adaptive functions. In the first place they occur during periods of low activity when we are in need of stimulation, and secondly they serve to provide suggestions about how we might behave in the future.

90% of the cases of spontaneous retrieval he could trace the retrieval cue. An association between the item "spontaneously" retrieved and the previous item of which the individual is aware, was almost always present. If this was the case, then our discussion of the mechanism of "spontaneous" retrieval, and its potential use, is quite redundant. The difficulties of investigating such phenomena cannot be underestimated, however, and the nature of the associations between previous events and "spontaneous" retrieval needs further examination.

3 The Psychological Present and the Conscious Activation of Memories

What you are aware of NOW, corresponds to the current contents of consciousness, or of primary memory in James's terms. The varieties of information which may be stored in this state of primary memory or conscious memory correspond exactly to the varieties of sensation which we can experience. Information being perceived or just perceived, is information in a state of activation and as such is being stored in conscious memory. This is not to say that "perception" is a unitary cognitive event which has consciousness as one of its consequences, for it is possible to argue that "perception" comprises a whole series of transformations of the sensory input and that consciousness may be applied to any number of these stages. We may be aware of transformations of the sensory input, but whether we can be aware of the untransformed input is questionable, for consciousness itself must be a stage of processing because it brings the benefits of experience to the new input. It may be impossible to perceive "objectively" and without any influences of experience, and as soon as we allow previous memories to influence our perceptions then we may be said to be transforming the input beyond its sensory representation. However, "perception" can consist of at least one stage prior to awareness, for the experiment described in Section 1.3.1 demonstrated that words can be recognized in the lexicon without achieving the state of being conscious memories.

The properties of information in its conscious state, that is, the information which gives us contact with the external world, are well known, and have been documented as the characteristics of Waugh and Norman's "primary memory". Thus, "primary memory" is described as having limited capacity, active selection for entry, categorized storage, and forgetting is by trace decay. The capacity limits have been defined as corresponding to the extent of the recency effect in the serial position curve of recall (Craik, 1968), and also to the difference in recall with no delay and 30 sec delay (Baddeley, 1970). These methods have suggested that the primary memory span is approximately three words. We can hold in consciousness just three words, whereas we can recall 7 ± 2 words from an immediate memory span. This difference might be evidence of the use of rules of encoding and retrieval which are stored in permanent memory. "Primary memory" is said to store words as semantic referents, rather than strings of phonemes (in 1968, Craik reported that the span was unaffected by word length), or associated ideas (Tulving and Patterson (1968) found that the span was unaffected by the semantic relationships of words). In order to categorize events in the world we need to attend selectively to some of their features, and this process of selection implies that the entry of a categorized item into primary memory is an active process: the presentation of an item to a passive subject will not produce a primary memory representation of that item. Attention is similarly required to maintain events in primary memory. Peterson and Peterson (1959) distracted subjects after they had categorically encoded an item, and reported that unless attention was redirected within a second or two then the probability of recall rapidly approached zero. It we can attend to an item, however meaningless, then the item will remain in primary memory, activated in a conscious state (Meunier *et al.*, 1972), but when attention is directed elsewhere and the activation is decreased, then recall is a function of the time between distraction and the re-direction of attention to the item. This is a function of what Craik and Watkins (1973) describe as the difference between maintenance rehearsal and elaborative operations. Repetitive or maintenance rehearsal in itself is sufficient to maintain an item at a level of activation necessary for immediate and perfect recall, but for recall at a later time, after attention has been directed elsewhere, a process of elaboration coding (Tulving and Madigan, 1970), or schematic assimilation (Bartlett, 1932) is necessary. We can remain aware of an event provided that nothing else is demanding activation to a conscious state, but events are easiest to remember when they have been related to other events which are already stored in categorized form.

The level of processing applied to an event recently perceived, in the sense intended by Craik and Lockhart (1972) and Craik and Tulving (1975), will determine the probability of recall from unconscious memory because it determines the probability of integrating the event with existing memories. If an elaboration level of processing is applied then the event will be more likely to be recalled than if a repetitive maintenance level of processing had been the strategy used. Non-elaborative rehearsal is sufficient to maintain an item in conscious memory, but will not lead to a stable encoding. Unless an item is well integrated with existing memories it will have a specific encoding, and fewer routes of access during retrieval. The encoding specificity principle, suggested by Thompson and Tulving (1970), holds that an event is effectively retrieved from memory via a restricted set of cues, and that the cues which are most effective are those which are an integral part of the encoding event. The most effective retrieval cues thus correspond to the event itself, as in a recognition paradigm. If an event is encoded in relative isolation from other events in memory, then fewer retrieval cues will be available. An event which is encoded specifically will be less likely to be recalled successfully than an event which has more routes of retrieval, whether these cues are provided by the context of the event or by the elaboration coding applied by the subject. Forgetting may then be considered as an example of encoding which is too specific, or the application of inappropriate retrieval plans. This effect was demonstrated in the experiment by Epstein and Wilder (1972).

3.1 The Volitional Retrieval of Unconscious Memories

Remembering is a skill, and as such shows the properties of other activities which can be described as skilful. Some activities need intimate control (the feedback loops control small sub-components of the whole event), and some activities require very little control (the feedback loop corresponds to the whole activity). When an activity is over-practised it tends to become automatized, and by this is meant the process by which conscious guidance is not necessary for successful execution. Differences in practice can also be observed in remembering. A "well-known" piece of information will be retrieved with less effort, and less attentional guidance, than a new or partially-encoded event. When asked the answer to the arithmetical question of "2 × 2 = ?", the solution appears without effort, as with questions of the variety "What is the capital city of France?". Both of these questions can be answered without a volitional memory search: the answers tend to appear in consciousness as soon as the question is stated. This phenomenon rather resembles riding a bicycle in that even after not having practised for a few years, the necessary control does not have to be programmed consciously for each component of the activity. In the case of cycling, the *intention* to move forward is sufficient for the muscular co-ordinations to operate, and sometimes in the case of remembering the *intention* to remember is sufficient. With less practised skills different effects can be observed. To the learner driver the simultaneous control of clutch, throttle and gear lever which is necessary to change gear may provide a task which requires too much processing capacity for the available resources. The attentional demand of the task exceeds the capacity available, and a less than skilful gear change is seen and heard. "What is the name of the West German Chancellor?", or perhaps "What is the capital city of Jordan?", or "What is the difference between an elm and a beech tree?", all indicate (to the writer at least) questions which require thought before the answers become available. The path of retrieval is nevertheless a mystery in that we do not experience the process of retrieval which is in operation: we are aware only of the product and some of the incorrect suggestions. We can attend to the problem, it seems, but the solution is provided for us by some process of which we are unaware.

The direction of attention to the problem area might itself be the mechanism by which possible solutions are offered. If we attend volitionally to features of the problem we activate the unconscious memories of those features, thereby changing their state to that of conscious memories, and their associates will also be activated by the structural process of spreading excitation. The solutions to factual questions are often provided by their associates stored in memory, and so excitation of the whole network would make a number of solutions available. The possibilities can then be reviewed and selected between once they are excited to their conscious mode.

Memory search tasks in the Sternberg paradigm (1966; see 1975 for a review) do not typically use well-encoded information in the sense that they are short-term tests of the use of episodic memory, rather than tests of the availability of information stored in semantic memory. Sternberg presented his subjects with a variable number of digits, followed after a pause by a digit to which the subjects responded "yes" or "no" according to whether or not it had appeared in the memory set. Increasing the size of the memory set increased the latency of the decision response, and there was no difference between positive and negative responses. Sternberg thus concluded that the comparison process whereby the probe item was matched against the memory set had the two properties of being serial (because of the linear increase in response time as the set size was increased) and exhaustive of all items in the set (because there was no difference between "yes" and "no" responses). These conclusions have been criticized as being unrepresentative of the "normal" operation of human memory, but whether this is so or not, one particular aspect of Sternberg's report is of importance here. Subjects were not aware of these processes of serial and exhaustive search, or of any search processes—the answer to their question of whether the probe item was old or new appeared to be presented to consciousness. The search was an un-conscious process and was not under volitional control. Only the *products* of memory search (and for that matter of thinking in general) are available to awareness. At the instant of testing, the subjects were presumably no longer holding the whole of the memory set in a state of conscious excitation, but this would depend upon the size of the set and might incidentally provide an explanation of the appearance of serial position effects in the responses to items. Items at the ends of the series typically gain faster responses than items in the centre (Corballis, 1967), and this may be a function of their preferred activation by a limited capacity device. The non-preferred items would then fail to be maintained to the level required for awareness, but their recency of activation would ensure that they would be usable within the period prior to complete dissipation of activation. What is activated is a word-concept: the sum of the attribute-associates which have previously been synthesized together to form a new entry in memory. Each of these attributes will have its own decay characteristics, and will return to its stable, unconscious mode independently of other attributes. We may be aware of the sound of a word after we have ceased to think about its meaning.

3.2 The Retrieval of Decaying Memories

The property of independent decay enables the model to account for the phenomenon of "short-term memory". If attributes of a memory are actively available after attention has been directed away then retrieval will still be possible using the original entry into conscious memory. We must remember not only the original arithmetical problem, and how far we have progressed with the task of finding the solution, but at a number of stages we will have to remember the product of an earlier manipulation and use it in a subsequent operation. We need to be able to retain the intermediate products without being conscious of them, for attention must be directed elsewhere, in the performance of new operations. Now, if the attributes of the intermediate product—acoustic, or imaged maybe—have not decayed beyond recognition when attention is elsewhere, then the task can be performed using the decay characteristics as a form of buffer memory. An event may be activated to an extent that it is in its conscious mode, or it may be totally inactive and still accessible in unconscious memory, or it may be in a third mode which is used for mental tasks. This third mode is neither conscious nor fully unconscious, but whereas the event is not the focus of attention, its attributes have not yet decayed in their excitation to the extent that they are not retrievable. When the excitation is dissipated, or the memory decayed, then no permanent trace may be available. In the performance of tasks such as mental arithmetic, it is often necessary to leave no permanent unconscious memory. Knowledge of the intermediate stages of processing is useless after completion of the task except in cases of error-seeking.

4 The Psychological Past and World Knowledge

Whereas some memories are personal and relate to our own actions and thoughts, other memories are held in common with other people, and relate to the concepts which we have learned about the shared world. This is the distinction between Tulving's (1972) episodic and semantic memory systems, but although the justifications for a structural or a functional distinction between these two systems are impoverished, Tulving has provided a useful descriptive concept. Our worlds are undoubtedly divided into personal and public components, with the public component (semantic memory) acquired through personal contact (episodic memory). We might therefore not only know the correct spelling of the word "asymmetry", but also how and where we learned it, as well as embarrassing instances of the use of its mis-spelled form. Alternatively, we may have forgotten the circumstances surrounding the acquisition of this information, and so all we would be left with would be an entry in what Tulving calls semantic memory. All knowledge is to some extent personal because we perceive it for ourselves, and the act of perceiving and encoding involves personal action. This personal intervention may then be forgotten and the event encoded as a general rule, but the act of forgetting is not necessarily a deletion of a discrete memory. Seen as the loss of an attribute of a memory the distinction between personal and public memories (or episodic and semantic memories) becomes entirely descriptive. We may have a memory corresponding, for example, to the word-concept "asymmetry". The attributes of this memory will be wide ranging, but will include such attributes as its meaning, its phonological form, its spelling (which may or may not be correct with relation to an accepted spelling), and a number of private attributes derived from our experience with the concept. Necessarily, the attributes of experience must form the initial basis of the memory, but once it has been integrated with the rest of the cognitive network, these attributes may be deleted without loss to the operation of the system. We do not need to postulate separate systems for the storage of episodic and semantic memories. For the performance of some tasks we will need to use the episodic memories, or personal attributes, of an event, and for other tasks the semantic memories, or public attributes will be necessary. This section concerns semantic memory, and involves the mnemonic systems which enable us to "know" that collie dogs do not have spark plugs.

4.1 Sentence Comprehension and the Operation of Semantic Memory

If subjects are asked at one time whether a chicken is a bird, and at another time whether a robin is a bird, the latter type of question gains the faster confirmation response. Chickens are apparently more difficult to identify as birds than are robins, and Smith *et al.* (1974) argue that this effect supports a model of sentence verification in which the typicality of the instance is the factor which determines the ease of response. Instances which are typical of a category are said to have more features in common with the category-concept, and so the verification conclusion is reached earlier than when the search for common features goes on for longer before the critical features are matched. Smith *et al*. distinguish between two types of features, and these might be described as semantic attributes or associates in the attribute theory of the structure of memory which was outlined above. Distinctive features are those which define the word and are the essential properties of the meaning of the concept indicated by that referent. For the word "birds", the defining features might include the list of "lay eggs", "have feathers", "have wings", "can eat", etc. Characteristic features are those features which are usually associated with instances of the concept, but which are not essential to the definition. "Birds" may have a set of characteristic features including "can fly", "have beaks", "perch in trees", "can sing", etc. Now, when we come to decide whether or not a robin is a bird we compare the features of "robin" with the features of "bird", and as there is general agreement the conclusion is reached quickly. If we are trying to decide whether a chicken is a bird, however, the overall comparison does not yield a one-to-one correspondence of features. Chickens are not typical birds: they do not often fly and they do not often perch in trees. The conclusion at this stage is "don't know", and Smith *et al*. propose that a second comparison is then performed. The second comparison involves only the defining features (which do match in our example) and it is only brought into operation when the combined comparison of defining and characteristic features fails to lead to a conclusion one way or the other. Atypical instances lead to longer decision times, therefore, because a second comparison process is necessary.

The semantic attributes of an entry in memory are separated into defining features and characteristic features by Smith *et al*., but the dividing line is far from clear. Language is not so well-defined as to allow the distinction between "what is", and "what is not". Categories of items stored in memory, and expressed through language, can best be described as being "fuzzy sets" (Hersh and Caramazza, 1976). The meanings of word-concepts are vague, and are often qualified in natural languages by what Lakoff (1972) describes as "linguistic hedges". How do chickens and bats and butterflies relate to the concept of birds? They all have some attributes in common with birds, but who is to decide that only chickens have the critical, defining features required by the Smith *et al*. model? The taxonomy of natural objects is at some stages arbitrary, and we recognize this through the use of linguistic hedges which indicate to the listener that we are using instances and concepts in a special way. It is possible to argue, for example that "technically speaking, a bat is a mammal, but loosely speaking it is a bird". In terms of the Smith *et al*. feature comparison model of instance allocation, the linguistic hedge "technically speaking" indicates the use of the defining features, whereas "loosely speaking" suggests a comparison using the characteristic features. With biological instances the problem of categorization is relatively simple for us because the taxonomy is well-defined and publically available even if we only rely on information we have been told (i.e. "bats are mammals"), but how should we decide what is a chair? Some things are built specifically for use as chairs, and have the defining characteristics by the intention of the builders, but some things which are built for other purposes also have the defining features of a chair (e.g. a coffee table). These objects only become chairs when they are perceived as having the necessary properties by a potential user. The vagueness of natural categories is best illustrated by the problem of baldness (Hersh and Caramazza, 1976), and is a problem posed by Greek philosophers as the paradox of *falatros*. The vagueness is one of deciding upon how many hairs a man must lose before he can be described as being bald. In some instances he will be definitely not bald, and in other instances definitely bald, but there exists a set of instances which are vaguely described and which do not fall clearly into one category or the other. Use of the concept of baldness is therefore imprecise, and to document its defining features, for a comparison of the type suggested by Smith *et al.*, would not be straightforward.

Natural objects have reference points against which new instances are judged, according to a series of experiments reported by Rosch (1975). Stimuli such as colours, numbers and lines of varying orientations were judged against other instances, and subjects preferred descriptive sentences of the form *A* is essentially *B* where "*B*" was an ideal colour, a number which was a multiple of 10, or a line in a primary orientation — horizontal, vertical or with an angle of 45° to the horizontal. Rather than "10 is roughly 11", subjects would prefer "11 is roughly 10" as a description of the relationship between the two numbers. In making a judgement about baldness we might expect that the decision be based upon imaginary ideal instances of "bald" and "not bald", against which the new instance is compared. The hedges available in our language allow us to communicate the idea that whereas someone is not actually bald he is getting there.

4.2 The Structure of Word Concepts

The model of instance categorization suggested by Smith *et al.* (1974), in which the features of the instance are matched against the features of the category, was proposed as an alternative to the network model of semantic memory suggested by Collins and Quillian (1969). The

salient principles of the Smith *et al.* model do not contradict those of
the Collins and Quillian model, however, and the feature comparison
can be accommodated by a network model. Collins and Loftus (1975)
have suggested an elaborated version of the original associative network
theory in which the network structure can combine with the comparison process to deal with most of the available evidence.

Collins and Quillian proposed that word concepts were organized in
a semantic memory structure in a hierarchical network with words
linked subordinately to encompassing categories (e.g. "bird" is linked
to "animal"), and linked superordinately to instances of the concept
(e.g. "bird" is linked to "canary", "robin", "ostrich", etc.). The words
in this lexical network are stored at the nodes and the properties of the
words are stored with them. The properties of "animal" will include
"eats", "breathes", "independently mobile", whereas the properties of
"birds" will include "has feathers", "can fly", "lays eggs", and the
properties of "canary" are "small", "yellow", "sings". In this way our
total knowledge of the world, as we have experienced it, can be represented in an ordered structure. New instances can be added quite
easily by creating a new entry below the appropriate node. When a
child learns that an ostrich is a bird, it is categorized below that node,
but something else must happen to account for the anomaly of a bird
which cannot fly. One of the properties of "ostrich" must be "can't fly",
and all exceptions to a property stored at a superordinate node must be
stored as individual properties. An objection to this notion of concepts
being defined by their properties has been raised in this form, to use an
example, "birds have wings, robins are birds, but what is a robin
if it happens to lose its wings in an accident"? The answer, quite
simply, is that particular robin is stored as a special instance of the
category "robins", just as ostriches are stored as special instances
of "birds". The defining feature may be lost, but this in itself forms
the basis of a new defining feature where the instance of the concept
may possess the property of not having a property which is held by
other instances.

In a development of the Collins and Quillian network model, Collins
and Loftus (1975) propose that the memory system has two components, a lexical network which stores the names of concepts, and a
semantic network which stores the properties of the concepts. It is not
clear how an item in the lexical network could be accessed entirely on
the basis of its phonological and orthographic attributes, as Collins and
Loftus suggest, without reference to its meaning, nor what advantage is
gained by the separation of the two systems. If an entry in lexical
memory can be activated by a phonological stimulus the meaning of the
stimulus can only be recognized by a link with the semantic network,

and Collins and Loftus suggest that each entry in lexical memory is connected to at least one entry in semantic memory. At this point the necessity for two systems disappears. If the connections between the two systems are as profuse as this, and they must be for the organism to recognize the meaning of words, then the lexical entry is no more than a property of the semantic entry. This is the attribute model earlier proposed here.

The information stored in semantic memory is for the large part unconscious, both in terms of time and content. We are aware of our memories only fleetingly and this needs to be the case if conscious activation is to be a state reserved for that information which is to be manipulated. If we are to add a new instance to a concept, or modify a property of an instance already in store, then and only then does that part of semantic memory need to be activated to its conscious state. The discussions in the present sections have concentrated on the structural organization of semantic memory, and on the word concept as the fundamental unit in this organization.

5 Concluding Remarks

Just as word concepts may be described as collections of properties, we are describing memories in general here as collection of attributes. The association of two events or attributes constitutes a memory, and the retrieval of an unconscious memory will itself constitute the formation of a new memory. When we retrieve information from memory we experience not only the retrieved information, but also the act of retrieval. We can remember, and we can remember remembering. In Tulving's model a retrieval from the public semantic system constitutes an entry in the more personal episodic system, and although we do not find it necessary to distinguish between semantic and episodic memories, other than descriptively, the principle of retrieval-as-re-entry is the same. In this case the two events which become associated are the information which is retrieved, and the context (time, place, other conscious events) of retrieval. The attributes which eventually constitute the memory trace will depend upon the mode of the information on presentation, as an indication of a structural-associative attribute, upon the manipulations performed upon the information by the perceiver, as an indication of cognitive-associative attribute, and upon the social environment of the presentation of the information, as an indication of a contextual-associative attribute.

As information is presented to us we may become aware of it (e.g. if we are attending and the stimulus is of sufficient intensity), and this perception constitutes the construction of a conscious memory, or primary memory in the sense intended by James. When this event passes from consciousness, and is no longer a part of that of which we are aware, the state of excitation of the memory may be said to be reduced. A passing from consciousness, or a reduction in the extent of activation are two ways of describing the same process: we become aware of events if their memories become activated to a certain critical state. Activation may result from a spread of activation from associated entries in the memory system, or it may result from the volitional retrieval of a memory. As with other skills, it appears to be the very intention to perform an act which produces it. With memory, the intention to retrieve a piece of information is often sufficient for it to appear in its conscious state. The intention to retrieve could act to produce diffuse activation within the domain of storage, with selection of the appropriate item as a second stage, but the solution of the problem of intention and volition is beyond the scope of current Psychology.

Memories sometimes achieve their conscious state spontaneously, or so it appears. Given that spontaneous retrieval does not follow the presentation of a retrieval cue (which would produce spreading activation), the problem remains as one of why we should remember old events which have nothing to do with current activity. It is possible that all memories are activated spontaneously and on a random basis, possibly as part of a maintenance routine, and that at a time of reduced cognitive activity this spontaneous activation is sufficient to exceed the threshold for awareness. This again is a problem outside of the realms of solution by current theory and practice.

The state of activation of a memory which we experience as conscious activation has evolved to serve a number of purposes, including the selective processing of information at the exclusion of other information, being necessary for the delayed achievement of goals and the associated problem solving activities. As a specific instance of selective processing and problem solving, the conscious state makes possible the selective encoding of new information in situations where the organism must learn to adapt to a new environment. Maintaining new, relevant, information in its conscious state for a short while gives sufficient opportunity to develop a permanent association which on subsequent occasions would become available on perception of the familiar characteristics of the problem.

Memory as a problem of consciousness is an area neglected at the expense of the investigation of the rules of abstracted verbal learning, but until we are prepared to admit this phenomenological attribute of memory processes then we will make only limited progress towards the goal of understanding the relationship between the structural and strategical limits of performance.

6 Acknowledgements

A number of readers have made very useful comments on the problems discussed here. Diz Breslaw, Michael Gruneberg, Elizabeth Loftus and Endel Tulving replied to issues and caused me to think again about many of them, but in particular I should like to thank Tom Carr and Donald Norman for their exhaustive and illuminating refereeing.

7 References

Baddeley, A. D. (1970). Estimating the short-term component in free recall. *British Journal of Psychology* **61**, 13–15.

Badderley, A. D. (1976). "Psychology of Memory." Harper and Row, New York.

Bartlett, F. C. (1932). "Remembering." Cambridge University Press, London.

Bradshaw, J. L. (1974). Peripherally presented and unreported words may bias the perceived meaning of a centrally fixated homograph. *Journal of Experimental Psychology* **103**, 1200–1202.

Brown, R. and McNeill, D. (1966). The "tip of the tongue" phenomenon. *Journal of Verbal Learning and Verbal Behavior* **5**, 325–337.

Collins, A. M. and Loftus, E. F. (1975). A spreading activation theory of semantic processing. *Psychological Review* **82**, 407–428.

Collins, A. M. and Quillian, M. R. (1969). Retrieval time from semantic memory. *Journal of Verbal Learning and Verbal Behavior* **8**, 240–248.

Corballis, M. C. (1967). Social order in recognition and recall. *Journal of Experimental Psychology* **74**, 99–105.

Craik, F. I. M. (1968). Two components in free recall. *Journal of Verbal Learning and Verbal Behavior* **7**, 996–1004.

Craik, F. I. M. and Lockhart, R. S. (1972). Levels of processing: a framework for memory research. *Journal of Verbal Learning and Verbal Behavior* **11**, 671–684.

Craik, F. I. M. and Tulving, E. (1975). Depth of processing and the retention of words in episodic memory. *Journal of Experimental Psychology: General* **104**, 268–294.

Craik, F. I. M. and Watkins, M. J. (1973). The role of rehearsal in short-term memory. *Journal of Verbal Learning and Verbal Behavior* **12**, 599–607.

Crowder, R. G. and Morton, J. (1969). Precategorical acoustic storage (PAS). *Perception and Psychophysics*, 365–373.

Dixon, N. F. (1971). "Subliminal Perception: The Nature of a Controversy." McGraw-Hill, London.

Epstein, W. and Wilder, L. (1972). Searching for to-be-forgotten material in a directed forgetting task. *Journal of Experimental Psychology* **95**, 349–357.

Gruneberg, M. M. (1970). A dichotonous theory of memory—unproved and unprovable. *Acta Psychologica* **34**, 489–496.

Gruneberg, M. M. and Monks, J. (1974). Feeling of knowing and cued recall. *Acta Psychologica* **38**, 257–265.

Gruneberg, M. M., Winfrow, P. and Woods, R. (1973). An investigation into memory blocking. *Acta Psychologica* **37**, 187–196.

Hart, J. T. (1965). Memory and the feeling of knowing experience. *Journal of Educational Psychology* **56**, 208–216.

Hersh, H. M. and Caramazza, A. (1976). A fuzzy set approach to modifiers and vagueness in natural language. *Journal of Experimental Psychology: General* **105**, 254–276.

James, W. (1890). "The Principles of Psychology." Macmillan, London.

Lakoff, G. (1972). Hedges: A study of meaning criteria and the logic of fuzzy concepts. Papers from the Eighth Regional Meeting, Chicago Linguistics Society. University of Chicago, Chicago.

Light, L. L. and Carter-Sobell, L. (1970). Effects of changed semantic context on recognition memory. *Journal of Verbal Learning and Verbal Behavior* **9**, 1–11.

Luria, A. R. (1969). "The Mind of a Mnemonist." Cape, London.

Melton, A. W. (1963). Implications of short-term memory for a general theory of memory. *Journal of Verbal Learning and Verbal Behavior* **2**, 1–12.

Meunier, G. F., Ritz, D. and Meunier, J. A. (1972). Rehearsal of individual items in short-term memory. *Journal of Experimental Psychology* **95**, 465–467.

Penfield, W. and Roberts, L. (1959). "Speech and Brain Mechanisms." Princeton University Press, Princeton, New Jersey.

Peterson, L. R. and Peterson, M. J. (1959). Short-term retention of individual verbal items. *Journal of Experimental Psychology* **58**, 193–198.

Rosch, E. (1975). Cognitive reference points. *Cognitive Psychology* **7**, 532–547.

Smith, E. E., Shoben, E. J. and Rips, L. J. (1974). Comparison processes in semantic memory. *Psychological Review* **81**, 214–241.

Sternberg, S. (1966). Memory scanning: new findings and current controversies. *Quarterly Journal of Experimental Psychology* **27**, 1–32.

Thompson, D. M. and Tulving, E. (1970). Associative encoding and retrieval: weak and strong cues. *Journal of Experimental Psychology* **86**, 255–262.

Tulving, E. (1972). Episodic and semantic memory. *In* "Organization of Memory" (Eds E. Tulving and W. Donaldson). Academic Press, New York.

Tulving, E. and Madigan, S. A. (1970). Memory and verbal learning. *Annual Review of Psychology* **21**, 437–484.

Tulving, E. and Patterson, R. D. (1968). Functional units and retrieval processes in free recall. *Journal of Experimental Psychology* **77**, 239–248.

Underwood, G. (1976a). "Attention and Memory." Pergamon Press, Oxford.

Underwood, G. (1976b). Semantic interference from unattended printed words. *British Journal of Psychology* **67**, 327–338.

Underwood, G. (1977). Attention, awareness and hemispheric differences in word recognition. *Neuropsychologia* **15**, 61–67.

Underwood, G. (1978). Attentional selectivity and behavioural control. *In* "Strategies of Information Processing" (Ed. G. Underwood). Academic Press, London.

Waugh, N. C. and Norman, D. A. (1965). Primary Memory. *Psychological Review* **72**, 89–104.

Wickelgren, W. A. (1973). The long and the short of memory. *Psychological Bulletin* **80**, 425–438.

Wickelgren, W. A. (1975). More on the long and the short of memory. *In* "Short-Term Memory" (Eds D. Deutsch and J. A. Deutsch). Academic Press, London.

6 Consciousness in Models of Human Information Processing: Primary Memory, Executive Control and Input Regulation

T. H. CARR

Department of Psychology,
Michigan State University

This paper discusses the uses to which a concept of consciousness has been put in models of human information processing. I will first review three information processing functions that various investigators have attributed to consciousness. Then I will briefly attempt to synthesize these functions as properties of a central mechanism involved in carrying out goal-directed tasks, remembering past events, and imagining events not actually encountered. The operation of this mechanism may not be the entirety of our conscious experience, but does appear to represent a part of what we commonly refer to as consciousness. Finally I'll borrow from a recent evolutionary argument pointing out the utility of such a mechanism in understanding the nature of human intelligence.

1 Information Processing Functions of Consciousness

For present purposes, consciousness will be described rather roughly as a changing body of introspectable mental activity. Consciousness is a potential phenomenon to be studied by information processing psychologists because this mental activity seems to be highly correlated with at least some aspects of the behaviour observed during task performance. Therefore one might ask whether particular mental operations or processing functions are subserved by consciousness (Chase, 1978; Kerr, 1973; Posner, 1973).

Some researchers who have addressed this question see consciousness as a kind of mental blackboard, attributing to it the functions of a theoretical construct called primary memory or short term store (Atkinson and Shiffrin, 1968, 1971; Crowder, 1976; Erdelyi, 1974; Waugh and Norman, 1965). Primary memory is regarded as a rather small amount of highly activated, readily available information which is kept alive in the mind—or held in consciousness—while the person is actually making use of it, and which fades out of consciousness or is replaced by new information quite rapidly as soon as the person stops using it. Ideas about the relation between primary memory and consciousness are often traced back to William James's (1890) discussion of the "stream of consciousness," in which the term primary memory was first used.

Other investigators see consciousness as an internal programmer or executive decision maker that plans and co-ordinates mental activity. This view originated from advances made in computer science in the last 25 years, especially the development of complex time-sharing systems. The best worked out example is Shallice's (1972) proposal that consciousness sets goals and activates behavioural action systems appropriate to accomplishing those goals.

The third position relates consciousness to attention, a limited-capacity central "switchboard" that regulates input from sensory pathways and memory retrieval mechanisms to response systems producing overt behaviour (Keele and Neill, in press; Posner, 1978a; Posner and Klein, 1973). The predominant theme of the huge literature on attention has been the limits of the human organism's ability to select information required for the accomplishment of a task at the expense of information irrelevant to that task. Therefore the idea of consciousness as an information selector is closely related to consciousness as an executive controller (Carr and Bacharach, 1976; Keele and Neill, in press).

2 Consciousness as a Mental Blackboard: Primary Memory

In 1890 William James drew a distinction between two states of memory. One was a quiescent or inactive state called secondary memory that characterizes all of one's knowledge and potentially rememberable experiences not being actively thought about at a particular point in time. Secondary memory represents the psychological past. The other state was called primary memory and consists of those mental contents of which one is currently aware, representing the psychological present. According to James the psychological present is extended somewhat in time because a mental event requires a short transition period to subside from the active primary state into the quiescent secondary state. This argument has had a strong influence on theories of cognition and consciousness.

2.1 Capacity Limitations in Memory and Performance

As psychologists began applying concepts drawn from information theory and computer science to human cognition (e.g. Broadbent, 1958; Cherry, 1953; Hyman, 1953; Miller, 1956; Welford, 1952), interest grew rapidly in two related phenomena that reminded some of the distinction made by James. First, as Miller (1956) pointed out, the number of unrelated digits or letters that can be reproduced verbatim after a single presentation (called the memory span), the number of categories that a person can keep distinct in making psychophysical judgments, and the number of items in the visual field that can be apprehended without counting one by one ("subitizing"), are all limited in a remarkably similar way to about 7 ± 2. Mandler (1975) has subsequently argued that the limitation is even greater, perhaps on the order of 5 ± 1, when linguistic items such as words are the stimuli to be processed. Second, as Welford (1952) and Broadbent (1958) discussed at length, people are also extremely limited in their abilities to perform more than one voluntary activity at a time. This limitation shows up in tasks as simple as pressing a button as rapidly as possible whenever a light comes on while pressing another button as rapidly as possible whenever a tone sounds and in tasks as complex as monitoring two conversations, one heard in the left ear and the other in the right, for some predefined set of target words. These two kinds of phenomena make one suspect that a bottleneck somewhere in the information processing system places severe constraints on the amount of information simultaneously processable (Broadbent, 1971; Kahneman, 1973; Keele, 1973; Kerr, 1975; Norman, 1976).

Noting that despite the small number of items in the memory span, the item heard last or most recently in the stimulus list is almost always correctly recalled, Waugh and Norman (1965) returned explicitly to the notion of primary memory in relating the limits on memory span to limits on judgment and simultaneous task performance. They speculated that:

> If we may assume that attending to a current item precludes reviewing a prior one, we can say that the span of immediate memory must be limited in large part by our inability to rehearse, and hence retain, the early items in a sequence while attempting to store the later ones. Our limited memory span would then be but one manifestation of our general inability to think about two things at the same time.
>
> (Waugh and Norman, 1965, p. 89)

Waugh and Norman performed a simple experiment designed to measure memory for digits from a spoken list as a function of both the amount of time and the number of other digits intervening between presentation and an attempt to recall. After hearing a list of 16 digits presented at a rate of either one or four items per second, the subject was given a probe digit and asked to recall the digit that had occurred immediately following the probe in the stimulus list. The results, shown in Fig. 1, showed that probability of correct recall fell off rapidly with number of intervening items until an asymptote was reached at about 12 items. The rate of decline in accuracy was approximately the same for the two presentation rates. These results led Waugh and Norman to

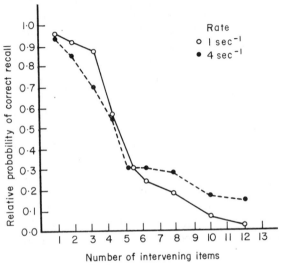

Fig. 1 Relative probabilities of correct recall of digit following the probe in probe recall experiment (Waugh and Norman, 1965).

propose that digits were recalled from two sources, a very limited primary memory which each presented digit must enter in order to be remembered at all, and a much larger and more stable secondary memory into which some digits are transferred and from which the digits may later be retrieved. The asymptotic level of performance was taken as an estimate of the number of digits transferred into secondary memory, while the rapidly declining preasymptotic function measured recall from primary memory. Because number of intervening items had a much larger effect on probability of correct recall than time since presentation, Waugh and Norman concluded that material is lost or forgotten from primary memory because it is displaced by other material, not because it decays spontaneously over time.

2.2 Process Dualism

Since Waugh and Norman's 1965 paper, the notion of process dualism, holding that human memory must be understood in terms of at least two qualitatively different stores or states of activation, has dominated information processing psychology. The best-elaborated model employing the Jamesian distinction is Atkinson and Shiffrin's (1968, 1971), in which primary memory is given the name short-term store and secondary memory is called long-term store. Though Atkinson and Shiffrin see decay over time as a critical factor in loss of material from short-term store or primary memory, the characteristics of the two stores and the functional relations between them are very much the same as those proposed by Waugh and Norman. As Atkinson and Shiffrin put it:

> One might consider the short-term store simply as being a temporary activation of some portion of the long-term store. In our thinking we tend to equate this short-term store with "consciousness," that is, the thoughts and information of which we are currently aware can be considered part of the content of short-term store.
>
> (Atkinson and Shiffrin 1971, p. 83)

While some process dualists have argued that primary memory maintains phonetic information only, it now seems clear that visual and semantic codes or internal representations can also reach this level of conscious activation (e.g. Baddeley, 1976; Crowder, 1976; Posner and Mitchell, 1967). It is important to note that memory codes are not isolated from the remainder of secondary memory as a result of entering the primary state. Neely (1977), for example, has demonstrated that consciously thinking about a category such as clothing can activate previously inactive codes associated with that category. Neely's subjects were given a prime or cue at the beginning of each trial consisting of the name of a category. The cue told them what to expect as the stimulus in a task requiring them to decide whether a pronounceable string of letters was a real English word. In the condition of greatest interest, one category was used as a cue for a different category. Subjects were told that if the category "buildings" was seen as a cue, they were most likely to get a word from the category "clothing". Facilitation for decisions about articles of clothing appeared if the decision stimulus was presented more than 500 msec after presentation of the cue, but not if the decision stimulus occurred less than 500 msec after the cue. Thus semantic information in secondary memory was being activated as a result of generating an expectation of a particular kind in primary memory, and the activation process required about 0·5 sec to take place. Other examples of spreading activation from one code to another in memory have been studied by Meyer *et al.* (1975) and McCauley *et al.* :1976), among others.

2.3 The Capacity of Consciousness

So far primary memory has been described as a limited capacity
memory system capable of maintaining a small amount of information
in a very high state of activation. Since the memory span has been
closely identified with primary memory, it is tempting to think of the
size of the memory span as a rather direct estimate of the capacity of
consciousness. On this basis one would conclude that consciousness
can encompass about four unrelated low frequency words, about six
unrelated high frequency words, or about seven to eight digits
(Crannell and Parrish, 1957; Watkins, 1977). Conscious apprehension
expands again for sequences of words forming meaningful sentences
(Ebbinghaus, 1885/1964).

However, Craik (1968) and Watkins (1977) have proposed that the
memory span is not a direct measure of primary memory at all, but is
instead the product of output from both primary and secondary memory. Watkins argued that retrieval from secondary memory is
made more or less difficult by stimulus characteristics such as frequency
or semantic connectedness, as indicated above, but that output from
primary memory should be much less affected by stimulus characteristics because the information is already highly activated and readily
accessible for response. By varying the number and location of high and
low frequency words in memory span stimulus lists, Watkins determined that no more than two or three items in the span list are ever
recalled entirely from primary memory. He concluded that the more
recently presented the item, the greater the relative contribution of
primary memory to its reproduction.

Looking back to Waugh and Norman (1965), one might think that
Watkin's (1977) estimate is still too large, and that recall of all items in a
memory span task may often be supported by information from both
states of memory. Because the decline in accuracy attributed to displacement by items entered more recently into primary memory is
evident between the first and second points on the graph in Fig. 1, it seems
that even two items can interfere with one another in consciousness. This
early decline is especially apparent with the faster presentation rate,
which allows less time for storage of information in secondary memory.
Rather than a bin that can hold some particular number of things, then,
primary memory appears to be a state of *relatively* high activation or
relatively high accessibility. Results from Waugh and Norman's probe
technique suggest that the *full* measure of conscious activation can be
given to only one item at a time. More than one item can be active
simultaneously in primary memory, but if so the items will be at less than
the highest level of activation possible (Shiffrin, 1975). Therefore, the

more events one is asked to remember from the recent past, the more one must supplement primary memory with retrieval from secondary memory in order to maintain perfect performance. This account predicts that memory span will contain a larger amount of information than the subject is consciously aware of at the time recall begins, but fails to explain what underlying process determines just how much larger span will be. A possible explanation has been offered by Graesser and Mandler (1978), and discussing their work will lead to the second function attributed to consciousness, executive control.

3 Consciousness as an Internal Programmer: Executive Control

Graesser and Mandler (1978) began with the size of the memory span for newly encountered word lists. They asked if a similar limitation applies to retrieving words from well-learned groupings according to a specified plan or to making comparative judgments about words along already-learned semantic dimensions. In one experiment, subjects were asked to name aloud as many instances of a category such as clothing, sports, or four-footed animals as they could in a 6-minute period. The output was tape-recorded and the protocols examined with respect to their distributions over time. As can be seen in Fig. 2, results

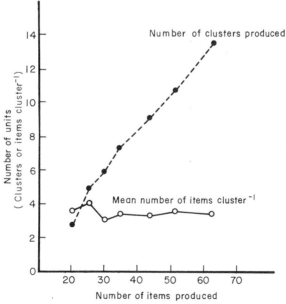

Fig. 2 Performance in category-member production experiment (Graesser and Mandler, 1978). Number of items per cluster and number of clusters are plotted against total number of category items produced during a 6-minute recall period.

showed that items were recalled in temporally-separated clusters averaging a little more than four items per cluster and that the total number of category members produced was a function of the number of clusters rather than their size. The smallest mean cluster size obtained in a single output period was 3·23 items and the largest was 7·59. Using rather different methods of calculation, Broadbent (1975) has obtained a similar range of cluster sizes in recall from secondary memory, though the modal cluster size was somewhat smaller. Thus the ability to retrieve and produce words from well-learned groupings in secondary memory seems to be limited in much the same quantitative way as memory span for groups of words just encountered for the first time.

In another experiment, Graesser and Mandler's subjects were given sets of randomly selected words ranging from 1 to 12 words per set. Their task was to find a "dimension, feature, or some attribute, based on meaning, that all the words shared" (p. 88) as rapidly as they could. After doing this to 40 different sets of words, subjects were presented with the words from all 40 sets one by one. Each word was accompanied by the dimension label the subject had given to the set which had contained the word in the categorization phase of the experiment. The task was to judge on a scale of 1–6 how well the label fit that particular word. Judgments of label fit are shown in Fig. 3. These data demonstrate quite clearly that regardless of set size, no more than about six items from a set were thought to fit the label applied to that set. Thus a limitation shows up in the ability to co-ordinate comparison of words along known semantic dimensions that is very similar to that seen in

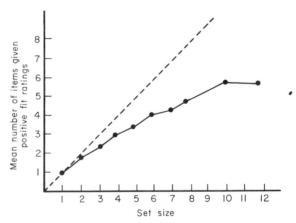

Fig. 3 Judgments of fit in semantic comparison and classification experiment (Graesser and Mandler, 1978). Number of items given a positive fit rating is plotted against set size. The dashed line has a slope of one and represents a perfect fit between all items in a set and the label applied to that set.

retrieval from secondary memory. Graesser and Mandler's (1978) experiments suggest that the phenomena described in the section on primary memory depend not only on the capacity of consciousness to hold information, but on its capacity to coordinate mental activity using that information as a data base. If this were true, then one might argue that consciousness is more than a primary storage system—its resources are also used for the executive control of task activity (Baddeley and Hitch, 1974). Let us now discuss how this executive control function might work.

3.1 The Programming Metaphor

In a previous paper, Mandler (1975) has likened consciousness to a computer programmer combining various operations of which his or her computer is capable in order to accomplish some unique calculation. For ease and convenience the programmer works for the most part in natural language—here Mandler may be referring to the inner voice we so often associate with conscious thought. Brain mechanisms that actually carry out the operations, however, cannot read natural language. Therefore consciously-constructed programs are compiled into a "machine language" that these brain mechanisms can understand. The machine-language translations of commands generated in consciousness then direct the operations required for the calculation, which occur outside of awareness. When the calculation is complete, its product becomes available to consciousness, providing an answer to the query originally posed in the natural-language program.

A simple demonstration has been used by Jaynes (1975, 1976), Miller (1962) and Nisbet and Wilson (1977) to make a similar point. Jaynes has people introspect upon their mental activity while adding two small numbers in the head. The reports of those introspections indicate that people are consciously aware of the two numbers, of the name of the required arithmetic operation, and after a brief time, of the answer. They are not aware of anything that could be described as performing the operation—once the information required by the problem is entered into consciousness the answer just seems to appear.

In the programming metaphor and the mental arithmetic demonstration, Mandler and Jaynes hold consciousness responsible for structuring a task to be carried out. This is the essence of executive control and has been discussed at length by Shallice (1972), who argues that executive control has two components. The first is goal setting, which can be defined at least for the purposes of experimentation as determining what action to initiate given some specific signal from the environment. The second is task organization, which can be defined as implementing a sequence of mental operations sufficient to accomplish the goal that has been set.

3.2 Goal Setting

In the definition of goal setting employed here, the question of motivation is substantially avoided. At issue are the mechanisms involved in selecting and responding to one signal for action at the expense of others, with commitment by the subject to enter into a task in which a certain set of signals is relevant essentially taken for granted. There are two fundamental aspects of setting a goal: deciding what signal is there and deciding what to do about it. I will briefly take up two experimental situations, the detection task and the secondary probe task, which allow the first of these decisions to be examined. I will then describe a particular version of the cueing or priming task which illuminates the second kind of decision.

3.2.1. *Deciding a signal is there*

The detection task enables a detailed analysis of determining that a signal of a certain kind is present. Subjects in this task are given a particular stimulus even as a target, such as a flash of light in an otherwise darkened visual field or a tone of a particular frequency in a background of white noise. In the simplest case, the subject's job is to give a single overt response, such as pressing a button, whenever the target occurs.

Posner *et al.* (in press) have argued that detection involves two operations that can interact with one another. In the first, called orienting, the subject is capable of making only certain non-arbitrary responses to the signal whose function is to obtain more information. In the second part of the process, called detecting, the subject becomes capable of communicating awareness of the signal by making any arbitrarily chosen overt response the experimenter and the subject care to agree on. For Posner and his colleagues, orienting involves the stimulus making known its presence to a central decision mechanism that has control over voluntary action. Detecting involves the decision mechanism acknowledging the stimulus by selecting and initiating some non-habitual behaviour.

Interactions between the two operations take place when the subject knows something in advance of the signal's occurrence that makes the occurrence more predictable, such as probable location in situations where it is possible for a visual signal to originate from several positions in space or probable modality when it is possible for either a visual or an auditory signal to occur. According to Posner *et al.*, this advance information allows the central decision mechanism to begin orienting before the signal actually occurs, rather than waiting for the signal to call attention to itself from some unknown sensory input pathway. If the advance information is accurate, detecting the signal is facilitated. If the information is misleading, detecting the signal is inhibited relative to having no information at all about the more likely location or modality (Fig. 4).

By eliminating all responsibilities other than perceiving a well-defined signal and initiating the response assigned to it, however, the detection task vastly over-simplifies the information processing environment in which goal setting ordinarily takes place. People are usually

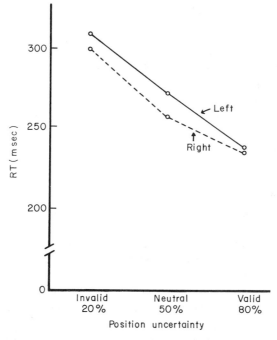

Fig. 4 Mean simple reaction time to a light occurring to the left or to the right of a central fixation point (Posner *et al.*, in press). Neutral point represents no advance information about location—the light could occur to the left or to the right with equal probability. "Valid" and "invalid" points represent respectively the benefit and the cost accruing when a cue was given in advance telling the subject that the light was 80% likely to occur in the valid position and only 20% likely to occur in the invalid position. "Right" and "left" represent the side of fixation the signal actually occurred on—it can be seen that subjects had a slight bias toward the right which was statistically independent of cue-related costs and benefits. Eye position was monitored to insure that subjects did not move their eyes during a trial. This means the results are due to orienting attention and not to orienting the eyes.

performing some other activity when an environmental signal requiring action occurs, and must interrupt that activity to process the signal (Deutsch and Deutsch, 1963; Simon, 1967). The secondary probe task adds these two characteristics to detection in order to study the process of changing one's activity in response to a change in action-demanding environmental conditions. In this task, subjects perform some ongoing activity on which they are told to concentrate, called the primary task. At various unpredictable points in the course of the primary task, a secondary stimulus or probe occurs to which the subject must give a response. The time or accuracy of responding to the probe is examined as a function of the kind of processing required at that point by the primary task, and this function compared to probe performance in the absence of the primary task, when the subject can devote full resources to the probe.

The general finding is that responses to probes are slower and less accurate during primary task performance than when probes occur as the only task activity. For example, rehearsing a newly encountered list of letters or words, one of the functions attributed to primary memory, produces decrements in probe performance (Johnston *et al.*, 1971; Logan, in press; Shulman and Greenberg, 1971; Stanners *et al.*, 1969). The longer the list or the harder the individual items are to remember, the larger the decrement. Tasks which vary in difficulty over time produce larger probe decrements at points of high difficulty and smaller decrements at points of low difficulty (Kahneman *et al.*, 1967). Results such as these have been taken to mean that detecting and responding to the probe requires the subject's limited central or conscious processing capacity and that when some other task occupies capacity probe detection becomes less efficient (Kahneman, 1973; Kerr, 1975; Posner and Klein, 1973).

This view has been criticized by McLeod (1978), who argues that if interference with probe performance were due to limitations on central or executive processing capacity, all probe tasks should show the same temporal patterns of interference from any particular primary task. It has been found that different kinds of probe tasks, such as responding to a visual rather than an auditory signal (Schwartz, 1976) or responding to a tone with a spoken word as opposed to a button push (McLeod, 1978), produce somewhat different temporal patterns of interference. Therefore McLeod maintains that secondary probe performance measures interference with specific input and response initiation operations and not with a central executive processor. This "either-or" interpretation does not seem warranted when all the available data are taken into account. The interactions cited by McLeod do demonstrate that input- and output-specific interference can occur between primary and secondary tasks. On the other hand, remarkably similar patterns of interference from speeded primary tasks are shown by secondary tasks as different in their input and output demands as pushing a button as rapidly as possible to a tone (e.g. Johnston *et al.*, 1971; Posner and Boies, 1971) and detecting the visual presentation of a Landolt C figure that need not be reported until the primary task has been comfortably completed (Ninio, 1974). Therefore it would seem that mental operations of a considerably more general nature, involving central decision and control processes, are also subject to interference that can be observed using the secondary probe technique (Posner, 1978a). From performance in the probe task, then, one can conclude that time is required to allocate attention to a newly occurring environmental signal for action, and that the more demanding the task one is already doing, the longer and more error-prone is the process of allocation.

3.2.2 *Deciding what to do about the signal*

Though more complex than detection, the probe task is still an over-simplification of goal setting. This is because the occurrence of a secondary stimulus always signals the same activity. In order to examine the additional problem of determining what activity to select given that more than one could be signalled, LaBerge *et al.* (1977) have employed a version of the cueing task discussed earlier in connection with Neely's demonstration of consciously-induced semantic activation. Subjects were presented with pairs of digits arrayed either vertically or horizontally. If a vertical array appeared, the subject was to decide whether the two digits were the same or different. In this matching task, the array $\frac{4}{4}$ would require a "yes" response and the array $\frac{4}{5}$ would require a "no" response. If a horizontal array appeared, the subject was to decide whether the two digits increased in value from left to right. In this ordering task, 4 4 would require a "no" response and 4 5 a "yes". The subject was given one of four different kinds of cues, 1800 msec before each array (Fig. 5). The neutral cue served as a warning signal but provided no information about the upcoming array. The pattern cue gave information about what digit was most likely to be seen. The task cue gave information about what task was most likely to be required. The fourth cue gave information about both pattern and task. Results, shown in Table I, indicated that both types of cueing facilitated performance. Collapsed over tasks, subjects were some 37 msec faster when told which digit would be most likely than when given no advance information about the digits to be seen. More important at this point in the discussion, subjects were some 43 msec faster when given advance information about the task to be performed.

Together, then, the detection, probe, and cueing tasks demonstrate that both aspects of goal setting—deciding that a signal is there and deciding what to do about it—take time. Both are facilitated by information provided in advance that makes either the presence of a signal or the action demanded by the signal more predictable. Further, the

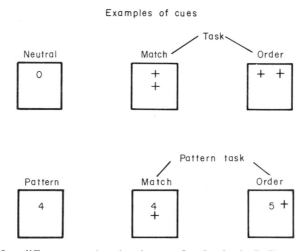

Fig. 5 The four different cues given in advance of a stimulus by LaBerge *et al.* (1977).

TABLE I *Reaction Time (msec) for "Yes" Responses in Cueing Experiment*[a]

	Pattern cue		No pattern cue	
	Matching task	Ordering task	Matching task	Ordering task
Task cue	387	497	432	546
No task cue	445	547	465	580
Advantage for task cue	58	50	33	34

[a] LaBerge *et al.* (1977).

detection and probe studies indicate that responding to an environmental signal for action draws on limited central processing capacity.

3.3 Task Organization

Once a goal for action is set, some sequence of mental operations must be implemented that will result in the goal's accomplishment. Such a sequence has been called a behavioural action system by Shallice (1972). Behavioural action systems are activated as units according to Shallice, with activation coming from two sources: sensory and memorial input providing data on which the system operates and a "selector input" generated consciously. The selector input is a command allowing the action system to take control of behaviour, and is reminiscent of a call to a sub-routine in a computer program. The action system will retain control of behaviour until either the goal is accomplished (Miller *et al.*, 1960) or consciousness transfers control to another action system, perhaps in response to a newly detected environmental signal (Carr and Bacharach, 1976; Deutsch and Deutsch, 1963; Newell, 1973).

If action systems are particular combinations of mental operations called up as sub-routine-like units, two issues arise. The first is how an action system comes to exist in the first place. This requires an examination of skill learning which will lead to the second issue, how the role of consciousness in controlling action systems might change at various levels of learning.

3.3.1 *Skill learning*

One old adage for which research on human performance has amassed considerable support is that "practice makes perfect"—or at least better. When confronted with a new task, whether primarily cognitive or primarily physical, it is nearly universal that the more times the task is carried out the faster and more accurate performance can be (Keele, 1973; Welford, 1976; Woodworth, 1938). Speaking specifically about physical skills, Keele (1968) and Keele and Summers (1976) have explained this phenomenon in terms of the establishment of an integrated motor program consisting of an ordered sequence of commands to muscles producing movements required by the activity. Early in learning, component movements of the activity are not well integrated and conscious attention must be used to select each movement in the proper sequence. As learning progresses the movements become better co-ordinated. Conscious control occurs at a higher and higher level of analysis until finally, once initiated, the whole activity runs off as a unit with no need for conscious intervention. An intuition for Keele's theory can be obtained by thinking back on learning to ride a bicycle, to type, or to pronounce the names of the characters in "War and Peace". On this view, skills are thought to be organized hierarchically, so that once a well-integrated program for a particular movement sequence is established, that program can be used as a unit in building more complex activities. Again an analogy can be drawn to the use of sub-routines in computer programming (Anderson, 1976, Ch. 6).

The programming metaphor can be applied to cognitive as well as physical skills. Establishing hierarchically organized structures via practice has been proposed to underlie perceptual recognition (Bindra, 1976; Gibson, 1969; LaBerge and Samuels, 1974) and the organization of secondary memory (Hayes-Roth, 1977). Richards and Reicher (1978) have argued that when an unfamiliar complex figure (e.g. Ⅎ or Ʌ) is first encountered, attention is required to keep track of the spatial relations among component features in order to perceive the figure accurately. With practice, however, higher-order representations are established in memory to which the component features are more or less securely associated. Presentation of the figure will then activate the higher-order representation as a unit, freeing conscious attention from the task of holding the features together in their proper organization. In the absence of conscious control, confusion may still occur when familiar figures near one another in the visual field contain features which, if exchanged between the figures, would result in the formation of some other familiar figure (Treisman, 1977). Much of the encoding of familiar figures, however, can go on without conscious assistance after sufficient practice (Kolers, 1975; LaBerge, 1973).

3.3.2 *Conscious control: when does task organization require capacity?*

In 1973 Posner and Klein reported a probe experiment in which subjects were presented with a warning signal followed after 500 msec by a letter of the alphabet. One second after this letter a second letter appeared. In half the blocks of trials the subject had to indicate as rapidly and accurately as possible whether the second letter was physically identical to the first. In the other blocks, the subject had to indicate whether the second letter matched whatever letter was three forward of the first letter in the alphabet (e.g. if the first letter was "C" and the second "F", the subject responded "same"). On half the trials in each block a probe tone occurred to which the subject had to press a key. The probe could occur at any one of eight points during the course of a primary task: 500 msec before the warning signal; 350 msec before the first letter; 50, 150, 300 or 500 msec after the first letter; and 150 or 300 msec after the second letter.

Fig. 6 shows reaction time to the probe in this experiment. The physical match condition produced very little interference relative to the first two probe points at 50, 150 or 300 msec after the first letter—and in other experiments reported in this paper, probe performance even improved at those three points. Posner and Klein argued that subjects were encoding the first letter during this period, and that encoding occurred without conscious involvement. Interference appeared 500 msec after the first letter, and reached a maximum 150 msec after the second letter. During this period Posner and Klein argued subjects were preparing the mental operations necessary to compare their internal representation of the first letter to the second letter and then actually carrying out the comparison.

The picture is quite different for the "add-three" condition. Here probe interference of striking magnitude appeared within 300 msec

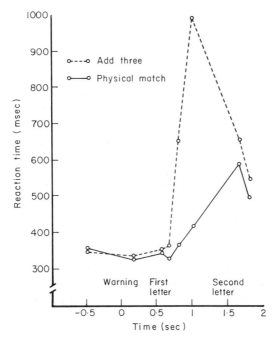

Fig. 6 Mean probe reaction time as a function of time of probe occurrence during the course of a letter-matching trial (Posner and Klein, 1973, Exp. 5). Time of occurrence on this graph is measured relative to the time of presentation of the warning signal.

after first letter presentation, peaked 200 msec later and was still somewhat greater than that observed in the physical match condition at both 150 and 300 msec after the second letter. Apparently encoding the first letter was also automatic in the "add-three" condition, as evidenced by the lack of interference during the first 150 msec following its occurrence, but as soon as the letter was identified a large investment of capacity was made in counting forward to the letter actually to be used in the matching decision. Once that letter was computed capacity was required to prepare for and perhaps to carry out the comparison operation.

As might be expected from the discussion of skill learning, then, encoding well-known letters seems to take place without conscious assistance, but preparing for and perhaps executing complex and relatively unfamiliar tasks such as counting through the alphabet or comparing two letters for identity requires some commitment of central processing capacity. Consistent with the programming metaphor, Posner and Klein speculated that with more practice, the alphabet counting task would become at least partially automated, reducing the tremendous probe interference observed for that condition in Fig. 6.

Further arguments that central control is needed to organize a complex but unfamiliar task have been offered by Logan (1978). In a series of experiments in which subjects searched for pre-specified targets in visually presented arrays of letters, Logan manipulated characteristics of the visual search task that are thought to affect particular mental operations but not others. His goal was to determine which of these operations require central processing capacity during execution and which do not. Following Sternberg's (1969) additive factors methodology, Logan varied the number of digits that had to be remembered in a concurrent memory span task, looking for interactions between the variables affecting specific operations in the search task and the size of the memory load imposed by the span task. We have already seen that larger memory loads appear to place larger demands on conscious storage and retrieval co-ordination capabilities—if executing a particular operation involved in the search task also requires central capacity, then variables that make that operation harder or easier should combine their effects with those of memory load in the form of an interaction. If the variables affecting a particular operation are statistically independent of memory load, one might conclude that the execution of that operation does not require conscious control. The additive factors method depends in part upon the assumption of serial processing stages, in which variables affecting the execution of a particular stage do not affect the code output to the next stage for further processing, but only the ease or difficulty with which that code is achieved. Because this assumption is often violated in skilled performance, there are other ways in which interactions between variable could occur than through their affecting the same stage or mental operation. However, the *absence* of interaction constitutes reasonable evidence that the variables do *not* affect the same operation.

Logan's results can be summarized quickly. Of all the parameters of the search task, only the number of targets—whose representations would presumably have to be maintained in a highly active state, drawing on space in primary memory—interacted with memory load.

However, this is not to say that memory load did not influence search performance. As Logan says:

> It was clear throughout the experiments that the visual task required attention—the main effect of memory load was quite reliable—yet there was no clear evidence that attention was involved in the *execution* of any stage's (or operation's) function. The components of the task seem automatic, but the task itself is not. Perhaps the stage structure of a task should be viewed as a temporary assembly of automatic, special-purpose processors organized by attention to deal with the task at hand . . . It may take attention, then, to *prepare* an appropriate sequence of structures, and *maintain* it until a stimulus has appeared.
>
> (Logan, 1978, p. 57)

The results of a study by Comstock (1975) are in accord with this conclusion. Reaction times to a temporally unpredictable probe tone were collected in the dual-task environment of Posner and Klein's (1973) physical match condition, and also in a single-task environment. All the visual events of the physical match task occurred as usual in the single-task environment, but subjects ignored them and responded only to the probe. Posner and Klein's results were replicated in the dual task (Fig. 6). In the single task, however, probe reaction times were about the same at all probe points. Most important, these times were faster than any of the times in the dual-task environment, even those to probes occurring before the warning signal when none of the operations of the matching task was actually being executed. It might be inferred that keeping the primary task organized required some capacity, which had to be committed even while the subject was supposedly resting between trials. Such an investment would be especially profitable at low levels of practice on a new task, whose programme or action system is not well-established and might be subject to disintegration if attention were removed entirely.

The obvious implication of these arguments is that operations which require capacity when unfamiliar and tasks whose organization requires capacity when new should become more and more automated with practice. Spelke *et al.* (1976) have put this proposition to a rather severe test by asking whether people could learn to read a short story and write words from dictation as well concurrently as each task could be done by itself. After about 40 hours of practice, reading speed, comprehension, and memory for story events were as high when the tasks were performed simultaneously as when reading alone. Spelke and her colleagues did not quite succeed in demonstrating that all the processing associated with dictation could also be carried on undiminished under dual task requirements. Dictation rate and accuracy were relatively unaffected, and after an initial deterioration handwriting quality was fairly normal as well. Late in practice dictated words could be categorized and the category name written instead of the word with considerable accuracy, but subjects were never able to remember the words they had written while reading as well as words written when dictation was the only task. Since the results were so impressive in every other respect, it might be speculated that memory would have come along had they only persevered. In this experiment, however, subjects rarely looked at the words they were writing while reading, but presumably did look at the words under dictation alone. Therefore the memory decrement may merely reflect the absence of a relevant source of information in the dual task situation rather than a last vestige of the limited capacity of conscious control.

4 Consciousness as an Information Selector: Input Regulation

4.1 Automaticity

It is now time to make a more formal statement about the notion of automaticity explored in the previous section. The term has been applied to two different kinds of processes, encoding a stimulus such as a letter or a word and organizing a task such as counting through the alphabet or searching an array for a target. Within the programming metaphor, these two kinds of processes can be seen as quite similar—a sub-routine must be established which is capable of accomplishing a certain goal, be it the simpler goal of activating a usable internal representation of some external stimulus, or the more complex goal of manipulating several such representations to ascertain relations among them (Anderson, 1976). The operation of such a sub-routine must be consciously controlled early in learning in order for information to flow through the sub-routine efficiently (Kolers, 1975; LaBerge, 1973; LaBerge and Samuels, 1974). Once fully established, the internal operation of the sub-routine is not dependent on conscious assistance or control. After activation, the sub-routine can run off automatically regardless of what is occupying consciousness during its execution.

Though much evidence exists for automatic encoding, it is not clear how much of human task organization is similarly automated. According to Shallice (1972) and Keele (1973), at least the *initiation* of an overt behaviour is always attended, even if the *operation* of the action system producing that behaviour is entirely automatic. Kerr (1975) has concluded from a review of the speech perception literature that comprehending spoken language—certainly one of the most practiced task activities—usually draws on central capacity. The same appears to be true for reading. The study by Spelke *et al.* (1976) shows that although people can learn to perform at least some kinds of complex linguistic tasks simultaneously with little interference, a great deal of specific practice is necessary to reach that state of automation. It may be that some involvement of attention occurs in most tasks requiring computations based on particular relations among multiple stimulus items.

4.2 Conscious Control of Information to be Processed

A tachistoscopic recognition experiment by Carr *et al.* (1978) can be used to illustrate this point. Strings of four letters were very briefly exposed and then replaced with a jumbled masking field. The subject's job was to determine which of two letters shown concurrently with the mask had occurred at a specified position in the stimulus string. This widely-used experimental paradigm was first developed by Reicher (1969), who found that letters were more accurately identified when presented as part of a word than as part of a random nonsense string (e.g. RDMA, EOTP) or even by themselves. Subsequent studies showed that orthographically regular but unfamiliar pseudowords (e.g. MARD, POTE) are also recognized better than nonsense strings, and sometimes just as well as words (Baron and Thurston, 1973; Manelis, 1974; Spoehr and Smith, 1975). Thus the "word superiority effect" could result from two different kinds of information, one provided by the predictable relations among any orthographically regular combination of letters and the other by the familiarity or meaning of combinations actually used as words in the language. Carr *et al.* wished to determine whether people have strategic control over which kind of information they rely on in this very demanding task.

Subjects were induced to expect only one type of stimulus in the experiment, shown that type for many trials, then surreptitiously shown an occasional stimulus of another type mixed in randomly with the expected stimulus type. When either words or nonsense strings were expected exclusively, the results were identical: accuracy on words was some 15% better than accuracy on nonsense or pseudowords, which did not differ. When pseudowords were expected, the more usual pattern of results was obtained. Accuracy on pseudowords was only slightly less than accuracy on words and significantly greater than accuracy on nonsense strings. Thus the recognition of familiar words appears to be supported by automatic encoding pathways that allow the words to be recognized considerably more efficiently in a masked tachistoscopic exposure than a collection of unrelated letters. Pseudowords, on the other hand, are unfamiliar and do not have such stimulus-specific automated codes. Unified internal representations can be obtained for pseudowords but they must be computed by more complex sub-routines that apply the rules of English orthography. These sub-routines seem to require some degree of conscious control in order to operate with any efficiency. If the perceiver does not know that pseudowords will occur and fails to attend to orthographic computation, pseudowords are treated like strings of independent letters and enjoy no recognition advantage over nonsense strings.

These results demonstrate the most fundamental proposition under-lying the role attributed to consciousness as an information selector or input regulator: the information extracted from a stimulus and used to control behaviour depends to a substantial degree on the expectations one entertains about that stimulus. Some kinds of potentially available stimulus information may not be extracted at all if one does not expect or intend to use them. Other kinds of information may be extracted along automatic encoding pathways, but the codes so activated go unused because the absence of attention prevents them from reaching decision and response mechanisms.

4.3 Generating and Testing Expectations: The Origins of Cost

As discussed earlier, Posner *et al.* (in press, Fig. 4) have shown that advance information about where a change in luminance is likely to occur has substantial effects on the time taken to detect the change. Benefit accrues when a light appears in an expected area and cost accrues when a light is presented elsewhere in the visual field. Expecta-tions about the nature of the stimulus also produce costs and benefits, as in Neely's (1977) experiment or the pattern cue condition of LaBerge *et al.* (1977). Posner and Snyder (1975) have conducted a systematic investigation of the time course of these effects using a single letter cue in advance of a pair of letters the subject had to match. In separate conditions the cue appeared in the matching array on either 20% or 80% of the trials. Some benefit occurred on accurately cued trials in the 20% condition, and Posner and Snyder attributed the benefit observed there to priming of automatic encoding pathways. In the 80% condi-tion, in which subjects reported actively attending to the cue in pre-paration for the array, a larger amount of benefit occurred on accu-rately cued trials as well as substantial cost on miscued trials. Though benefit began to accrue as soon as the cue was presented, costs did not appear for some 300–500 msec. In an analysis much like that applied to detecting luminance changes, Posner and Snyder concluded that atten-tion is oriented toward the encoding pathway corresponding to the expected letter and that this process takes time. After orientation, letters different from the expected letter cannot gain access to decision and response systems until attention is reoriented from the expected pathway to the unexpected pathway.

In a detailed study of the capacity demands of processing the cue in a letter matching task, McLean (1977) and McLean and Shulman (1978) have modified this idea about how an expectation works. McLean added a secondary probe task to the standard cued letter matching paradigm. On half the trials, subjects received single letters as cues followed either 100 msec or 500 msec later by two letters to be matched. On the other trials, a probe tone occurred either 100 or 500 msec after the cue. The matching array was presented as soon as the subject responded to the probe. Fig. 7 compares cost in the letter

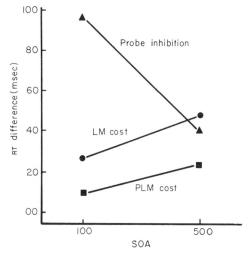

Fig. 7 Probe inhibition and letter matching cost in McLean's (1977) study of the attention demands of processing the cue in a letter-matching task. SOA (stimulus onset asynchrony) represents time between presentation of cue and presentation of the two letters to be matched on unprobed trials or the probe on probed trials, which were mixed randomly. LM cost is cost occurring on unprobed trials and PLM cost is cost occurring on probed trials. In both cases, cost increases over SOA, while probe inhibition decreases.

matching task at 100 and 500 msec following the cue to interference with probe detection at the same times. As in the experiments of Posner and Snyder (1975), letter matching cost is minimal at 100 msec but rises substantially by 500 msec. Probe interference, however, shows an opposite time course. It appears that central processing capacity is invested in generating an expectation before any letter matching cost accrues, but once the expectation has been generated central capacity can be devoted at least momentarily to another task without destroying the expectation. Rather than pointing an attentional spotlight towards an input pathway, McLean argues that expectations should be regarded as hypotheses about upcoming stimulus events that are generated consciously, maintained until needed, and tested against the actual stimulus event when it occurs. Viewed in this way, expectations about stimuli are task-specific as well as stimulus-specific. They consist of priming decision mechanisms not only to carry out a certain kind of decision, such as a same-different judgment about letters, but to make that decision about a *particular* letter, such as an "A" instead of a "B". Carrying out this preparation requires conscious control and large amounts of probe interference result. Once the preparation is accomplished, much less capacity is needed to maintain the preparation and probe interference diminishes. Presumably, however, a probe given just after the matching array appears would suffer interference as in Posner and Klein's (1973) experiment, at least at low levels of practice

5 Conclusion: What Do We Gain by a Concept of Consciousness?

5.1 Consciousness as a Means of Supporting New Behaviour

At times suggestions have been made that consciousness is the sum total of all the information processing going on at a given point in time. A less encompassing claim has been made that no identifiable mechanisms of attention can be separated from some "remainder" of the information processing apparatus (Neisser, 1976). Though it is somewhat difficult to say precisely what this means, one interpretation is that however else one claims the mind works, it does represent a single, unitary entity in its operation. Yet in the last two sections considerable evidence has been reviewed in favour of a different view. As Posner argues, investigations of the time course of information flow:

> give rise to models in which information can be represented in [visual], phonetic and semantic information processing systems (LaBerge & Samuels, 1974; Posner & Rogers, 1978). Chronometric studies show that each of these systems can be isolated from the others in the sense that subjects can respond to information in one code independently from information derived in another code. It is unnecessary to view these systems as serial stages in the processing of information. Instead they should be thought of as complex isolated systems that can deal with information in independent codes within the same nervous system.
>
> (Posner, 1978b)

In Section 2 evidence was reviewed that information in each of these codes can potentially exist in at least two different states of activation in the mind, referred to as primary and secondary memory. By introducing the notion of priming or partial activation in Sections 3 and 4 this memorial dichotomy was changed into a continuum. One might say that codes representing information in the mind can take a range of states of activation from essentially zero to some maximum. The closer a code is to maximum activation the more conscious it is and the more readily accessible is its information for any (perhaps arbitrary) purpose. The results of Waugh and Norman (1965) indicate that the amount of information that can be maintained in the highest state of activation is strictly limited, perhaps to one code. The codes active at any point in time can all potentially influence overt behaviour (Conrad, 1974; McKay, 1973; Treisman, 1969). However, access to less activated codes is less efficient, making it harder to use these codes in guiding behaviour. This can be seen in nearly all the phenomena reviewed here, from the decreasing probability of correct recall as digits fade from primary memory to the difficulty people have in performing more than one task at a time when the task is new to them. Less activated codes can be used most profitably only in well-automated processing sequences. Therefore consciousness might be regarded as a gateway to novel manipulations of information. On this view consciousness can select and maintain a small amount of information to be processed in some unique fashion, and control the step-by-step execution of that processing until the operations involved have been integrated into a new sub-routine through practice.

The idea that internal representations can be more or less conscious depending on how highly they are activated may seem at odds with Underwood's arguments in this volume for a dichotomous view: memories are either conscious or unconscious. Though the evidence for varying degrees of activation is strong (Fischler and Bloom, 1977; Ashcraft, 1977; Collins and Loftus, 1975; Fischler and Goodman, in press; Posner and Snyder, 1975; Wally and Weiden, 1973; Warren, 1976), the evidence that people can consciously apprehend only a small amount of information is even stronger, as was shown in Section 2. However, there is nothing in this evidence that compels one to believe that all information of which one is conscious is equally activated. We have all had the experience of being "vaguely aware" of something, be it an environmental stimulus to which we eventually turn our attention or some past experience partially called to mind by present events that we are eventually able to remember more fully. Thus codes within the scope of introspection may vary in degree of activation, some codes may lie on the fringes of conscious apprehension, and others may be outside of awareness yet activated sufficiently to influence performance, all at the same moment in time. Despite the continuity of possible levels of activation, a general claim can still be made that consciousness serves roughly to separate mental activity into two quite different—though not necessarily homogenous—states. The less automated and more closely controlled or regulated is the task to be performed, the more evidence will be seen for a dichotomy of memorial states. The less conscious control is exerted, the wider can be the scope of conscious (or partially conscious) apprehension and the more easily one can find evidence for codes at continuously varying levels of activation.

5.2 A Mechanism for General Rather than Specific Intelligence?

One possible gain from having a concept of conscious function that emphasizes control over novel processing has been proposed by Rozin, who finds it useful in understanding the evolution of intelligence:

> As is the case with virtually all complex biological systems, intelligence should be organized in a hierarchical manner, out of component "subprograms." Within an evolutionary framework, these subprograms, which can be called *adaptive specializations*, usually originate as specific solutions to specific problems in survival, such as prey detection . . . At the time of their origin, these specializations are tightly wired into the functional systems they were designed to serve and are thus inaccessible to other programs or systems in the brain. I suggest that in the course of evolution these programs become more *accessible* to other systems and, in the extreme, may rise to the level of consciousness and be applied over the full realm of behavior or mental function . . . It is suggested that part of the process of learning and education can be considered as bringing to consciousness some of the limited-access programs, the "cognitive unconscious," already in the head.
>
> (Rozin, 1976, 245–246)

Rozin is arguing that consciousness is responsible for applying already existing mental operations to new stimulus material or in new task situations outside the original ecological context in which the operation evolved. Thus consciousness, the gateway to novel manipulations, may represent a mechanism by which we are able to adapt our finite repertoire of information processing capabilities to new situations voluntarily rather than waiting for evolution to do the job for us.

6 Acknowledgements

Preparation of this review was supported by NIH Postdoctoral Fellowship 1-F32-HD05157 from the National Institute of Child Health and

Human Development (USA) taken at the University of Oregon under the sponsorship of Dr Michael I. Posner and by the Department of Psychology at the University of Nebraska, Omaha where I taught during the 1978–79 academic year. I would like to thank Mike Posner, Harold Hawkins, Verne Bacharach, Gordon Shulman, Steve Keele, Joelle Presson, Tom Killion, Gordon Logan, Geoff Underwood, Tim Shallice, Denise Frieder Carr and two anonymous reviewers for their very helpful comments, criticisms and discussion.

7 References

Ashcraft, M. H. (1976). Priming and property dominance effects in semantic memory. *Memory and Cognition* **4**, 490–500.

Atkinson, R. C. and Shiffrin, R. M. (1968). Human memory: A proposed system and its control process. *In* "Advances in the psychology of learning and motivation research and therapy" (Eds K. W. Spence and J. T. Spence), Vol. 2. Academic Press, New York.

Atkinson, R. C. and Shiffrin, R. M. (1971). The control of short-term memory. *Scientific American* **225**, 82–91.

Baddeley, A. D. (1976). "The psychology of memory." Basic Books, New York.

Baddeley, A. D. and Hitch, G. (1974). *In* "The Psychology of learning and motivation" (Ed. G. H. Bower), Vol. 8. Academic Press, New York.

Baron, J., & Thurston, I. (1973). An analysis of the word superiority effect. *Cognitive Psychology* **4**, 207–228.

Bindra, D. (1976). "A theory of intelligent behavior." John Wiley, New York.

Broadbent, D. E. (1958). "Perception and communication." Pergamon, Elsford, New York.

Broadbent, D. E. (1971). "Decision and stress." Academic Press, New York.

Broadbent, D. E. The magic number seven after fifteen years. *In* "Studies in long term memory" (Eds A. Kennedy and A. Wilkes). John Wiley, London.

Carr, T. H. and Bacharach, V. R. (1976). Perceptual tuning and conscious attention: Systems of input regulation in visual information processing. *Cognition* **4**, 281–302.

Carr, T. H., Davidson, B. J. and Hawkins, H. L. (1978). Perceptual flexibility in word recognition: Strategies affect orthographic computation but not lexical access. *Journal of experimental Psychology: Human Perception and Performance* **7**, 674–690.

Chase, W. G. (1978). Elementary information processes. *In* "Handbook of learning and cognitive processes" (Ed. W. K. Estes), Vol. 5. Lawrence Erlbaum Associates, Hillsdale, New Jersey.

Cherry, E. C. (1953). Some experiments on the recognition of speech, with one and two ears. *Journal of the Acoustical Society of America* **25**, 975–979.

Collins, A. M., and Loftus, E. F. (1975). A spreading-activation theory of semantic processing. *Psychological Review* **82**, 407–428.

Comstock, E. M. (1975). Limited-capacity central attention mechanisms. Doctoral dissertation. University of Massachusetts, Amherst.

Conrad, C. (1974). Context effects in sentence comprehension: A study of the subjective lexicon. *Memory and Cognition* **2**, 130–138.

Craik, F. I. M. (1968). Two components in free recall. *Journal of Verbal Learning and Verbal Behavior* **1**, 996–1004.

Crannel, C. W. and Parrish, J. M. (1957). A comparison of immediate memory span for digits, letters, and words. *Journal of Psychology* **44**, 319–327.

Crowder, R. G. (1976). "Principles of learning and memory." Lawrence Erlbaum Associates, Hillsdale, New Jersey.

Deutsch, J. A. and Deutsch, D. (1963). Attention: Some theoretical considerations. *Psychological Review* **70**, 80–90.

Ebbinghaus, H. (1964). "Memory: A contribution to experimental psychology." Dover, New York. (Originally published, 1885.)

Erdelyi, M. H. (1974). A new look at the New Look: Perceptual defense and vigilance. *Psychological Review* **81**, 1–25.

Fischler, I., and Bloom, P. A. (1977). Contextual facilitation of word retrieval in reading. Paper presented to the American Psychological Association, San Francisco, California.

Fischler, I. and Goodman, G. O. (1978). Latency of associative facilitation in memory. *Journal of Experimental Psychology: Human Perception and Performance* **4**, 445–270.

Gibson, E. J. (1969). "Principles of perceptual learning and development." New York: Appleton-Century-Crofts, New York.

Graesser, A. and Mandler, G. (1978). Limited processing capacity constrains the storage of unrelated sets of words and retrieval from natural categories. *Journal of Experimental Psychology: Human Learning and Memory* **4**, 86–100.

Hayes-Roth, B. (1977). Evolution of cognitive structures and processes. *Psychological Review* **84**, 260–278.

Hyman, R. (1953). Stimulus information as a determinant of reaction time. *Journal of Experimental Psychology* **45**, 188–196.

James, W. (1890). "The principles of psychology", Vol. 1. Holt, New York.

Jaynes, J. (1975). Invited address. George Peabody College, Nashville, Tennessee.

Jaynes, J. (1976). "The origins of consciousness in the breakdown of the bicameral mind." Houghton Mifflin, New York.

Johnston, W. A. Greenberg, S. N., Risher, R. P. and Martin, D. W. (1970). Divided attention: A vehicle for monitoring memory processes. *Journal of Experimental Psychology* **83**, 164–171.

Kahneman, D. (1973). "Attention and effort." Prentice Hall, Englewood Cliffs, New Jersey.

Kahneman, D., Beatty, J. and Pollack, I. (1967). Perceptual deficit during a mental task. *Science* **157**, 218–219.

Keele, S. W. (1968). Movement control in skilled motor performance. *Psychological Bulletin* **70**, 387–403.

Keele, S. W. (1973). "Attention and human performance." Goodyear, Pacific Palisades, California.

Keele, S. W. and Neill, W. T. (in press). Mechanisms of attention. *In* "Handbook of perception" (Eds E. C. Carterette and M. P. Friedman), Vol. 9. Academic Press, New York.

Keele, S. W. and Summers, J. J. (1976). The structure of motor programs. *In* "Motor control: Issues and trends." (Ed. G. E. Stelmach). Academic Press, New York.

Kerr, B. (1973). Processing demands during mental operations. *Memory and Cognition* **4**, 401–412.

Kolers, P. A. (1975). Memorial consequences of automatized encoding. *Journal of Experimental Psychology: Human Learning and Memory* **1**, 689–701.

LaBerge, D. (1973). Attention and the measurement of perceptual learning. *Memory and Cognition* **1**, 268–276.

LaBerge, D., Petersen, R. and Norden, M. J. (1977). Exploring the limits of cueing. *In* "Attention and performance" (Ed. S. Dornic), Vol. 6. Lawrence Erlbaum Associates, Hillsdale, New Jersey.

LaBerge, D. and Samuels, S. J. (1974). Toward a theory of automatic information processing in reading. *Cognitive Psychology* **6**, 293–323.

Logan, G. (1978). Attention in character-classification tasks: Evidence for the automaticity of component stages. *Journal of Experimental Psychology: General* **107**, 32–63.

McCauley, C., Weil, C. and Sperber, R. (1976). The development of memory structures reflected by semantic priming effects. *Journal of Experimental Child Psychology* **22**, 511–518.

McKay, D. (1973). Aspects of the theory of comprehension, memory, and attention. *Quarterly Journal of Experimental Psychology* **25**, 22–40.

McLean, J. (1977). Strategic and ballistic aspects of attention. Master's thesis. University of Oregon, Eugene.

McLean, J. and Shulmann, G. (1978). The construction and maintenance of expectancies. *Quarterly Journal of Experimental Psychology*, **30**, 441–454.

McLeod, P. (1978). Does probe RT measure central processing demand? *Quarterly Journal of Experimental Psychology* **30**, 83–89.

Mandler, G. (1975). "Mind and emotion." John Wiley, New York.

Manelis, L. (1974). The effect of meaningfulness in tachistoscopic word perception. *Perception and Psychophysics* **16**, 183–192.

Meyer, D. E., Schvaneveldt, R. W. and Ruddy, M. G. (1975). Loci of contextual effects on visual word recognition. *In* "Attention and performance" (Ed. P. M. A. Rabbitt), Vol. 5. Academic Press, London.

Miller, G. A. (1956). The magical number seven, plus or minus two: Some limits on our capacity for processing information. *Psychological Review* **63**, 81–97.

Miller, G. A. (1962). "Psychology: The science of mental life." Harper and Row, New York.

Miller, G. A., Galanter, E. and Pribram, K. H. (1960). "Plans and the structure of behavior." Holt, New York.

Neely, J. H. (1977). Semantic priming and retrieval from lexical memory:

Roles of inhibitionless spreading activation and limited-capacity attention. *Journal of Experimental Psychology: General* **106**, 226–254.

Neisser, U. (1976), "Cognition and reality." Freeman, San Francisco.

Newell, A. (1973). Production systems: Models of control structures. *In* "Visual information processing" (Ed. W. G. Chase). Academic Press, New York.

Ninio, A. (1974). The rate of expenditure of effort in RT tasks of varying difficulty. Doctoral dissertation. The Hebrew University, Jerusalem, Israel.

Nisbet, R. E. and Wilson, T. D. (1977). Telling more than we can know: Verbal reports on mental processes. *Psychological Review* **84**, 231–259.

Norman, D. A. (1976). "Memory and attention" (2nd edn.). Wiley, New York.

Posner, M. I. (1973). "Cognition: An introduction." Scott-Foresman, Glenview, Illinois.

Posner, M. I. (1978a). "Chronometric explorations of mind." Lawrence Erlbaum Associates, Hillsdale, New Jersey.

Posner, M. I. (1978b). Mental chronometry and the problem of consciousness. Invited address presented as part of a lecture series, "On the Structure of Thought". Dalhousie University, Halifax, Nova Scotia.

Posner, M. I. and Boies, S. J. (1971). Components of attention. *Psychological Review* **78**, 391–408.

Posner, M. I. and Klein, R. M. (1973). On the functions of consciousness. *In* "Attention and performance" (Ed. S. Kornblum), Vol. 4. Academic Press, London.

Posner, M. I. and Mitchell, R. (1967). Chronometric analysis of classification. *Psychological Review* **74**, 392–409.

Posner, M. I. and Rogers, M. G. K. (1978). Chronometric analysis of abstraction and recognition. *In* "Handbook of learning and cognitive processes" (Ed. W. K. Estes), Vol. 6. Lawrence Erlbaum Associates, Hillsdale, New Jersey.

Posner, M. I. and Snyder, C. R. R. (1975). Attention and cognitive control. *In* "Information processing and cognition: The Loyola Symposium" (Ed. R. L. Solso), Lawrence Erlbaum Associates, Hillsdale, New Jersey.

Posner, M I., Snyder, C. R. R. and Davidson, B. J. (in press). Attention and the detection of signals. *Journal of Experimental Psychology: General.*

Reicher, G. M. (1969). Perceptual recognition as a function of meaningfulness of stimulus material. *Journal of Experimental Psychology* **81**, 275–281.

Richards, J. T. and Reicher, G. M. (1978). The effects of background familiarity in visual search: An analysis of underlying factors. *Perception and Psychophysics* **23**, 499–505.

Rozin, P. (1976). The evolution of intelligence and access to the cognitive unconscious. *In* "Progress in psychobiology and physiological psychology" (Eds J. M. Sprague and A. N. Epstein). Academic Press, New York.

Schwartz, S. P. (1976). Capacity limitations in human information processing. *Memory and Cognition* **4**, 763–768.

Simon, H. (1967). Motivational and emotional controls of cognition. *Psychological Review* **74**, 29–39.

Shallice, T. (1972). Dual functions of consciousness. *Psychological Review* **79**, 383–393.

Shulman, H. G. and Greenberg, S. N. (1971). Perceptual deficit due to division of attention between memory and attention. *Journal of Experimental Psychology* **88**, 171–176.

Spelke, E., Hirst, W. and Neisser, U. (1976). Skills of divided attention. *Cognition* **4**, 215–230.

Spoehr, K. T. and Smith, E. E. (1975). The role of orthographic and phonotactic rules in perceiving letter patterns. *Journal of Experimental Psychology: Human Perception and Performance* **1**, 21–34.

Stanners, R. F., Munier, G. F. and Headley, D. B. (1969). Reaction time as an index of rehearsal in short term memory. *Journal of Experimental Psychology* **82**, 566–570.

Sternberg, S. (1969). The discovery of processing stages: Extensions of Donders' methods. *In* "Attention and performance" (Ed. W. G. Koster), Vol. 2. North Holland, Amsterdam.

Treisman, A. M. (1969). Strategies and models of selective attention. *Psychological Review* **76**, 282–299.

Treisman, A. M. (1977). Focused attention in the perception and retrieval of multidimensional stimuli. *Perception and Psychophysics* **22**, 1–11.

Wally, R. E. and Weiden, T. D. (1973). Lateral inhibition and cognitive masking: A neuropsychological theory of attention. *Psychological Review* 284–302.

Warren, R. E. (1977). Time and the spread of activation in memory. *Journal of Experimental Psychology: Human Learning and Memory* **3**, 458–466.

Watkins, M. J. (1977). The intricacy of the memory span. *Memory and Cognition* **5**, 529–534.

Waugh, N. C. and Norman, D. A. (1965). Primary memory. *Psychological Review* **72**, 89–104.

Welford, A. T. (1952). The "psychological refractory period" and the timing of high speed performance: A review and a theory. *British Journal of Psychology* **43**, 2–19.

Welford, A. T. (1976). "Skilled performance: Perceptual and motor skills." Scott-Foresman, Glenview, Illinois.

Woodworth, R. S. (1938). "Experimental psychology." Holt, New York.

7 Sensory Deprivation

G. F. REED

Department of Psychology,
York University, Ontario

1 Introduction

During the early 1950s a group of psychologists at McGill University, under the direction of D. O. Hebb, published a series of reports regarding the effects on human subjects of restricted environmental variation (Heron *et al.*, 1953; Bexton *et al.*, 1954;). For several reasons, their findings aroused immediate, world-wide interest. They inaugurated a surge of research by psychologists and psychiatrists which was to continue for two decades under the rubric of "sensory deprivation" (SD). This chapter will be primarily concerned with the cognitive changes associated with experimental SD and their theoretical implications. It will not consider attitude changes or affective concomitants. Nor will it include the various psycho-analytic formulations which have been brought to bear upon SD. And, finally, it will not cover the anecdotal experiences of explorers and lone mariners and aviators which have traditionally been cited in relationship to SD (Brownfield, 1965). However intrinsically interesting such material is, its relevance to the study of sensory deprivation is only tenuous at best.

The most dramatic finding of the McGill group and one which initially surprised the researchers themselves, was that some SD subjects reported having experienced vivid hallucinations. Clinicians were not slow to appreciate the implications of this, and it was suggested that SD conditions were capable of producing "model psychoses", an idea which was naturally seized upon by the popular press. The subsequent media coverage was augmented by the fact that findings of this kind could be intepreted as having direct relevance to two other areas of contemporary public concern—space travel and "brain-washing". Governmental support and other forms of research funding rapidly became available, and although the McGill programme ceased in 1954, other SD research programmes were established at several centres in North America, Europe and Japan. Understandably, different investigators tended to focus upon various aspects of SD, whilst several introduced quite different experimental conditions from those used in the original studies.

The McGill group had at first described their procedures as involving "decreased variation in the sensory environment"; later, they used the term "perceptual isolation". Their technique consisted of isolating individual subjects for several hours or days in a laboratory cubicle. The subject lay on a couch, wearing translucent goggles which prevented pattern vision, and cardboard cuffs which restricted tactile stimulation. External sounds were masked by padded earphones which carried a low hum from an amplifier and the ventilating equipment. This remained as the standard set-up, but an increasing number of variations were introduced. J. P. Zubek, one of the McGill group, continued SD investigations in Manitoba, but used a much more sophisticated isolation chamber. At the National Institute of Mental Health at Bethesda, J. C. Lilly studied the reactions of subjects to prolonged immersion in water at body temperature, a technique subsequently employed by his associate, J. T. Shurley at Oklahoma City VA Hospital. J. A. Vernon, at Princeton, subjected volunteers to conditions of total darkness and silence, as did the Human Research Office team (Monterey), headed by T. I. Myers. P. Solomon's group at Harvard and the Boston City Hospital used, among other techniques, confinement in a tank-type respirator.

Thus, many procedures for the modification of input have been employed, and attempts to categorize them have not met with universal acceptance. A basic classificatory dichotomy proposed by Kubzansky (1961) restricts the term "sensory deprivation" to procedures aimed at the absolute reduction of input intensity, and the term "perceptual deprivation" to those which allow only invariant and unpatterned input. (The McGill set-up attempted to produce the second situation, whilst the water-immersion technique employed by Lilly and Shurley is usually cited as the most stringent example of the first.) Even this simple classification presents problems (Rossi, 1969), and meanwhile investigators have employed a variety of other terms—Brownfield (1965) lists 25 different labels which have been used in the research literature. The question as to whether the experimental effects can be attributed to modifications in sensory input or whether they reflect perceptual changes remains unresolved. Probably this is a meaningless question; it is difficult to see how sensation could be distinguished from perception in this context. But certainly the major effects reported seem to be functions of central processing rather than of sensory limitation *per se.* And, of course, it is clearly not feasible to impose sensory deprivation over all modalities in the human subject if he is to remain conscious and functioning normally. In short, the term "sensory deprivation" (SD) is a misnomer, although in accordance with precedent it will be used as a generic title throughout this chapter. (Suedfeld and others have recently urged, as a substitute for "sensory deprivation" and its variants, the term "restricted environmental stimulation technique". This would certainly represent a more accurate and yet inclusive description of the methods employed. And as Suedfeld (personal communication) has pointed out it offers several peripheral advantages; it escapes the adverse connotations acquired by previous terms, and lends itself to a rather nice acronym.)

By the mid-1960s the SD "Movement", if it may be so-called, was generating well over 100 articles each year in English-language professional journals (psychology, psychiatry, physiology and medicine), as well as books and unpublished conference papers, technical reports and academic theses. There have been several review papers of various levels of insight and range of coverage. Zubek (1964) offers a sound overview, whilst the critical review by Kenna (1962) is a model of succinctness, clarity and acuity. Of several books on the subject, the two most authoritative are "Sensory Deprivation" (the proceedings of the 1958 Harvard symposium, published in 1961) edited by P. Solomon *et al.*, and "Sensory Deprivation: Fifteen Years of Research" (published in 1969) edited by J. P. Zubek. These two texts, each excellent in its own way, may be seen as milestones in the development of the SD movement; they make interesting comparative reading. The first reflects the flowering of the early or pagan period, the golden years. Much of it consists of original experimental reports and case studies. The perceived parameters are still clear, and there is an overall tone of surety and optimism. The second was written about a decade later, and thus represents the end of the movement's middle or Gothic period. There is still confidence, but the contributors are now more concerned with theory formulation. They are faced in their reviews with the task of bringing some order to the field. Far from presenting the results of individual studies, they are overwhelmed by the mass of data in the literature accumulated during the 1960s, much of it conflicting, and by the emergence of new variables and methodological problems unforeseen by their predecessors.

Indeed, the sheer richness and diversity of the literature may well have contributed to the decline in SD investigations. To a large extent, the diversity was due to the introduction of new experimental settings as outlined above. There was also an increasing variability in the procedures used for eliciting subjects' reports and test performances.

The variance attributable to individual differences was becoming more evident. And related to this, several investigators had reported the differential effects of anticipatory set (Jackson and Kelly, 1962; Reed, 1962) and of suggestion (Kandel *et al.*, 1958; Jackson and Pollard, 1962). It became increasingly difficult to identify and disentangle the web of emerging variables. It became harder to judge whether a result was in fact due to SD *per se*, or to some experimental artifact. Generalization became precarious, because findings were increasingly divergent, and comparisons between the welter of studies were hedged with qualifications.

The number of experimental SD investigations began to decline in the late 1960s, although some research continued in specialized areas. For example, The University of Manitoba Sensory Isolation Laboratory was active until Zubek's tragic death in 1974. But its research focussed increasingly upon "unimodal" SD (the work of Zubek and his colleagues in this area has been elegantly reviewed recently by Harper and Bross, 1978). There are still many articles published each year which are indexed under sensory or perceptual deprivation. But few of these describe human experimental research as such. For the most part they report animal studies or are speculative essays applying SD findings to problems in child development, gerontology, hospital practices and psychopathology. Suedfeld (1975), for instance, has turned his attention to the possible beneficial effects of SD, and is currently studying its therapeutic application to such problems as stopping smoking. The current stage in the development of the SD movement, in other words, is one where core work has almost ceased but where both theories and procedures have moved into applied areas.

The causes of the movement's decline at the centre include the conceptual problems discussed above. But there were also pragmatic reasons. By its very nature, SD investigation is notoriously time- and resource-consuming. Each experimental session may involve several days of continous observation, whilst space and equipment demands usually enforce the running of only one subject at a time. And under such conditions as have been generally used, the data pay-off is meagre. Because the independent variable is SD, which subsumes the isolation of the subject, the amount of data yielded from a session is necessarily limited. Experimental intervention *during* the session obviously counteracts the very situation under study, whilst prolonged testing or interviewing *after* the session may fail to catch many experimental effects which have already dissipated.

But there were further, extra-professional reasons for the waning of standard SD investigations. Public curiosity about the reactions of man to the stresses of space travel had been answered—the exploration of space had begun, and men had demonstrated that they could cope successfully with the unknown. At the same time, public alarm about "brain-washing" had begun to dissipate. That alarm had been crucially a response to the successful political indoctrination of American POWs by the Chinese during and after the Korean war. The American public's bewilderment and anxiety in that regard were overshadowed by other alarms and another war. SD, in short, was no longer "relevant".

And, finally, even the original interest-provoker—the production of hallucinations as a main effect of SD—had not lived up to its dramatic promise, as we shall see.

2 The Cognitive Effects of SD

Despite the rich confusion of the literature several "themes" are detectable, which may be summarized as follows.

2.1 The Inability to Maintain Attention

The SD effect most consistently reported is a rapid decline in the ability to maintain focussed attention upon ideational content, to follow a particular line of thought. This has been reported regardless of the conditions and methodologies employed. Thus, the original McGill subjects found themselves unable to concentrate upon a given topic (Scott, 1954; Bexton *et al.*, 1954. Scott *et al.*, 1959). Those who had initially resolved to use their enforced solitude constructively, e.g. by searching for solutions to problems, or by reviewing their academic knowledge, found that they were unable to do so. They rapidly lost their concentration, allowing their thoughts to wander. The same finding has been reported from other laboratories using "perceptual deprivation" techniques (Goldberger and Holt, 1958; Smith and Lewty, 1959; Courtney *et al.*, 1961), and from those using tank-type respirators (Wexler *et al.*, 1958; Davis *et al.*, 1960). To a somewhat lesser extent, the same holds true for studies using the "sensory deprivation" conditions of silence and darkness (Zubek *et al.*, 1960).

2.2 Deterioration in logical thinking

As might be expected, the inability to concentrate is succeeded by a generalized deterioration in organized thinking. Subjects report the emergence of free floating fantasy and diffuse daydreaming, which replace logical coherence. For instance, all the subjects studied by Scott *et al.* (1950) found it increasingly difficult to organize their thoughts, those of Davis *et al.* (1960) and Courtney *et al.* (1961) reported feelings of "mental clouding", and thinking was distorted in all those described by Smith and Lewty (1959). Similar findings are reported by Shurley (1953), Myers *et al.* (1962), Ruff *et al.* (1961) and Ohkubo and Kitamura (1965).

The deterioration and the preceding one are presumably part of the same process. But they may be conceptually differentiated by saying that a loosening in linear organization develops into the loss of analytic function and the weakening of directed access to schematic structures.

Cognitive impairment as a result of SD procedures has been reported quite consistently. What cannot be determined from the published subjective reports is the *degree* of impairment. This is partly due to the varying levels of sophistication of the reports themselves, and partly to the methods used to elicit them. Some investigators have asked their subjects to report "any unusual experiences", whilst others have specifically enquired as to whether difficulties in concentration or logical thinking had been encountered. Yet others have merely recorded spontaneous observations, without attempting to explore them. Very few have conducted detailed phenomenological enquiries. These methodological differences are compounded by profound individual differences between subjects, both in degree of cognitive disturbance and its experiential concomitants, and in the extent and specificity of subsequent reportage.

Psychometric attempts to identify and measure the precise areas of cognitive performance affected by SD have been disappointing. The inconsistency amongst test results has been documented and discussed by Schultz (1965) and Suefeld (1969). Clearly, many of the contradictions are due to the varying types of conditions and methodologies referred to above. Some order was brought to the area by the introduction of more sophisticated experimental design in the work of Zubek (Zubek *et al.*, 1962); but difficulties still remained. Where test-re-test techniques have been used, there arise the problems of test and subject reliabilities. Where comparisons have been made between performances by experimental and control subjects there are problems of inter-group differences in intellectual ability, set and motivation. And group sizes in the majority of studies would have rendered statistical control of these differences unsatisfactory. Meanwhile, to make matters more complicated, most investigators have used different batteries of tests, although certain tasks (Koh's block designs, mental arithmetic, Digit Symbol Substitution and word naming) have been used in a number of studies.

In view of the above, any attempt to generalize about the effects of SD upon the performance of objective cognitive tests is on shaky ground. If one excludes those findings which have not attained statistical significance, those which have not been replicated and those which have been contradicted by other reports, very little is left. That little would include verbal fluency, abstract reasoning, and Digit Symbol Substitution—all being tasks in which significant deterioration of performance has been found to be associated with *perceptual* deprivation.

Much more consistency is to be found among reports of performances on memory tasks under SD Significant impairment has been observed when such tasks utilize nonsense syllables and geometric patterns. But substantial decrements have not been reported in performances on the standard digit span test, nor on recall tasks involving meaningful material. Indeed, a number of studies have reported actual improvements in the recall of verbal passages upon retest after SD.

Suedfeld (1969) has made a valiant attempt to produce conceptual order among the diverse reports of cognitive test results, and continues to seek experimental support for a model which accounts for SD phenomena in terms of arousal level and task complexity (Suedfeld and Landon, 1970). But overall, whereas deterioration in logical thinking as a consequence of SD has been amply evidenced by subjects' reports, its examination by the use of objective tests has yielded relatively little that is clear-cut or consistent.

2.3 Heightened Awareness of Imagery, and Perceptual Anomalies

As we have noted, what initially surprised the original McGill workers were their subjects' spontaneous reports of imagery so vivid that the investigators took it to be hallucinatory. References to heightened imagery have featured in almost all subsequent studies, and there have been a number of reviews of such findings, the most thorough of which was that of Zuckerman (1969a). More than a quarter of the studies in West's (1962) authoritative book on hallucinations are to do with hallucinogenic phenomena experienced under SD conditions. But despite the plethora of studies, a number of problems remain unresolved, and there is still a need for systematic investigation. As is characteristic of SD research, difficulties of interpretation are due to variations in set-up and procedures (as observed above) and to inconsistencies in terminology and theoretical assumptions. In particular, terminological inaccuracy has bedevilled this aspect of SD work from the beginning, probably because the early investigators were experimental psychologists who lacked the clinical expertise to identify and discriminate between the types of experience reported by their subjects. Subsequent clinical investigators tended to belong to one or another of the psycho-analytic persuasions; they were more concerned with ego function and the content of experience. Most were either unwilling or unequipped to elicit the formal phenomenological detail necessary to distinguish between, e.g. imagery, illusions, hallucinations, pseudo-hallucinations, functional hallucinations and delusional percepts (c.f. Kenna, 1962; Reed, 1972). To avoid the inevitable differences of opinion as to the nature of what was being reported, it became the practice to merely lump experiences under the neutral headings of "reported visual sensations" (RVS) or "reported auditory sensations" (RAS). But this practice, of course, is a "cop-out" which begs every associated question of theoretical interest.

An unavoidable difficulty is that the evidence must be inferred from verbal reports which are functions of subjects' articulateness, motivation and willingness to respond. Differential effects of expectancy or set have been reported in some studies (Myers and Murphy, 1962) whilst there is a high probability (although little evidence) that the nature of imagery is related to personality variables. This applies particularly to cognitive characteristics related to the individual's acceptance of his imagery and his ability to identify it as such (Reed, 1972). At the same time, reporting may be facilitated or inhibited by experimental procedures. There is some evidence that situations which encourage continual reporting during isolation are more productive than those where reports are elicited only *after* the experimental session. But it seems likely that the opportunity for continuous reporting modifies the experimental situation. Again, investigators have differed in the way they have handled post-isolation interviewing. If a subject is not encouraged to report his subjective experiences, does his failure to so report indicate that he has experienced no imagery, or simply that he does not feel called upon to report it?

A problem of considerable theoretical importance is the question of the varying levels of consciousness of subjects during the SD sessions, Especially during the first few hours of SD, subjects tend to drift off to sleep, and an interesting feature is that they become increasingly unsure whether they are fully awake, sleepy or actually asleep. It seems highly likely that many RVSs and RASs in SD studies are actually dreams or hypnopompic/hypnagogic experiences. Attempts to confirm this in detail by examination of EEG recordings have not proved conclusive, because of the difficulty of determining when a phenomenon is experienced, as opposed to when it is reported (Zuckerman and Hopkins, 1966).

SD imagery in both vision and audition (and, to a lesser extent, in other modalities) can be categorized in terms of structuredness and of meaningfulness or "interpretability". Zuckerman's (1969a) "A" category includes "primitive" RVSs, such as spots and flashes of light and simple geometric forms. "A" category RASs include all kinds of interpretable noise. "B" category RVSs include all meaningful objects and scenes, whilst among RASs this category is restricted to the sounds of human voices, human presence or music. "A" type experiences have been consistently reported in the SD literature. In those studies where "B" type experiences have been reported they develop out of the "A" type. In other words, there is typically a progression from diffuse, primitive perceptual experiences to more structured, complex and meaningful ones.

Some "A" type experiences can be attributable to equipment faults (e.g. light leaks, earphone crackle or building noise). In such cases, obviously, we may be dealing not with imagery or perceptual anomalies but with perceptions which are veridical with external stimuli. In most cases, "real" stimuli may be present, but ones which are interoceptive or proprioceptive in origin. In both sorts of instance, the subject may be reporting simple veridical perception; or he may elaborate or structure his experience and thus be subject to illusion.

We may now return to a consideration of the early reports of hallucinations consequent upon exposure to SD conditions. The crucial point here is that the classical definition of hallucination as "perception without an object" is insufficient. The absence of an object is certainly necessary, but to be classified as an hallucination, the experience must possess those phenomenological attributes which differentiate perceptions from images (Jaspers, 1962). The criteria include (a) objective quality, (b) appearance in external objective space ("out-thereness"), (c) definition and detail, (d) vividness, (e) constancy and (f) independence of voluntary control. Furthermore, the subject must feel conviction that his "perception" has an external source. If he is prepared to attribute it to his imagination or describes it in "as-if" terms, then he is not reporting an hallucination.

The original McGill procedures did not include the elicitation of sufficient detail to determine whether the experiences reported could validly be classified as "hallucinations". When phenomenological criteria were introduced in subsequent studies, reports of hallucinatory phenomena decreased sharply. It now seems likely that many of the apparently bizarre McGill experiences could have been classified in terms of "normal" psychological phenomena such as illusions, dreams, hypnagogic, hypnopompic and eidetic imagery. (The situation is, in fact, very reminiscent of the sad decrease in the incidence of high-scoring ESP subjects after the introduction of experimental criteria by the American Psychological Association.)

In summary, there is little evidence for any direct association between SD conditions and pathological hallucinatory experiences. But there is ample and consistent evidence that SD subjects experience after-images, misperceptions, illusions, daydreaming, fantasizing and imagery of various types.

2.4 Temporal Disorientation

There has been less examination of time experiences under SD conditions than might be expected. After all, prolonged SD is essentially a *boring* situation, and boredom is traditionally associated with consciousness of the passage of time. Furthermore, many investigators have failed to observe the distinction between the *experience* of duration (feelings about the passage of time) and *estimation* of duration (judgements in terms of objective clock-time).

However, such findings as have been published show considerable consistency. Where temporal *experience* is concerned, subjects' spontaneous comments suggest that time loses its significance. Seven of Reed's (1962) 20 subjects described a feeling of "timelessness" during a SD session of less than 1 hour. All 10 of the subjects described by Cohen *et al.* (1961) lost all conception of time during 2 hours in a dark soundproof chamber. Similar experiences have been reported by Goldberger and Holt (1958) and Zubek and MacNeill (1967).

The majority of studies which have examined temporal *estimations* (Lilly and Shurley, 1955; Lilly, 1956; Shurley, 1960; Walters and Quinn, 1960; Banks and Cappon, 1962) have reported that subjects underestimate time. This finding is quite predictable in the light of Sturt's (1925) work, as well as the more recent and much more sophisticated formulation of Ornstein (1969). Both these investigators have postulated that the duration of a period of time is judged according to the number of "mental events" (Sturt) or "filtered contents of consciousness" (Ornstein) occurring within it. The more events experienced during the period in question, the longer is its subjective duration. In SD where external events at least are restricted, underestimation of duration would be anticipated.

Some interesting problems remain, however. Firstly, there seems to be little relationship between subjective feelings and judgements, although this has not been studied in detail. It would appear that a subject may feel that time is passing very slowly and yet estimate an elapsed period as being less than clock time. Thus, Banks and Cappon (1962) and Cohen *et al.* (1961) report almost universal underestimation by their subjects but no clear relationships between experiences and estimates. Secondly, there appear to be changes relative to the length of time passed in SD, although once again the effects upon experience as opposed to judgement are unclear. Smith and Lewty (1959) reported that time tended to be underestimated during the early part of a session but was usually overestimated after several hours. Pollard *et al.* (1963) found a significant tendency to underestimation among their 24 subjects. But this tendency disappeared when the subjects were exposed to a second SD session a week later. Thirdly, personality variables play a part, as might be expected. Reed and Kenna (1964) compared the performances of 10 subjects whose MPI scores were 30 and above with 10 subjects whose MPI scores were 20 or below. They were required to estimate when 15 min had passed under normal conditions and under SD conditions of brief duration. No significant differences were found between the groups under normal conditions. Both groups underestimated under SD conditions, but significantly larger errors were made by the extroverts than by the introverts. Murphy *et al.* (1962) found that measures of time estimation could be used as predictors of the ability to endure prolonged SD exposure. The subjects who dropped out before the completion of a 96-hour session had, earlier in the session, *over*estimated the passage of time significantly more than those who subsequently completed the session. Within the "early release" group there was a significant negative correlation between degree of overestimation and the number of hours endured.

In summary, from a mass of findings of bewildering variety, a number of consistent "themes" may be detected referring to the effect of SD upon cognitive activities. These themes include an increasing inability to maintain concentration, to focus attention upon a given line of thought. Probably consequent upon this there emerges a deterioration in logical, analytical thought with linguistic representation. This deterioration is paralleled by an increase in unwilled imagery, reported mainly in relation to vision but occurring in all modalities. The inability to concentrate implies a weakening of time-based activity whilst failures in logical thinking imply impairment in sequential operations. These temporal failures are reflected in distortions of time experience as well as judgement of the passage of time.

3 SD Effects and Cognitive Psychology

An observation worth recording is that, despite the element of drama which is still attached to SD, its main cognitive effects are not particularly surprising in the light of modern psychological theorizing. Far from being taken as evidence for the production of "model psychoses", they would be those predicted by contemporary cognitive psychology. This in itself documents the radical changes in emphasis in the study of cognitive processes which have occurred during the last 20 years. But perhaps it should be added that the SD studies may themselves have contributed to those changes.

Nowadays, perception would generally be regarded as a constructive process (Neisser, 1967), which involves sampling, matching and hypothesis-formulating (c.f. Reed, 1972; Gregory, 1974). Perception is not a mechanism which passively encodes and translates whatever information is provided by the environment. Input is operated upon in terms of what is already in the cognitive system. It is selected, classified and integrated with existing schemata, and the identification and assessment of events is as much a question of conceptualization as of perception. This approach assumes, of course, that perception is continuously *active*, and that normal cognitive functioning requires ongoing stimulation.

It was not by accident that SD studies were pioneered at McGill. Hebb's (1949, 1955) theory had postulated that for optimal functioning the central nervous system requires constant stimulation and varying input. Having reviewed the neurophysiological evidence for this, he argued that continual brain activity constitutes a behavioural drive. Stimulation has a "cue" function and an "arousal" function, but the first cannot exist without the second. Hebb's theory had led him to predict that prolonged exposure to decreased stimulation and restricted environmental variation would produce perceptual/cognitive disorganization. Although he modestly asserted, in his introduction to Heron (1961), that the theoretical situation of SD left him "completely at sea", it is obvious that SD findings offered massive support for his prediction, even though his neurophysiological speculations had been disconfirmed.

Given that the cognitive system operates to impose structure and meaningfulness upon input, it also maintains an overall level of activity. It seems reasonable, then, to suggest that any diminution of activation at the input stage will be compensated by reciprocal increases in the contributions of other parts of the system. For example, if visual input is restricted to random or primitive stimuli, the system will operate towards imposing meaningfulness by making increased reference to schematic material already available within itself. Thus illusions and/or imagery at various levels will be experienced. And what if there are *no* visual stimuli from external sources? Firstly, there may well be *endogenous* stimuli available—"phosphenes" or random retinal firings. But in the total absence of visual input, presumably cognition can proceed without visual reference. On the other hand, Zuckerman's (1969) summary indicates that there is no difference in the incidence of RVSs between studies where subjects were confined in darkness and those using diffuse, unpatterened visual stimulation.

Perhaps we should remind ourselves at this juncture that SD is a situation which offers little information, but encourages the search for meaningfulness. During their waking hours, SD subjects are constrained to search for clues, to reflect upon them and to try to make sense of whatever is available. There is simply nothing else for them to do. It is quite possible that they have similar perceptual experiences in everyday life, but that their conscious awareness of these is dissipated by the press of "real" events. For the same reason, they are unlikely to record such experiences under normal conditions. And even should they do so, there is no reason why they should recall or, indeed, verbalize them subsequently. In SD experiments, the subject may be "set" to register his imaging and reflect upon his subjective experiences. Subsequently, he is encouraged or required by active interrogation to recall and verbally report his experiences or, as in some Russian studies of isolation, to log them in a diary (Gagarin and Lebedev, 1970).

So far, we have been discussing the perceptual anomalies associated with SD. But what of the disorganization of thinking which we have noted to be also characteristic of deprivation experiments? What has been discussed above may be referred to as perceptual consciousness—the awareness of our commerce with the outside world, our hypotheses as to the significance of input. The reports of cognitive impairment have reference to difficulties in maintaining a line of thought, of arranging thoughts in appropriate sequences, of pursuing logical arguments, etc. All of these problems refer to the conscious consideration of material *within* the system, as opposed to operations performed on *input* to the system. The SD situation is designed to modify input, but why should it affect the mode of operation of pre-existing processes and cognitive structures? It could be argued that the perceptual anomalies constitute "false leads" which cloud or divert logical thought sequences. But this cannot be the whole story; in everyday life we can concentrate, arrange our thoughts in logical sequence and solve problems despite the distractions and diversions of input from the environment. Another way of tackling the question might be to approach logical thinking as a complex skill, as Bartlett (1958) suggested. Successful performance of an "open" motor skill is contingent upon sensitivity to feedback information. In SD the subject's search for meaningfulness is hampered by the absence of reality checks; in other words, he is denied feedback. Like the rifleman who is deprived of knowledge of results, his performance may remain consistent but his score will get steadily worse. Unfortunately, this argument is also insufficient. In the first place, the SD subject's "performance" does not remain consistent. It rapidly becomes diffuse and notably inconsistent. Not only can he no longer hit the bullseye, he cannot remember what the target is. Furthermore, when the task is a mental problem or review, feedback is usually intrinsic to the task itself. Only in formal problems is knowledge of results externally available. In such instances only the final step—the "answer"—may be presented; and this is merely confirmatory.

The study of imagery is currently much more active than it was during the main period of SD researches. Paivio (1971) in particular has examined the functional distinctions between the imaginal and the verbal constituents of symbolic process. Imagery and perception are conceived as *parallel-processing* systems, whereas verbal thinking processes information *sequentially*. For instance, it seems that units of visual information are stored as discrete entities, the hierarchical organization of which is spatial. Verbal material, on the other hand, is dynamically schematized and is processed temporally. Thus, SD effects may be conceptualized as reflecting a change in the normal balance of the two symbolic systems. SD conditions favour the dominance of the imaginal mode of processing at the expense of the verbal mode.

One plausible answer to our question, therefore, is that in SD conditions a change in mode of information-processing occurs, which involves some impairment in the sequential ordering of information. In terms of conscious awareness, this is reflected in the experiences of disorientation and clinical depersonalization reported by some SD subjects (Reed and Sedman, 1964). What might underly this shift in functional balance is still open to question, but one possibility will be considered shortly.

4 Neurological Findings and Psychological Theories

There has certainly been no dearth of theorizing in regard to the effects of SD, but as Kenna (1962) concluded, "There has been a tendency to seek theoretical explanations of the often inconsistent findings in the speculative areas of neurology, communication theory, psychoanalysis and perceptual theory without first considering the resources of more conventional formulations". As far as cognitive changes of the sort discussed here are concerned, the most popular source of "explanation" has been neuroanatomy. Psychologists—at least those of the "hard-nosed" variety—have characteristically looked first to the neuro-sciences for intellectual support and solace. We seem to find comfort or assurance in psychological models which can be seen to be identical to, or at least isomorphic with neurological "realities". In some cases psychological theorizing has been precipitated by advances in the neuro-sciences. (Ironically, in some ways the reverse has also occurred; there is clearly a symbiotic relationship between the two disciplinary areas.)

In the case of SD, psychological theorizers found a new field of neurological discovery ready at hand. This was the work associated with Magoun and Rhines, (1946) and then most notably with Lindsley (1958) regarding the *reticular formation* of the lower brain stem. Very briefly, it was being discovered that the functions of the reticular formation are more diversified than had been traditionally presumed. It responds to different sensory modalities and facilitates or inhibits their interactions. The ascending reticular activating system (ARAS) may be regarded as sampling and monitoring both input and output, and adjusting their relations to an appropriate level of balance (Lindsley, 1961). Because its response level is projected upon the cortex it presumably influences perception. And its regulatory function gives it a central role in arousal, attention and the changes between wakefulness and sleep. Where the normal balance between input and output is disturbed, as in SD, then its function may account for behavioural changes. "If one deprives the reticular system of its sensory input, it meets an unfamiliar situation, and only within limits can it adjust to this change" (Lindsley, 1961, 193–4). It is not surprising, therefore, that the reticular formation was seized upon as providing a sound physical base for psychological speculation.

It may be suggested that if theorizing about SD had peaked a decade later another area of neurological investigation might well have been seized upon as a base—the "split-brain" work of Roger Sperry and his associates. Psychological hypotheses would doubtless have focussed upon the possible relationship between SD effects and the differing functions of the two cerebral hemispheres. As it is, to my knowledge, there has been no detailed discussion of such a relationship in the psychological literature. Perhaps the time is ripe to initiate such discussion; certainly there would appear to be obvious parallels between some SD phenomena and the functions which appear to be characteristic of the right hemisphere.

The original split-brain research was conducted by Myers and Sperry in the early 1950s, during the same period as the original McGill investigations of SD. But the work of most relevance to the present concern began in 1960 with the first study of cerebral commisurotomy in man, and its psychological results (Gazzaniga *et al.*, 1962, 1963). Since then there have appeared many studies reporting differences in specialized function between the left (or as it used to be called, the dominant) hemisphere and the right (or minor) hemisphere. There is overall consistency among these findings, as well as between the generalizations drawn from them. The findings have been reviewed by many authorities (Zangwill, 1961; Milner, 1971; Sperry, 1973; Nebes, 1974). In summary, it is claimed that the left hemisphere (LH) is notably superior to the right in tasks involving naming and verbal processing, whereas the right hemisphere (RH) seems to operate in auditory but non-verbal tasks such as the recognition and recall of melodies and chords. The LH is superior in the processing of abstract, logical and linguistic tasks, whereas the RH is superior in the performance of tasks involving spatial relationships. The LH handles problems analytically and objectively, whereas the RH functions more holistically and intuitively. In recall tasks, the LH uses an analytic approach, recalling more details but with less overall coherence than the RH, which shows superiority in holistic recall, particularly of faces and pictorial material.

There have been many attempts to conceptualize these differences in hemispherical specialization. Bogen (1977) has urged the identification of differences in how material (tests, tasks, etc.) is processed, rather than emphasis upon the material itself. He differentiates between the "propositional" nature of LH functioning as opposed to the "appositional" functioning of the RH. LH activity seems to be related to the consideration of sequential order, whereas RH activity excels in part–whole relationships. Gordon and Bogen (1974) had hypothesized that the LH is specialized for processing *time-ordered stimulus sequences*, and the RH for *time-independent stimulus configurations*. Similarly, Nebes (1977) points to differences between the hemispheres in terms of information-processing strategies. He stresses the analytic and sequential nature of LH functioning as opposed to the holistic character of RH activity, which utilizes imagery rather than language. (A caveat must be introduced here. Bogen and Nebes are recognized authorities in this field, and their widely-cited views have become very influential. But the very elegance of their arguments raises some questions. Neurophysiological and psychological findings seldom lend themselves to such clear-cut generalizations as these arguments assume. There is not the space here for any detailed examination of the evidence upon which the generalizations are founded, although some general observations will be made later in this section.)

In short, there is some consensus that the RH operates in a holistic, intuitive manner, utilizing configurational relationships and imagery; it is inferior in analytical, verbal and logical operations and in time-sequential functions. *And this list includes exactly those characteristics which we observed to be typical of SD effects.* It seems at least plausible, then, that SD conditions in some way facilitate or enhance the contributions of the RH to cognitive activity, whilst diminishing or inhibiting those of the LH.

If the above suggestion is provisionally accepted, does it contribute anything to the consideration of SD in relation to consciousness? The answer must be that it certainly opens a floodgate to a new wave of speculations. As it happens, questions related to consciousness have particularly exercised those concerned with split-brain studies. Many writers have detected in the specialized functions of the RH a concatenation reflecting the subjective, creative and humanistic aspects of thinking. It has been a short step to claiming for the RH a role as the seat of mysticism, the suppressed alternative to materialism, objectivity, the scientific approach, logic and the Protestant work ethic. As Nebes (1977) wryly observes, "The right hemisphere has thus been enthusiastically embraced by counterculture groups as their side of the brain . . . " (104–5). Blakemore (1977) adds the ironical twist, "There is a growing vocal movement that calls (presumably with its left hemisphere) for the liberation of its right . . ." (p. 164). From this position it has been an even shorter step to equate RH functioning with *a second consciousness.* This suggestion has been made quite explicitly by Sperry (1964), "Everything we have seen so far indicates that the surgery has left each of these people with two separate minds, that is, with two separate spheres of consciousness." Sperry's conclusion is confirmed by Gazzaniga (1967), "All the evidence indicates that separation of the hemispheres creates two independent spheres of consciousness within a single cranium . . ." Even the escape term— "spheres of"—is absent in the title of a later well-known paper by Gazzaniga (1977), "One brain—two minds?" Meanwhile, Bogen's (1969) elegant and influential paper was basically a recruitment of evidence to support Wigan's (1844) assertion that, "The mind is essentially dual, like the organs by which it is exercised" (p. 4).

This line of thought certainly leads to an exciting range of possibilities. But before we become *too* excited, it will be as well to examine the steps implicit in at least *some* forms of the argument:

(1) Consciousness (or mind) is identical with an anatomical structure or organ.
(2) That structure is the brain.
(3) The brain has two sides, each of which has now been shown to have its own specialized functions.
(4) *Therefore*, the individual possesses two consciousnesses.

Each of these steps contains at least one basic assumption which invites examination.

The first step presumes acceptance of the most extreme form of the "identity" hypothesis. Without venturing into the most venerable and fiercely debated area of philosophical controversy, it may at least be noted that the identity position has been forcibly rejected by many of the most eminent of contemporary neuro-scientists. But there are many supporters of the identity position who would not take such an uncompromisingly reductionist stance as the present one—for instance, those who equate consciousness not with a physical *organ*, but with a physical *process* (Shallice, 1972) or those who take the neo-Marxist view that consciousness is the dynamic interaction between the brain and the environment (Rose, 1976). Consciousness has been taken to be a property, a function, a process, a state or merely the outcome of ways of using words. What it surely cannot be is a *thing*—an anatomical structure, organ or mechanism.

The second step involves the assumption that given that consciousness *is* an anatomical structure, then the structure is the brain. Furthermore, the argument refers not to the brain in its entirety, but only to certain components of the brain—the cerebral hemispheres. This suggests a somewhat cavalier dismissal of, e.g. the role of the brainstem in attention and information processing (c.f. Kahneman, 1973). But even if the argument had reference to the whole brain, it could not be accepted without question. A more plausible formulation, it might be suggested, would be that the structure in question is the entire central nervous system.

The third step presents a different sort of problem. The statement itself is amply supported by evidence, and is not so open to logical, philosophical or metaphysical questions. What are in doubt are its implications, and here some notes of caution must be sounded. Firstly, the nature of the sources of evidence should be borne in mind. By far the most productive studies have been examinations of the performances of unilaterally brain-injured patients or epileptic patients after surgical intervention. To date, studies of hemispherical specialization in normal subjects have of necessity been limited to a very narrow range of perceptual and motor functions. Secondly, even in split-brain patients there is communication between the separated hemispheres and overlap in their operations. In the normal individual, the two sides of the brain do not simply communicate or work with each other. They are complementary components of the same system; under normal conditions, their operations are synchronized and integrated. It has not been seriously claimed that the healthy person's hemispheres are discrete organs, which happen to be yoked in parallel. Yet this is the inference which might be drawn from some discussions.

The fourth and crucial step is surely a simple *non sequitur*. Having assumed the applicability of the previous statement to normal people, it is now asserted that each hemisphere has its own consciousness. In other words, each individual rejoices in *two* consciousnesses. There is a semantic and definitional problem involved here, of course, but what is mainly in doubt is the facile equation of "modes of activity" with "consciousness". Consciousness, it may be argued, reflects, facilitates or parallels cognitive activities. It is probably isomorphic with the varying modes and deployments of those activities. But that is not to say that it *is* the activities themselves. The hemispheres differ in the ways they contribute to the processing of information. But that statement is a far cry from the assertion that each hemisphere is itself a different consciousness, or even that each is *associated* with a different consciousness. One does not require a number of flashlights to illuminate the various objects or activities in a darkened room.

5 Conclusion

The experimental study of humans in severely restricted environments is currently out of fashion; the SD movement is now past its heyday. But its reports constitute a rich storehouse of information. It would be a pity if its contents were not sifted and applied to the study of other problems. The examination of consciousness is but one enterprise which might fruitfully draw upon SD material.

Evidently, SD reports cover all *levels* of consciousness from drowsy and "twilight" states to heightened awareness. Indeed, many theorists have used various models of arousal in their approaches to SD effects (Zuckerman, 1969b). Again, on Tart's (1969) definition, SD effects include a variety of altered *states* of consciousness, albeit the SD versions are in no way pathological and, as we have seen, are amenable to analysis in terms of normal cognitive functioning. It is unfortunate that basic SD research declined before individual differences in ASC, could be thoroughly investigated. As mentioned earlier, the decline also took place before the resurgence of interest in imagery, but SD reports include a wealth of material of relevance to the study of conscious imagery, its development and its relationship with dreams and fantasy.

Again, it is a pity that the SD work was done before the current wave of interest in consciousness among cognitive psychologists. As Shallice (1972) has pointed out, the study of consciousness and its mapping in information-processing terms is a prerequisite for satisfactory cognitive theorizing. Shallice's proposed model assumes that the brain contains a large set of action systems, each of which has a "selector input". The latter determines whether its action system is to become dominant and, if so, sets its goal. These two properties correspond to those of consciousness. Shallice's action systems are similar to the TOTE units of Miller *et al.* (1960), and it could be suggested that in SD there are insufficient input parameters available for normal processing to occur.

In an elegant and thought-provoking contribution, Mandler (1975) points out that current cognitive theorizing has focused on consciousness of the perceptual or encoding side of information flow. The evidence from SD studies should be of provocative interest in the examination of the *output* side.

Finally, the present account has emphasized temporal phenomena, an aspect sadly neglected by previous SD reviewers. Time experiences are examined elsewhere in this volume. Their implications may hold an important key to the problems of consciousness, as suggested in a provocative chapter in Ornstein (1972).

In has been pointed out here that there seem to be uncannily close parallels between the most consistently reported SD phenomena and those functions claimed by many authorities to represent differential hemispheric functioning. This raises the intriguing possibility that SD conditions may in some way facilitate activity of the right hemisphere whilst inhibiting that of the left. What process or mechanism might account for such an effect is beyond the scope of this chapter, but closer examination is clearly invited. Meanwhile, however, a modest suggestion has been advanced here, which may be argued with or without reference to hemispheric specialization. SD conditions drastically reduce meaningful input, whilst discouraging or excluding verbalization. The former restriction may encourage the imaginal mode of cognitive processing, whilst the latter may simultaneously inhibit the verbal mode. As argued earlier, this shift in the balance of information-processing modes would involve impairment in sequential processing. And this temporal disorganization would be accentuated by the absence of objective time-markers. This straightforward proposal, it will be noted, accounts satisfactorily for the four clusters of cognitive phenomena identified above as being characteristic of SD effects.

6 References

Banks, R. and Cappon, D. (1962). Effect of reduced sensory input on time perception. *Perceptual and Motor Skills* **14**, 74.

Barlett, F. C. (1958). "Thinking: An Experimental and Social Study." George Allen and Unwin, London.

Bexton, W. H., Heron, W. and Scott, T. H. (1954). Effects of decreased variation in the sensory environments. *Canadian Journal of Psychology* **8**, 70–6.

Blakemore, C. (1977). "Mechanics of the Mind." Cambridge University Press, Cambridge.

Bogen, J. E. (1969). The other side of the brain, II: An appositional mind. *Bulletin of the Los Angeles Neurological Society* **34**, 135–62.

Bogen, J. E. (1977). Some educational implications of hemispheric specialization. *In* "The Human Brain" (Ed. M. C. Wittrock). Prentice-Hall, Englewood Cliffs, New Jersey.

Brownfield, C. A. (1965). "Isolation: Clinical and Experimental Approaches." Random House, New York.

Cohen, S. I., Silverman, A. J., Bressler, B. and Shmavonian, B. (1961). Problems in isolation studies. *In* "Sensory Deprivation" (Eds P. Solomon *et al.*). Harvard University Press, Cambridge, Mass.

Courtney, J., Davis, J. M. and Solomon, P. (1961). Sensory deprivation: The role of movement. *Perceptual and Motor Skills*, 191–9.

Davis, J. M., McCourt, W. F. and Solomon, P. (1960). The effect of visual stimulation on hallucinations and other mental experiences during sensory deprivation. *American Journal of Psychiatry* **116**, 889–92.

Deikman, A. J. (1971). Bimodal consciousness. *Archives of General Psychiatry* **25**, 481–9.

Gagarin, Y. and Lebedev, V. (1970). "Psychology and Space." (Translated by B. Belitsky.) MIR, Moscow.

Gazzaniga, M. S. (1967). The split brain in man. *Scientific American* **217**, 24–9.

Gazzaniga, M. S. (1977). One brain—two minds? *In* "Current Trends in Psychology" (Ed. I. L. Janis). William Kaufmann, Los Altos, California.

Gazzaniga, M. S., Bogen, J. E. and Sperry, R. W. (1962). Some functional effects of sectioning cerebral commissures in man. *Proceedings of the National Academy of Science* **48**, 1765.

Gazzaniga, M. S., Bogen, J. E. and Sperry, R. W. (1963). Laterality effects in somesthesis following cerebral commissurotomy in man. *Neuropyschologia* **1**, 209–15.

Goldberger, L. and Holt, R. R. (1958). Experimental interference with reality contact (perceptual isolation): Method and group results. *Journal of nervous and mental Disorders* **127**, 99–112.

Gordon, H. W. and Bogen, J. E. (1974). Hemispheric lateralization of singing after intracarotid sodium amylobarbitone. *Neurology, Neurosurgery and Psychiatry* **37**, 727–38.

Gregory, R. L. (1974). Perception as hypothesis. *In* "Philosophy of Pyschology" (Ed. S. C. Brown). Macmillan, London.

Harper, D. W. and Bross, M. (1978). The effect of unimodal sensory deprivation on sensory processes: A decade of research from the University of Manitoba. *Canadian Psychological Review* **19**, 128–44.

Hebb, D. O. (1949). "The Organization of Behaviour." John Wiley, New York.

Hebb, D. O. (1955). Drives and the C. N. S. (conceptual nervous system). *Psychological Review* **62**, 243–54.

Heron, W. (1961). Cognitive and physiological effects of perceptual isolation. *In* "Sensory Deprivation" (Eds P. Solomon *et al.*). Harvard University Press, Cambridge, Mass.

Heron, W., Bexton, W. H. and Hebb, D. O. (1953). Cognitive effects of a decreased variation to the sensory environment. *American Psychologist* **8**, 366.

Jackson, Jr, C. W. and Kelly, E. L. (1962). Influence of suggestion and subject's prior knowledge in research on sensory deprivation. *Science* **132**, 211–12.

Jackson, Jr, C. W. and Pollard, J. C. (1962). Sensory deprivation and suggestion: a theoretical approach. *Behavioural Science* **7**, 332–42.

Jaspers, K. (1962). "General psychopathology." (Translated by J. Iloenig and M. Hamilton.) Manchester University Press, Manchester.

Kahneman, D. (1973). "Attention and Effort." Prentice-Hall, Englewood Cliffs, New Jersey.

Kandel, E. J., Myers, T. I. and Murphy, D. B. (1958). Influence of prior verbalization and instructions on visual sensations reported under conditions of reduced sensory input. *American Psychologist* **13**, 334.

Kenna, J. C. (1962). Sensory deprivation phenomena: critical review and explanatory models. *Proceedings of the Royal Society of Medicine* **55**, 1005–10.

Lilly, J. C. (1956). Mental effects of reduction of ordinary levels of physical stimuli on intact, healthy persons. *Psychiatric Research Reports* **5**, 1–9.

Lilly, J. C. and Shurley, J. T. (1955). Experiments in solitude in maximum achievable physical isolation with water suspension of intact, healthy persons. *In* "Psychophysiological Aspects of Space Flight" (Ed. B. E. Flaherty). Columbia University Press, New York.

Lindsley, D. B. (1958). The reticular system and perceptual discrimination. *In* "Reticular Formation of the Brain." (Eds H. H. Jasper *et al.*). Little Brown, Boston.

Lindsley, D. B. (1961). Common factors in sensory deprivation, sensory distortion, and sensory overload. *In* "Sensory Deprivation." (Eds P. Solomon *et al.*). Harvard University Press, Cambridge, Mass.

Magoun, H. W. and Rhines, R. (1946). An inhibitory mechanism in the bulbar reticular formation. *Journal of Neurophysiology* **9**, 165.

Mandler, G. (1975). Consciousness. *In* "Information Processing and Cognition: The Loyola Symposium" (Ed. R. L. Solso). Lawrence Erbaum Associates, Hillsdale, New Jersey.

Miller, G. A., Galanter, E. H. and Pribram, K. (1960). "Plans and the Structure of Behaviour." Holt, New York.

Milner, B. (1971). Interhemispheric differences in the localization of psychological processes in man. *British Medical Bulletin* **27**, 272–7.

Murphy, D. B., Hampton, G. L. and Myers, T. I. (1962). Time estimation error as a predictor of endurance in sustained sensory deprivation. *American Psychologist* **17**, 389.

Myers, T. I. and Murphy, D. B. (1962). Reported visual sensation during brief exposure to reduced sensory input. *In* "Hallucinations" (Ed. L. J. West). Grune and Stratton, New York.

Myers, T. I. Murphy, D. B., Smith, S. and Windle, C. (1962). "Summary Results of the HumRRO program." US Army, Monterey, California.

Nebes, R. D. (1974). Hemispheric specialization in commissurotomized man. *Psychological Bulletin* **81**, 1–14.

Nebes, R. D. (1977). Man's so-called minor hemisphere. *In* "The Human

Brain" (Eds. M. C. Wittrock *et al.*). Prentice-Hall, Englewood Cliffs, New Jersey.

Neisser, U. (1967). "Cognitive Psychology." Appleton-Century-Crofts, New York.

Ohkubo, Y. and Kitamura, S. (1965). Studies on sensory deprivation: III. Part 1. Introductory remarks and general methods. *Tohoku Psychologia Folia* **23**, 53–5.

Ornstein, R. E. (1969). "On the Experience of Time." Penguin, Harmondsworth.

Ornstein, R. E. (1972). "The Psychology of Consciousness." W. H. Freeman, San Francisco.

Paivio, A. (1971). "Imagery and Verbal Processes." Holt, New York.

Pollard, J. C., Uhr, L. and Jackson, C. W. (1963). Studies in sensory deprivation. *Archives of general Psychiatry* **8**, 435–54.

Reed, G. F. (1962). Preparatory set as a factor in the production of sensory deprivation phenomena. *Proceedings of the Royal Society of Medicine* **55**, 1010–14.

Reed, G. F. (1972). "The Psychology of Anomalous Experience." Hutchinson University Library, London.

Reed, G. F. and Kenna, J. C. (1964). Personality and time estimation in sensory deprivation. *Perceptual and Motor Skills* **18**, 182.

Reed, G. F. and Sedman, G. (1964). Personality and depersonalization under sensory deprivation conditions. *Perceptual and Motor Skills* **18**, 659–60.

Rose, S. (1976). "The Conscious Brain." Vintage Books, New York.

Rossi, A. M. (1969). General methodological considerations. *In* "Sensory Deprivation: Fifteen Years of Research" (Ed. J. P. Zubek). Appleton-Century-Crofts, New York.

Ruff, G. E., Levy, E. Z. and Thaler, V. H. (1961). Factors influencing the reaction to reduced sensory input. *In* "Sensory Deprivation" (Eds P. Solomon *et al.*). Harvard University Press, Cambridge, Mass.

Schultz, D. P. (1965). "Sensory Restriction: Effects on Behaviour." Academic Press, New York.

Scott, T. H. (1954). "Intellectual Effects of Perceptual Isolation." Ph.D. dissertation. McGill University.

Scott, T. H., Bexton, W. H., Heron, W. and Doane, B. K. (1959). Cognitive effects of perceptual isolation. *Canadian Journal of Psychology* **13**, 200–9.

Shallice, T. (1972). Dual functions of consciousness. *Psychological Review* **79**, 383–93.

Shurley, J. T. (1960). Profound experimental sensory isolation. *American Journal of Psychiatry* **117**, 539–45.

Shurley, J. T. (1963). The hydro-hypodynamic environments. *In* "Proceedings of the Third World Congress of Psychiatry", Vol. 3. University of Toronto Press, Toronto.

Smith, S. and Lewty, W. (1959). Perceptual isolation using a silent room. *Lancet* **2**, 342–5.

Solomon, P., Kubzansky, P. E., Leiderman, P. H., Mendelson, J. H. Trumbull.

178   *G. F. Reed*

R. and Wexler, D. (Eds.) (1961). "Sensory Deprivation." Harvard University Press, Cambridge, Mass.

Sperry, R. W. (1964). "Problems Outstanding in the Evolution of Brain Function." American Museum of Natural History, New York.

Sperry, R. W. (1973). Lateral specialization of cerebral function in the surgically separated hemispheres. *In* "The Psychophysiology of Thinking" (Ed. F. J. McGuigan). Academic Press, New York.

Sturt, M. (1925). "The Psychology of Time." Kegan Paul, London.

Suedfeld, P. (1969). Changes in intellectual performance and in susceptibility to influence. *In* "Sensory Deprivation: Fifteen Years of Research" (Ed. J. P. Zubek). Appleton-Century-Crofts, New York.

Suedfeld, P. (1975). The benefits of boredom: Sensory Deprivation reconsidered. *American Scientist* **63**, 60–9.

Suedfeld, P. and Landon, P. B. (1970). Motivational arousal and task complexity: support for a model of cognitive changes in sensory deprivation. *Journal of Experimental Psychology* **83**, 329–30.

Tart, C. T. (1969). Introduction. "Altered States of Consciousness: A Book of Readings" (Ed. C. T. Tart). John Wiley, New York.

Walters, R. H. and Quinn, M. J. (1960). The effects of social and sensory deprivation on autokinetic judgments. *Journal of Personality* **28**, 210–19.

West, L. J. (Ed.) (1962). "Hallucinations." Grune and Stratton, New York.

Wexler, D., Mendelson, J., Leiderman, P. H. and Solomon, P. (1958). Sensory deprivation: A technique of studying psychiatric aspects of stress. *Archives of Neurology and Psychiatry* **79**, 225–33.

Wigan, A. L. (1844). "The Duality of the Mind." Longman, London.

Zangwill, O. L. (1961). Asymmetry of cerebral hemisphere function. *In* "Scientific Aspects of Neurology" (Ed. H. Garland). Livingstone, London.

Zubek, J. P. (1964). Effect of prolonged sensory and perceptual deprivation. *British Medical Bulletin* **20**, 38–42.

Zubek, J. P. (Ed.) (1969). "Sensory Deprivation: Fifteen Years of Research." Appleton-Century-Crofts, New York.

Zubek, J. P., Aftanas, M., Hasek, J., Sansom, W., Schludermann, E., Wilgosh, L. and Winocur, G. (1962). Intellectual and perceptual changes during prolonged perceptual deprivation: Low illumination and noise level. *Perceptual and Motor Skills* **15**, 171–98.

Zubek, J. P. and MacNeill, M. (1967). Perceptual deprivation phenomena: Role of the recumbent position. *Journal of Abnormal Psychology* **72**, 147–50.

Zuckerman, M. (1969). a) Hallucinations, reported sensations, and images. b) Theoretical formulations: 1. *In* "Sensory Deprivation: Fifteen Years of Research" (Eds J. P. Zubek *et al.*). Appleton-Century-Crofts, New York.

Zuckerman, M. and Hopkins, T. R. (1966). Hallucinations or dreams? A study of arousal levels and reported visual sensations during sensory deprivation. *Perceptual and Motor Skills* **22**, 447–59.

8 Time and Consciousness

R. A. BLOCK

*Department of Psychology,
Montana State University*

1 Introduction: Approaches to Time and Consciousness

Consciousness is permeated by a succession of temporally-defined events and temporal relationships between events. Stated somewhat differently, "the nature of experience itself is far more involved with time than anything else" (Orme, 1969, p. 2). For this reason, it is not surprising that theoretical and empirical work on time and consciousness was done by some of the first psychologists in the late 1800s and that the topic is currently receiving increasing interest. Most psychological studies of consciousness were conducted either before 1920 or after 1960 (Ornstein, 1977), but the annual number of psychological studies of time shows a fairly continuous acceleration (Zelkind and Sprug, 1974). Notable psychological attempts to relate time and consciousness include those by James (1890), Boring (1933/1963), Schaltenbrand (1967) and Ornstein (1969, 1977).

This chapter presents a selective review of relationships between consciousness and several related kinds of temporal experience, such as simultaneity and successiveness, short temporal experiences, longer temporal experiences and temporal perspective (cf. Ornstein, 1969). The emphases are on empirical evidence and theories based on such evidence. The review includes a consideration of temporal experience in both "ordinary" waking consciousness and several categories of altered states of consciousness. There are many possible approaches to the study of time and consciousness, but this review assumes a cognitive, or information processing, approach. Cognitive approaches to temporal experience have been promoted by James (1890), Boring (1933/1963), Frankenhaeuser (1959), Fraisse (1963), Ornstein (1969), Michon (1972) and many others. Cognitive approaches to consciousness have been promoted by many other theorists in recent years (see

Ch. 7). Abundant evidence suggests that a cognitive approach is the most parsimonious and integrative approach to take in relating consciousness and temporal experience.

In the literature on temporal experience, a persistent controversy has revolved around the relative merits of "internal-clock" and "cognitive" approaches (Michon, 1972; Ornstein, 1969). Most theorists have argued that one of these two kinds of approaches is necessary and sufficient to explain temporal experience, while the other is neither necessary nor sufficient; however, different theorists do not agree on which approach is better. One cause of the nearly exclusively dichotomous reasoning has been the rather implausible assumptions made by both kinds of theorists. Some internal-clock theorists have assumed that one simple biological (usually, neural) mechanism underlies all human temporal experience. On the other hand, some cognitive theorists have assumed that biological processes play little or no role in temporal experience.

Internal-clock theories have roots in older philosophical and psychological discussions of the "time sense", but almost all recent varieties of them have been influenced by the seminal work of François (cited by Hoagland, 1933) and Hoagland (1933, 1951). In Hoagland's words:

> Measurements of the estimations of short durations indicate the existence of a master chemical clock of a specific nature. . . . Longer intervals of time appear to be judged in terms of the velocities of other master chemical reactions . . . which determine cyclic diurnal rhythms. Large scale conceptions of duration evidently depend upon slowly accumulating irreversible effects in the internal environment composing the body humors.
>
> (Hoagland, 1933, p. 283)

Hoagland's only assertion that is directly supported by his evidence is that a master chemical clock mediates estimations of short durations. His data, which are remarkably shabby considering the specific nature of his assertions, were obtained from just three subjects. All showed increased body temperature, two as a result of influenza and one as a result of diathermy. When asked to count at the rate of 1 per sec, they counted more rapidly as body temperature increased.

Since Hoagland's original proposal, many researchers have engaged in a fruitless search for a specific internal-clock mechanism. However, only Hoagland's assertion regarding short durations has received much empirical testing. Some experiments in which body temperature was either manipulated, or observed during normal diurnal variation, support an internal-clock hypothesis, while others do not (O'Hanlon *et al.*, 1974; Ornstein, 1969). Inconsistent findings have also been reported in studies of heart rate (Bell and Provins, 1963), cortical alpha rhythm frequency (Legg, 1968) and other physiological variables. Generally, studies measuring counting, tapping, handwriting and other motor tasks support an internal-clock approach more consistently than studies employing verbal estimation, production, reproduction and other more symbolic tasks. Ornstein's conclusion is typical of some recent cognitive theorists' criticisms of internal-clock approaches:

> The argument is not that increases in body temperature (or the speeding up of a "biological clock" with a drug) do not lengthen time experience, but rather that these manipulations are more parsimoniously considered as affecting cognitive processing rather than altering one of the maze of possible "chronometers".
>
> (Ornstein, 1969, p. 34)

In other words, it is foolish to attack all internal-clock approaches by questioning the reliability of reported effects. But it is equally foolish to cling to the belief that all human temporal experiences are mediated by an internal clock or even several clocks. In recent years there has been a distinct shift of the "Zeitgeist" away from internal-clock approaches and toward cognitive approaches. There is now abundant evidence that cognitive processes play a central role in temporal experience, and the present review emphasizes this evidence. What is needed is a conciliation of the two approaches, with further research into the questions of how physiological variations affect cognitive processes and how information-processing activities affect physiological processes (Kahneman, 1973).

2 Temporal Experiences in "Ordinary" Consciousness

2.1 The Psychological Moment: Fine Structure of Consciousness

When the fine structure of consciousness is considered, a recurring question is whether consciousness is continuous or intermittent. Of course, no awareness accompanies some physiological conditions, such as dreamless sleep, coma and some epileptic seizures; but the question can be asked nevertheless regarding "ordinary" waking consciousness. Phenomenologically, there is wide agreement that consciousness is continuous, and James's (1890) metaphor of consciousness as a "stream" certainly seems reasonable. However, some experimental studies suggest that consciousness might actually be intermittent.

In 1898 Richet (cited by Fraisse, 1963) proposed a basic oscillation in the nervous system. However, Stroud (1955, 1967) is usually acknowledged as the originator of an explicit intermittency hypothesis.

(The proposed intermittency has often been related to the cortical alpha rhythm, but evidence supporting such a specific physiological assertion is meagre and inconsistent.) Stroud's basic assumption was that time is represented as a discrete, rather than a continuous, variable. Thus, his hypothesis is usually called the "discrete-moment" hypothesis. It says that information is processed in temporally distinct, or non-overlapping, integrations and that the temporal order of information within each integration is not preserved. In other words, events that occur within a single moment are experienced as simultaneous, while events that occur in different moments are experienced as successive. An alternative proposal, the "travelling-moment" hypothesis (Allport, 1968), says that information is not processed in non-overlapping integrations, but rather in a continuously moving temporal "window". All events separated in time by less than the span of the moving window, or travelling moment, are experienced as simultaneous; events separated by greater than the span are experienced as successive. In order to evaluate these two hypotheses, empirical studies concerning the duration of the psychological moment, as well as those concerning phenomena of simultaneity and successiveness, need to be considered.

Different sensory systems transduce and transmit information at slightly different speeds, so that an experience of successiveness can occur when stimuli in different sensory modalities are physically simultaneous. When simultaneous stimuli are presented in the same modality, an expected event may be experienced as occurring earlier than an unexpected one. Most experiments on simultaneity, however, have used stimuli presented in the same modality and expected to about the same degree. In one early study, Hylan (1903) successively presented six letters that formed a word, and all observers reported them as simultaneous if the total presentation duration was less than about 90 msec. Stroud (1955) reviewed a number of different kinds of studies, including some concerned with motor as well as perceptual phenomena, and concluded that the duration of a moment was between 50 and 200 msec. White (1963) found that judgments of the number of stimuli in a rapid sequence were underestimates, and he inferred from them that the duration of a moment was about 140–170 msec. Allport (1968) used a successive oscilloscope display of 12 lines that could be cycled at various rates, and he found that all 12 lines were reported to be simultaneously present when the cycle period was decreased to about 70–100 msec. Efron (1970, 1972) measured the duration of visual and auditory perceptions by asking observers to adjust a brief index stimulus, which was presented in a different modality from a control stimulus, so that it seemed to be simultaneous with either the onset or the offset of the control stimulus. He found that the interval between onset and offset of the index stimulus was adjusted to be about 130 msec with any auditory or visual control stimulus duration less than about 130 msec. Efron concluded that the duration of the perception of a stimulus less than about 130 msec is constant.

Some theorists have regarded these and other similar findings, which are consistent with the hypothesis of a discrete moment of about 50–200 msec, as evidence that a fairly constant biological pacemaker, or internal clock, underlies human temporal experience. Some other findings, however, complicate and contradict both the discrete-moment hypothesis and the internal-clock hypothesis. Allport (1968) obtained phenomenological evidence rejecting the discrete-moment hypothesis in favour of the travelling-moment hypothesis. When subjects observed his rapidly cycling oscilloscope display of lines, they reported that a shadow appeared to move in a direction that was the same as the sequence of lines. This effect is predicted by the travelling-moment hypothesis, but it is the opposite of what is predicted by the discrete-moment hypothesis. Estimates of the duration of a moment are also affected by stimulus variables, such as the luminance of the visual stimuli used (Allport, 1968; Efron and Lee, 1971). Efron and Lee asserted that these findings make even the travelling-moment hypothesis, "less interesting theoretically, since the duration of the alleged 'moment' [is] primarily determined by stimulus parameters rather than by temporal parameters of any neurophysiological sampling mechanism" (p. 374).

Other experiments reveal that successiveness may be experienced under certain conditions when the interval between two brief stimuli is as short as 2 msec (Exner, cited by James, 1890; Hirsh, 1959). In addition, trained subjects could make judgments of temporal order of two stimuli with 75% accuracy when the interval between the stimuli was as short as 20 msec (Hirsh and Sherrick, 1961). These findings seem to be inconsistent with the discrete-moment hypothesis, the travelling-moment hypothesis and any other hypothesis that attempts to explain both the experience of simultaneity and the experience of successiveness by referring to the duration of a moment in which information is integrated. It may be that these findings are obtained only under ideal conditions, using trained observers, repeated stimulus presentations and so on. Another possiblity is to conclude, as Baron (1971) did, that, "there is no evidence . . . for a periodic psychological moment which has anything to do with successiveness discrimination" (p. 206). It seems to me, however, that psychological moment hypotheses, which were originally proposed to explain experiences of simultaneity, should also be able to explain experiences of successiveness. This viewpoint was implicit in the work of Robinson *et al.* (cited by Robinson and Pollack, 1971), who proposed an "overlapping-moment" hypothesis. It retains the notion of discrete moments, which can explain experiences of simultaneity, but it says that there is a substantial overlapping of successive moments. In that regard, it is like the travelling-moment hypothesis, except that it regards the movement of the travelling window as discontinuous in time. Experiences of simultaneity are related to the duration of the moment, while experiences of successiveness are related to the relatively short (several milliseconds) time period during which successive moments do not overlap. Another solution to the problem of explaining the evidence on experiences of successiveness may be to modify the travelling-moment hypothesis. It might be assumed that the trailing edge of the travelling window is blurred over a few milliseconds and that successiveness is experienced when this edge "passes by" successive stimuli separated by more than a few milliseconds. Experiences of simultaneity would still be related to the duration of the moment.

All of the moment hypotheses discussed so far have proposed a relatively stimulus-independent intermittency or scanning process, and none of them seems completely satisfactory. A radically different kind of approach would be to assume that both the experience of simultaneity and the experience of successiveness are based on comparisons of the duration and overlapping of the initial registration of events—the activation of perceptual traces—in some central location. Specifically, Efron (1963) presented evidence indicating that the left cerebral hemisphere of most individuals is intimately involved in experiences of simultaneity and successiveness. (This notion is explored further in Section 3.8 of this review.) Regardless of the ultimate resolution of these complex issues, it is clear that phenomena of the psychological moment do not indicate the existence of an internal-clock mechanism. Rather, these phenomena are apparently based on dynamic aspects of the human information-processing system. A more complete understanding of the dynamic processes that are involved requires additional research.

2.2 Sensory Information Storage and the Indifference Point

Some researchers have attempted to determine psycho-physical functions describing judgments of durations ranging from fractions of a second to many years. Michon (1975) provided an excellent theoretical integration of some of the findings. Of relevance here is Michon's (1967) finding that judgments of durations between about 100 and 500 msec increase approximately with the square root of the actual durations, while judgments of durations between about 500 msec and 2 sec increase linearly. Thus, different processes apparently underlie experiences of durations less than 500 msec and those greater than 500 msec. Michon (1975) ascribed the difference to, "the transition from immediate memory to short term memory" (p. 304). It is notable that the transitional time period (about 500 msec) corresponds closely with the most typically obtained "indifference point" (Fraisse, 1963; Woodrow, 1951). The indifference point, which is sometimes called the "indifference interval", is a time period that is, on the average, neither overestimated nor underestimated. What is usually called "Vierordt's Law" was apparently first discovered by Höring (cited by Fraisse, 1963), who was a student of Vierordt. It refers to the finding that relatively short time periods tend to be overestimated while relatively long time periods tend to be underestimated compared to physical, or clock, time. The indifference point is usually found to be about 500–700 msec, although estimates range from about 300 msec–5 sec or longer (Woodrow, 1951). Many studies show that the indifference point can be affected by various factors, especially the range of time periods used, and that it varies from subject to subject and from task to task. Some well-designed studies have found no indifference point at all. Early theorists related the indifference point to the duration of physiological processes underlying heart rate, walking rate and so on. Fraisse (1963) speculated that the indifference point is related to reaction time and the "complete perceptual process" (p. 126). In modern cognitive terminology, it seems that Fraisse was referring to the processing of information in the sensory information storage systems. Blumenthal (1977) provided a recent review of "buffer delays" (in sensory information storage) that makes the relationship between the transitional time period and information storage systems more explicit. He asserted that the indifference point "may be an artifact of an intrinsic buffer delay. That is, short events may be prolonged subjectively by the holding action of buffer processes and slightly longer events may be constricted subjectively by the same process" (p. 64). Support for Blumenthal's assertion comes from the frequent finding that brief stimuli which are more intense seem longer in duration than those which are less intense (Berglund *et al.*, 1969). One possible explanation is that intense stimuli take longer to decay from sensory information storage than weak stimuli.

2.3 Very Short Duration Experiences

Many other studies have investigated variables that affect very short duration experiences. (For present purposes, "very short" duration experiences are those typically resulting from stimulus durations of less than about 1 sec.) At least two additional cognitive processes must be considered in attempts to explain the findings: pre-attentive processes through which a stimulus contacts a memorial representation; and processes of selective attention, which may involve time-sharing between attention to stimulus information and attention to the passage of time itself. These processes are probably intimately related; the nature of the relationship is made explicit in the theoretical account that follows.

When a stimulus occurs for a very short duration, the experienced duration of the stimulus depends on the observer's familiarity with it. A recent series of experiments (Avant and Lyman, 1975; Avant *et al.*, 1975) found a lengthened experience of duration of an unfamiliar non-word (e.g. EIO) compared to a familiar word (e.g. DIG), a familiar word compared to a familiar letter (e.g. I) and an inverted word (e.g. ƆIႺ) compared to an upright word. Since these differences were found with stimulus durations of 10–30 msec, it follows that two different types of stimuli presented for an equal duration less than that of the psychological moment may produce different duration experiences. Regarding the findings of Efron (1970, 1972), which were discussed in Section 2.1, Avant *et al.* said that "while the real-time duration of the processing of a single perceptual unit may be no briefer than 130 msec . . . the *apparent or subjective duration* of shorter presentations is not constant" (p. 253, their italics). Further, the differences were found even when identification of the stimuli was at chance level. A tentative hypothesis is that the experienced duration of a brief presentation of a stimulus depends on the time taken for the stimulus to contact a memorial representation.

With somewhat longer but still very short durations, a number of different stimulus variables lengthen duration experience, including increased numerosity of pattern elements (Mo, 1971), increased area and decreased perimeter of a figure (Cantor and Thomas, 1977) and higher frequency of occurrence of words in a language (Warm and McCray, 1969). Although some of the effects seem to contradict the findings of Avant and his colleagues (Avant and Lyman, 1975; Avant *et al.*, 1975), an important difference is the much shorter durations used by Avant. As Avant and Lyman note, with durations that allow identification (full recognition) of a stimulus, other cognitive activities may occupy a greater proportion of the duration. This kind of notion has been clarified by Thomas and his colleagues (Thomas and Weaver, 1975). They developed and tested a mathematical model of experienced duration of visual stimuli in which attention is shared between two parallel processors, a temporal information processor ("timer") and a non-temporal information processor ("visual information processor"). As visual information increases, more attention is allocated to the visual information processor; as visual information decreases, more attention is allocated to the timer. When more attention is allocated to one processor, the other becomes more unreliable. Thus, experienced duration is assumed to be a weighted average of the information encoded by each processor.

2.4 Longer Temporal Experiences: Durations and Intervals

A clarification of the distinction between the terms duration and interval seems necessary at this point. The term "duration" refers to "the time during which something exists or lasts", while the term "interval" refers to "a space of time between events" (Webster's New Collegiate Dictionary, 1977). The more neutral term "time period", or simply "period", is used here to refer in a general way to either a duration or an interval.

The distinction is both historically and theoretically necessary in order to understand diverse temporal phenomena involving longer time periods. Historically, phenomena related to intervals have been a concern of psychologists primarily studying memory, while phenomena related to durations have been a concern of psychologists primarily studying time. To my knowledge, only Michon (1975) has attempted to integrate these topics, and his discussion was limited. A comprehensive synthesis of the two separate lines of research is clearly needed.

Some recent memory research has focused on the nature of memory attributes and processes mediating judgment of recency, temporal position and spacing (lag). A "recency" judgment involves the estimation of an interval between a past event and the present occurrence of an equivalent event. A "temporal-position" judgment, which is similar to a recency judgment, involves the estimation of the temporal location of a past event on a scale representing a given sequence of events. A "spacing" ("lag") judgment involves the estimation of an interval between two past events. In memory research on these judgments, the events to be judged are typically embedded in a sequence of similar events. In contrast, some psychological research on time has focussed on the nature of the processes mediating judgment of duration. When longer duration experiences are studied, researchers typically use cohesive sequences of events. Distinctive events mark the beginning and end of the durations, and a distinctive cognitive context is present throughout each. The distinctive cognitive context is what unifies long durations, so that even long time periods can be properly called durations.

Given these clarifications, an attempt can be made to synthesize diverse studies of longer temporal experience.

2.5 The Psychological Present: Contents of Consciousness

James (1890) proposed that humans "are constantly conscious of a certain duration—the specious present—varying in length from a few seconds to probably not more than a minute" (p. 642), with longer durations conceived by adding and shorter durations by dividing portions of the specious present. A metaphor James used was that of "a saddle-back, with a certain breadth of its own on which we sit perched, and from which we look in two directions into time" (p. 609). His statement that the nucleus of the specious present "is probably the dozen seconds or less that have just elapsed" (p. 613) contained the seeds of a controversy about the temporal extent of the phenomenon. Boring (1933/1963) said that the "conscious present can certainly include a rhythmical grouping that occupies a second or a second and a half, and that with somewhat less 'immediacy' . . . may extend to include a rhythm of a quarter or perhaps even half a minute" (p. 135). Fraisse (1963) said that the "psychological present", as he called it, enables us to "perceive units of change which . . . are elements from which we construct the unity of our whole psychological life" (p. 98). From a cognitive viewpoint, it seems clear that the psychological present is related to the temporal dynamics of short-term memory. Unrehearsed information is "lost" from short-term memory over a period of about 10–20 sec. This is an upper limit, and for practical purposes the psychological present may be limited to about 5 sec (Fraisse, 1963; Woodrow, 1951). Some memory theorists equate the contents of short-term memory with the contents of consciousness (see Ch. 7). Thus, the direct awareness of succession or continuous change—what James (1890) called the "stream" of consciousness (p. 607)—pervades short-term memory, which is thought to relate information from the sensory information storage and long-term memory systems. When attention is focused on discrete events, there is apparently an automatic awareness of their durations. Under uninformed ("incidental learning") conditions, subjects can make somewhat accurate judgments of event duration when the events are no longer within the psychological present (Hintzman, 1970). Awareness of rhythm seems to be an awareness of durations of events and of intervals between related events in the psychological present (Fraisse, 1963).

If an event is repeated in two similar contexts, we seem to be frequently (perhaps always, if the contexts are similar enough) aware of and able to judge the approximate recency of the first occurrence of the event. It has been proposed that judgment of recency is based on the decreased "strength" (Hinrichs, 1970) or "fragility" (Wickelgren, 1974) of the retrieved representation, or memory trace, of an event. However, evidence from studies in which judgments of the temporal position of events were requested seriously discredits these hypotheses (Hintzman and Block, 1971; Hintzman *et al.*, 1973; Tzeng *et al.*, 1979). Instead, a "contextual-association" hypothesis is supported. It proposes that judgment of recency is based on retrieval of contextual information associated with the earlier occurrence. Automatically-retrieved contextual information may produce an awareness of the approximate recency of the event, as well as of other attributes such as its duration and sensory modality. In other words, awareness of recency is apparently the result of an implicit comparison of the context associated with the previous occurrence and the context prevailing during the present occurrence. It must be noted that we are ordinarily not automatically aware of an interval separating two unrelated events. Judgments of spacing between two remembered, but unrelated, events that occurred in a sequence of similar events are usually very inaccurate (Hintzman and Block, 1973; Hintzman *et al.*, 1975; Underwood, 1977). However, if one event creates a unique cognitive context and another event terminates that context, we may properly speak of the experience of duration. A judgment of the duration of a sequence of events no longer within the psychological present may be mediated by an effortful memorial reconstruction of certain aspects of the conscious contents during the duration (see Section 2.9).

2.6 Short, Long and Very Long Temporal Experiences

In evaluating research and proposing theories concerning longer temporal experiences, a general issue is whether different processes mediate experiences of time periods of different lengths. For present purposes, "short" time periods are those within the psychological present, or up to about 10 or 20 sec; "long" time periods are those from about 10 or 20 sec to a few hours; and "very long" time periods are those longer than a few hours.

First, consider whether or not experiences of durations of different lengths are mediated by different processes. Abundant psycho-physical evidence shows that judgments of durations ranging from a few tenths of a second to a few minutes can be described by a power function. The exponent of the function varies between about 0·7 and 1·3, but averages about 1·1, across experiments (Eisler, 1975, 1976; Michon, 1975). Simply stated, such duration judgments are approximately veridical, since the exponent is probably not significantly different from 1·0.

Based on this evidence, Michon hypothesized that the transition between short-term and long-term memory is not observable in the duration judgments of normal subjects. To my knowledge, Michon has not overlooked any evidence showing a discontinuity at durations of about 10 or 20 sec. An exception mentioned by Michon is the case of "H.M.", which is often cited as evidence for a distinction between short-term and long-term memory. A bilateral hippocampectomy was performed on H.M. to relieve his frequent epileptic seizures, and the resulting deficit has been described as an inability to transfer new information from short-term to long-term memory. An experiment conducted by Richards (1973) revealed that different power-function exponents are needed to characterize H.M.'s judgments of durations less than about 20 sec (an exponent of 1·05) and his judgments of longer durations (an exponent of 0·44). Richards extrapolated the data in order to remark that, "one hour to us is like 3 minutes to H.M." (p. 281). With the exception of H.M., however, we can evaluate research on duration experiences without distinguishing between those using short and those using long durations, since there is no evidence that the underlying processes differ. There are few studies using very long durations, and to my knowledge no one has investigated durations between a few minutes and a few hours. However, a study by Crombag *et al.* (cited by Michon, 1975) found that judgments of duration are linear and approximately veridical in the range from about 5–80 h. Results of this study suggest that processes mediating judgment of long and very long durations do not differ. Thus, there is no evidence that different processes mediate judgments of durations between about 500 msec and 80 h.

A related question is whether or not processes underlying judgment of an interval between events differ depending on the length of the interval. Experiments investigating judgment of spacing between two equivalent or related events reveal no discontinuity in such judgments over a range of onset-to-onset intervals from 5–130 sec (Hintzman and Block, 1973; Hintzman *et al.*, 1975). Similarly, Hinrichs and Buschke (1968) and Hinrichs (1970) found no discontinuity in recency judgments across onset-to-onset intervals from 3–45 sec. Apparently no distinction between processes involved in judging short and long intervals (such as, short-term and long-term memory processes) is necessary. The observed psycho-physical relationship relating judgment of recency and actual recency could be described by either a logarithmic or a power function, with the former fitting the data slightly better. The exponent of the best-fitting power function was 0·46. This exponent is clearly different from the exponent of about 1·1 that is usually found for judgments of durations of similar length. Thus, judgment of an interval between events must be based on different processes than those involved in judgment of duration. This conclusion is supported by an earlier study of the apparent recencies of "real-world" events (Cohen *et al.*, 1954). Subjects were asked to indicate subjective temporal positions of past events on a line from "birth" to "now". They found a logarithmic function for events within the past 6 months; intervals closer to "now" were judged disproportionately longer than more remote intervals. For events which occurred more than about a year previously, judgments were related to actual temporal position in a linear way. Cohen *et al.* suggested that a process of calculation based on calendar dates could explain the linear relationship. Other theorists have suggested that judgment of recency or temporal position of events which occurred months or years previously are mediated by logical inferences based on direct or indirect associations with well known calendar dates, distinctive temporal "landmarks", seasons of the year, and so on (Linton, 1975; Underwood, 1977). Thus, judgments of very long intervals seem to be based on different processes than judgments of shorter intervals.

2.7 Experienced and Remembered Duration

Following James (1890), some theorists have emphasized the need to distinguish between duration experiences in passing—referred to here as "experienced duration"—and duration experiences in retrospect—referred to here as "remembered duration". In fact, James proposed that apparently contradictory effects could occur:

> *In general, a time filled with varied and interesting experiences seems short in passing, but long as we look back. On the other hand, a tract of time empty of experiences seems long in passing, but in retrospect short.*
>
> (James, 1890, p. 624, his italics)

In an attempt to explain effects such as these, James proposed that experienced duration lengthens when "we grow attentive to the passage of time itself" (p. 626), while remembered duration lengthens with "the multitudinousness of the memories which the time affords" (p. 624). Fraisse (1963) proposed that "direct time judgments [are] founded immediately on the changes we experience and later on the changes we remember" (p. 234).

Experiments typically have studied either experienced duration or remembered duration by informing a subject either before or after the time period that the experimenter is requesting a duration judgment. Some researchers have studied only remembered duration in order to avoid attempts of some subjects to be accurate by counting, tapping and so on. When experienced duration is studied, subjects are usually asked not to count or tap unless, of course, counting or tapping rate is the dependent variable of interest. The psychological effect of such instructions on both conscious and unconscious processes is admittedly not known, but most subjects seem to be quite willing and able to comply. In some recent studies, experienced duration has been compared with remembered duration in the same experiment. Hicks *et al.* (1976) found that the experienced duration of a 42-second time period was shorter when more information was processed, but remembered duration was not affected by the manipulation. Miller *et al.* (1978) found that the experienced duration of a 32- to 54-second time period spent rehearsing verbal information was lengthened as the number of previous study trials was increased, but remembered duration was shortened. Both of these studies suggest that cognitive control processes, which presumably require conscious involvement, differ depending upon whether the focus is on experienced duration or remembered duration. It seems that James (1890), Fraisse (1963) and others were justified in making such a distinction.

Until recently, many researchers and theorists have failed to realize the importance of distinguishing between experienced and remembered duration. An effect of this negligence has been a general confusion, with different studies seeming to find opposite or contradictory effects of certain variables on duration judgments. When one adds to this confusion the misleading and vague terminology used to describe effects found using different duration judgment methods, the net effect is apparent chaos. When careful distinctions are made, though, somewhat orderly relationships emerge.

2.8 Experienced Duration: Awareness of Passing Time

In addition to the experiments already described, many others have been conducted examining experienced duration. Let us consider some of the more suggestive findings and reasonable hypotheses regarding experienced duration. Some theorists have attempted to explain experienced duration by postulating an internal clock, or pacemaker, mechanism that generates regularly-spaced "pulses". Most of these models are implicitly based on the discrete-moment hypothesis, which is inferior to other moment hypotheses for reasons discussed earlier in this review (Section 2.1). The best-known model of this kind is Treisman's (1963). He proposed a counter that records the number of pulses between two events, one defining the start and another the end of a time period. The total number of pulses is then deposited in a store, which can be accessed by a comparator (decision mechanism) in making a duration judgment. In my opinion, this kind of model obscures a number of aspects of the cognitive processes mediating experienced duration. It also is subject to the same kind of criticism to which other internal-clock hypotheses are subject, since it fails to explain adequately the effects of information-processing manipulations on experienced duration.

There are a number of older studies of experienced duration that are difficult to explain by referring to an internal-clock mechanism. The most extensive of these was Loehlin's (1959) study of experienced duration of a 2-minute period spent performing one of 16 different kinds of tasks. He concluded that "time may seem long during an interval because the activity is boring, because attention is being paid to the passage of time, because the activity is unfamiliar, or because [the subject] is relatively passive" (p. 16). Loehlin's review of previous studies generally supported his conclusions about the importance of these factors.

More recently, Hicks and his colleagues (Hicks *et al.*, 1976, 1977) have used quantitative variations in information-processing activities to investigate hypotheses about experienced duration. Summarizing their findings, as well as those of others, they concluded that:

> Events on which [experienced duration] is based require attention (processing capacity) for storage. Stimuli requiring no processing can increase experienced duration by increasing the number of events in storage. Stimuli requiring processing can decrease experienced duration because fewer of the events defining duration are stored.
>
> (Hicks *et al.*, 1977, p. 443)

The proposal is reminiscent of that of Thomas and his colleagues regarding experienced duration of very short intervals (see Section 2.3). A problem with this kind of hypothesis is that it does not adequately specify the nature of the "events defining duration". In other words, when a person attends to the "passage of time itself" (James, 1890, p. 626), what are the momentary contents of consciousness? Surely attention to clocks should not be equated with attention to time, and in most experiments subjects do not have access to clocks anyway. A proposal that may represent an initial move in the direction of greater specificity is that attending to the passage of time means attending to changes in cognitive context—that is, certain aspects of the contents of consciousness. This hypothesis is clarified following a discussion of remembered duration.

2.9 Remembered Duration: Awareness of Past Time

A wide variety of factors have been found to affect remembered duration. However, hypotheses have tended to focus on a single kind of variable and to attempt a parsimonious explanation in terms of processes presumably causing an effect of that variable on remembered duration. What is needed is an hypothesis that integrates all reliable findings in a coherent way. Block and Reed (1978) recently discussed four kinds of hypotheses that seem to have some generality—"informational", "attentional", "event-memory" and "contextual-change" hypotheses. To some extent these are overlapping hypotheses, since they all recognize that we must consider processes involved in encoding information during a duration, storing information between the time of encoding and the time of retrieval, and retrieving information at the time the duration is remembered. However, the relative emphases differ.

Informational and attentional hypotheses emphasize information-processing activities during encoding. Informational hypotheses propose that the most important consideration is the amount of information presented and processed during the duration. Support for this kind of hypothesis comes from Vroon's (1970) findings that if overt responding to presented information was not required, remembered duration lengthened when there was a greater amount of information presented; but if overt responding was required, remembered duration shortened when there was a greater amount of information processed. Attentional hypotheses propose that the most important consideration is the selectivity of attention required by the information-processing task (Underwood, 1975). For example, Underwood and Swain (1973) found that a prose passage which required more attention for analysis was remembered as longer in duration than one which required less attention. One weakness of informational and attentional hypotheses is that they must rely on other hypotheses for an explanation of the role of memory storage and retrieval processes in remembering duration. It is not obvious how a person remembers the amount of information presented and processed or the amount of attention demanded by the information-processing task performed during the duration.

Event-memory and contextual-change hypotheses emphasize memory retrieval processes, in addition to encoding and storage processes. Event-memory hypotheses propose that the most important consideration is the process of covert retrieval of memory representations of stimulus events that occurred during the duration. Ornstein's (1969) "storage size" hypothesis is the most well known event-memory hypothesis. It asserts that remembered duration is a cognitive construction based on a covert assessment of "the size of the storage space" of representations of stimulus events "*remaining in storage*" (p. 104, his italics). The hypothesis was proposed in order to explain his findings that remembered duration lengthened with an increase in the number of stimulus events, the complexity of a stimulus or a sequence of stimuli, and the assumed complexity of coding of a stimulus.

The contextual-change hypothesis is similar to the storage-size hypothesis, except that it maintains that encoding, storage and retrieval of contextual information—rather than stimulus information—is the critical factor. The basic proposal is that remembered duration is a cognitive construction mediated by a covert assessment of the remembered amount of change in cognitive context during the duration (Block, 1978; Block and Reed, 1978). The four kinds of hypotheses were tested by Block and Reed, and they interpreted the results of their two experiments as consistent only with the contextual-change hypothesis. In their first experiment, a duration spent processing information at a "deep" (semantic) level was not remembered as longer than one spent processing information at a "shallow" (structural) level, even though the former task increased memory for stimulus events and presumably demanded more attention. In their second experiment, a duration spent alternately performing shallow and deep processing was remembered as longer than one spent processing information at a single level, even though the amount of information presented and processed was equivalent in the two conditions. The contextual-change hypothesis explains both of these findings by assuming that a unique cognitive context is associated with each kind of information-processing task (Underwood, 1977); when different kinds of tasks are performed, the cognitive context changes accordingly. In addition, several studies (Block, 1974, 1978; Block and Reed, 1978) obtained both duration judgments and memory judgments regarding the contents of the duration. The results indicated that retrieval processes involved in remembering stimulus events that occurred—such as those involved in judgment of number of events, recall or recognition of events and assignment of recognized events to the correct duration—do not mediate remembered duration. Since the contextual-change hypothesis does not emphasize memory for stimulus events, these findings are not unexpected.

The contextual-change hypothesis emphasizes change in aspects of the cognitive context, which are presumably part of the contents of consciousness. These contextual aspects probably include conspicuous environmental stimuli, internal sensations, characteristics of the task being performed and cognitive and affective reactions to the task (cf. Hintzman *et al.*, 1973). One model of memory asserts that experiences are encoded in a propositional format (Anderson and Bower, 1973). In this model, contextual aspects are assumed to be encoded directly in propositions, but new propositions are encoded only when some change occurs. Such a change might be a result of awareness of new incoming information, new contextual aspects, or both. Ordinarily these two kinds of causes are related, since processing information usually produces changes in affective reactions, "cognitive strain" and other contextual aspects. The encoding, storage and retrieval of non-contextual information, such as concerning stimulus events that occurred during a duration, may play a role in remembered duration if the accessibility of contextual associations in memory is affected. However, the evidence suggests that the primary emphasis must be on encoding, storage and retrieval of contextual information.

To illustrate the integrative nature of the contextual-change hypothesis, consider how it might explain the effects of some variables on remembered duration. When the number of stimulus events presented during a time period is increased, a person attends to the more rapid change of contextual elements correlated with "cognitive strain" (cf. Hintzman et al., 1973), and remembered duration is lengthened accordingly. A similar explanation is offered to explain the lengthened remembered duration of a time period containing a more difficult stimulus detection task (Underwood and Swain, 1973). However, if a person must actively generate a rapid sequence of responses, there is little residual processing capacity (attention) for encoding contextual changes, and remembered duration is shortened (Vroon, 1970). When a more complex stimulus is presented, contextual elements associated with different interpretations of the stimulus change more frequently (cf. Block, 1974), and remembered duration is lengthened. Finally, the first of two equal durations is remembered as being longer, perhaps because contextual elements correlated with affective reactions such as boredom change more rapidly at the start of a new experience, such as an experiment (Block, 1978; Block and Reed, 1978; Hintzman et al., 1973).

A contextual-change hypothesis on remembered duration also has implications for hypotheses on experienced duration. Perhaps references to attention to time itself that are found in the literature on experienced duration can be understood in terms of attention to changes in contextual aspects of consciousness. Performing a task that requires relatively little information processing allows a person to allocate more attention to encoding contextual aspects. In addition, such a task produces relatively large changes in contextual aspects involving emotions such as boredom. On the other hand, performing a difficult information-processing task seems shorter in experienced duration because fewer contextual aspects are attended to and thereby encoded. To state this proposal somewhat differently, a relatively idle, "empty" duration seems long in passing because of increased attention to changes in contextual information. It seems short in retrospect—especially after a delay—because there are fewer retrieval routes to contextual information as a result of the relative lack of memories of stimulus events. Opposite effects are found for a relatively busy, "filled" duration for exactly opposite reasons. It remains to be seen whether the contextual-change hypothesis can succeed in integrating phenomena of experienced and remembered duration in the way described here.

2.10 Temporal Perspective: Past, Present and Future Time

The concept of "temporal perspective", "temporal horizon" or "temporal orientation" has been used to refer to all-encompassing philosophical and metaphysical viewpoints on time. Various theorists have described the concept somewhat differently. Fraisse (1963) characterized it as "the way in which we behave in relation to three aspects of time: the past, the present, and the future" (p. 153). Ornstein (1969) referred to it as "philosophical, social, cultural constructions of the world and their effects on the interpretation of time experience" (p. 23). Gorman and Wessman (1977) defined it as "the degree to which a person, group, or society conceptualizes events removed from the present situation" (p. 228). From a cognitive viewpoint, an important point is that the contents of consciousness ordinarily consist of remembrances of past events, responses to present events and anticipations of future events. It is usually difficult to separate these components, since the normal performance of any task depends on all three of them. However, individual and cultural differences in cognition must be acknowledged. Some people and some cultures place relatively more or less emphasis on each of the three components, and resulting differences in the overall conception of time may be substantial. Furthermore, an individual's temporal perspective changes dramatically as he or she experiences certain altered states of consciousness, since memory, information-processing and planning functions are altered.

In psychological literature on time, questions about temporal perspective of most people in ordinary waking consciousness have been addressed mostly by those concerned with developmental, personality, and social factors. Few cognitive psychologists have been concerned with these kinds of issues, although a basic understanding of cognitive processes involved in temporal perspective would seem to be a prerequisite to an understanding of individual differences in cognition. Little can be said, however, about relationships between temporal perspective and cognitive aspects of temporal experience discussed in this review.

As a pre-requisite to an understanding of altered temporal perspective,

LeShan's discussions of normal temporal perspective are particularly useful. Most humans are assumed to operate most of the time from a metaphysical viewpoint he called the "Sensory Reality" (LeShan, 1974) or "sensory modes of being" (LeShan, 1976). Regarding temporal perspective, the basic laws, or limiting principles, are that every event has a cause which occurs before the event; that events in the past can be remembered but not changed; and that events in the future can be anticipated and influenced (LeShan, 1976, 88–91). Ornstein (1977) called this the "linear mode", in which "time is directional, a duration carrying us from the past into the future" (p. 103). Many people would not be aware of the possibility of other realities or modes of being regarding time unless altered states of consciousness were experienced. It is to temporal experiences in certain altered states of consciousness that we now must look for an understanding of the experience of alternate realities.

3 Temporal Experiences in Altered States of Consciousness

3.1 Approaches to Time in Altered States of Consciousness

Any reasonably comprehensive discussion of relationships between time and consciousness must consider temporal experiences associated with altered states of consciousness. There are two main reasons why this is important. First, a full understanding of temporal experiences in "ordinary" waking consciousness may not be possible without considering implications from experiences of "non-ordinary" states of consciousness. Second, any discussion of differences between altered states of consciousness and ordinary waking consciousness or of differences among various altered states of consciousness must include an account of alterations in temporal experience.

Although attempts have been made to identify discrete states of consciousness, a definitive listing seems remote. In fact, some definitions of the concept of altered states of consciousness in terms of continuous, quantitative variations obviously preclude such a listing, which assumes that there are discrete, qualitatively different states. At present, we can only speak of certain general categories of altered states of consciousness, with each category being distinguished by the use of certain techniques or the presence of certain conditions. Although it is probably a mistake to equate techniques or conditions and altered states of consciousness, given our present lack of understanding of altered states it is easiest to organize a discussion around general kinds of techniques or conditions. This review discusses several of the more common categories of altered states of consciousness. Within each category, only those aspects of temporal experience that have been studied experimentally are discussed. In general, few studies have investigated changes in experiences of simultaneity, succession and very short durations; while many studies have investigated changes in the psychological present, longer duration experiences and temporal perspective.

3.2 Sleeping and Dreaming

Researchers have attempted to answer several related questions about temporal phenomena associated with sleeping and dreaming. One question concerns processes underlying judgments of the duration of dreamless sleep periods, which are generally associated with the absence of rapid eye movements. It is generally agreed that the remembered duration of dreamless sleep periods is not related to the experienced duration of such periods, since there is usually no awareness during non-rapid-eye-movement periods. Studies (Noble and Lundie, 1974) in which subjects were awakened at various intervals after sleep onset reveal some degree of accuracy in judging the duration of non-rapid-eye-movement periods, although the absolute error is considerable. Since only brief fragments of mental activity are sometimes reported upon awakening from even long non-rapid-eye-movement periods, it seems that people make inferences about duration based on other cues. Such cues ordinarily include external stimuli; but in the absence of any change in external stimuli, people rely on internal cues noticed upon awakening, such as general feelings of restedness or fatigue, stomach and bladder sensations and the apparent recency of pre-sleep events (Boring and Boring, 1917).

Some people claim to be able to awaken at any pre-selected time. Five studies conducted over 40 years ago (Tart, 1970) lend some support to this possibility, although they reveal nothing about the underlying processes. Tart investigated some subjects who believed that they could successfully awaken at any pre-selected time. Most of them reported doing so on six experimental nights at home. He then instructed three of the more successful individuals to awaken at various times while sleeping in the laboratory. The results confirmed a substantial ability in these subjects. There were no obvious physiological correlates of successful awakenings, such as sleep stage upon awakening. One confounding effect, however, was a substantially increased frequency of awakening. Interestingly, one person who in this case apparently misunderstood or forgot the pre-selected time of 01.23 hours, awoke at 02.22 hours, about a minute after mumbling in his sleep, "Wake at 2:23"! Zung and Wilson (1971) used a more representative sample of subjects, and they found about 32% awakenings within ± 10 minutes of a pre-selected time between 02.00 and 05.00 hours. This accuracy is equivalent to the accuracy of waking estimates of comparable durations (Webb and Ross, 1972). In general agreement with Tart's findings, successful awakenings were independent of prior sleep stage, as well as the particular pre-selected time. In an attempt to explain their findings, Zung and Wilson proposed a "specific arousal system" that is unrelated to the 90-minute sleep cycle of alternating rapid- and non-rapid-eye-movement periods. In my opinion, their findings suggest the operation of subconscious (dissociated) information-processing mechanisms. The processes that underlie this phenomenon are still unknown, and it is also not known why only relatively few individuals apparently are able to awaken consistently at any pre-selected time. It might be revealing to study the temporal abilities of such persons in ordinary waking consciousness. It is possible that they simply represent an extreme portion of a normal distribution of temporal abilities.

Other investigators have studied the experienced duration of dream periods, which are generally associated with rapid eye movements. Although many people apparently believe that dreams last only a few seconds, electrophysiological records show that rapid-eye-movement periods last up to 1 hour. In one study (Dement and Kleitman, 1957), subjects were awakened either 5 or 15 minutes after the onset of rapid eye movements, and they were over 80% accurate in discriminating between the two time periods. In another study (Dement and Wolpert, 1958), subjects who had been showing rapid eye movements for a few minutes were exposed to an external stimulus, such as a spray of cold water, and then were awakened after a certain interval. In 10 instances in which the stimulus was incorporated into an ongoing dream, "the amount of dream action in the interval between the modifying stimulus and the awakening did not vary far from the amount of action that would have been expected to take place during an identical time in reality" (p. 550). Of course, it is possible, and perhaps even common, for an "ordinary" temporal sequence of events to be distorted, reversed or telescoped in dreams (Sturt, 1925), and some dreams may seem "timeless" (Cohen, 1954). It is not known to what extent these effects are produced by memory retrieval processes upon awakening, but it is unlikely that temporal distortions during dreams can be entirely explained in this way. One intriguing explanation is suggested by evidence indicating that in most people there is both greater activation of the right cerebral hemisphere and greater independence or reduced communication between the two hemispheres during rapid-eye-movement sleep (Bakan, 1977–78). Since the right cerebral hemisphere seems to be less involved in the analysis of temporal sequences than the left hemisphere, distortions of temporal sequences in dreams are understandable. Ordinarily, however, sequences of dream events are remembered upon awakening as having occurred in approximately "real-time", and processes involved in experiencing and remembering duration of dreams are probably not radically different from those mediating experienced and remembered duration of awake periods. In other words, awakened persons probably rely on retrieval of aspects of dream content in much the same way that awake persons rely on retrieval of certain aspects of conscious content in judging duration.

3.3 Daydreaming

Like nocturnal dreaming (i.e. rapid-eye-movement) periods, day-dreaming periods tend to recur in an approximately 90-minute cycle in adult humans. This cyclic variation in consciousness apparently involves changes in present-centredness as well as duration experience. Recent work on daydreaming has begun to clarify the nature of these changes. For present purposes, "daydreaming" is defined as any conscious activity that is not related to immediate external information-processing demands. This definition emphasizes that daydreaming is stimulus-independent or task-irrelevant mentation. Daydreaming draws attention away from processing incoming information, so that consciousness shifts toward reconstructing the past or anticipating the future, often in ways involving considerable fantasy. One effect of this different orientation of attention seems to be a shortening of duration experience. To my knowledge, the only study investigating the relationship between daydreaming and temporal experience is that of Wheeler (1969). He found that subjects who reported more stimulus-independent mentation, especially of an emotionally positive nature, during a boring signal-detection task tended to remember the task duration as shorter than did other subjects. One possible explanation is that the daydreamer is encoding fewer changes in contextual information, either because certain elements of the cognitive context (such as those involving feelings of boredom) are changing less rapidly or because less attention is being allocated to existing changes. It is also possible that memories of daydream content become less accessible once consciousness has returned to task-relevant information, perhaps for reasons similar to those underlying state-dependent retrieval effects. Regardless of the ultimate explanation, daydreaming may be beneficial in tolerating long periods of repetitious, monotonous activity (such as assembly-line work) because of the shortening of duration experience it apparently produces.

3.4 Sensory Deprivation and Sensory Overload

During the past 20 years, there has been some interest in possible alterations in temporal experience resulting from what is usually called "sensory deprivation". There are a number of older anecdotal reports given by people isolated in caves and other remote environments, many of which suggest that a shortening of duration experience accompanies isolation. Virtually all of the experimental evidence has been obtained by researchers primarily concerned with sensory deprivation rather than temporal experience, and they have made little effort to comment on the broader implications of their findings. Some psychologists primarily interested in temporal phenomena have attempted to relate sensory deprivation studies of temporal experience to the old controversy about the relative effects of filled and unfilled intervals (Doob, 1971, 117–118). It is apparent that only in a very narrow definition of an unfilled, or "empty", interval—one devoid or nearly devoid of changes in *external* stimuli—can a period of sensory deprivation be said to represent an "empty" interval. All subjects, in fact, report that conscious mental activity continues during most of the deprivation period, and electrophysiological recording supports such introspective reports. Nevertheless, it is quite reasonable to determine whether gross reductions in external stimulus information affect temporal experience. Of particular relevance here are introspective reports and empirical findings indicating that many subjects experience altered states of consciousness, especially under certain conditions and durations of sensory deprivation.

Different kinds of environments have been used in sensory deprivation research, but the most commonly used are the isolation room or cubicle and the water-immersion tank. Forgays and McClure (1974) found that experienced duration—measured by repeated production of 30-minute intervals—was longer during a period spent in a tank than during a period spent in a cubicle. Unfortunately, as in many sensory deprivation studies, a non-deprivation control was not used, so no conclusions could be made about changes in duration experience produced by sensory deprivation relative to more ordinary environmental conditions.

It is, however, usually concluded that experienced duration is shortened in sensory deprivation relative to more normal environmental conditions (Doob, 1971). The actual experimental evidence is meagre and inconclusive. Banks and Cappon (1962) reported that the duration of a period of "reduced sensory input" was underestimated more than that of a period spent reading or filling out questionnaire forms; but they did not describe the "reduced sensory input" environment, indicate what temporal judgment method was used or report the mean judgments. Vernon and McGill (1963) obtained both prospective and retrospective estimates of duration of a sensory deprivation period up to 96 hours long. Prospective estimates—repeated productions of 60-minute intervals—averaged about 81% of the actual duration. Retrospective estimates—verbal estimates of the total time period—were also underestimates, averaging about 92% of the actual duration. Unfortunately, no firm conclusions about relative duration experience are possible, since no control condition was used. To my knowledge, no well-controlled study comparing temporal experience in sensory deprivation and more normal environmental conditions has been conducted. The shortening of duration experience in sensory deprivation must be considered to be a hypothesis that needs to be adequately tested.

In spite of the lack of any definitive conclusion regarding relative effects of deprivation, duration judgments have proved to be useful to some sensory deprivation researchers. Murphy *et al.* (cited by Myers, 1969) reported a significant negative correlation between the degree of overestimation of the first 4 hours of deprivation and the number of hours of deprivation endured. The "early release" subjects gave a mean verbal estimate of 7·7 hours, while the "long staying" subjects gave a mean estimate of 5·1 hours. Surprisingly, both types of subjects verbally over-estimated the duration. Regardless of this inconsistency with other findings, it appears that duration judgments can be used to predict endurance of sensory deprivation.

A related question is whether duration experience is altered during "sensory overload" conditions, which produce some of the same effects as sensory deprivation conditions. One report (Ludwig, 1972) suggested that "disturbances in sense of time" may occur and that the effect may be related to alterations in consciousness experienced by some subjects. However, the reported evidence on temporal experiences consisted entirely of excerpts of retrospective accounts given by three subjects. Further research is clearly needed on the effects of sensory deprivation and sensory overload, with the use of a more normal environmental condition as an appropriate and necessary control and with greater use of a variety of temporal judgment methods.

3.5 Hypnosis

The term "hypnosis" is used here to refer to a range of altered states of consciousness that a sufficiently suggestible person may be enabled to experience as a result of the use of any of a number of different techniques. Let us first consider temporal experience in a typical hypnotic state—that is, one induced by customary techniques, but with no specific suggestions regarding temporal experience. Some early investigations (Cooper and Erickson, 1959) suggested that duration is judged more accurately during hypnosis than during "ordinary" waking consciousness; however, many of the experiments lacked a proper control condition. In contrast, some well-designed studies found no significant difference. For example, Stalnaker and Richardson (1930) asked subjects to produce durations of 1, 2 and 3 minutes during both a hypnotic "trance state" and an ordinary "waking state". There were no significant differences in mean estimation error, even though it was suggested to subjects that their estimations during hypnosis would be more accurate. There was also no significant lengthening or shortening of experienced duration during hypnosis. More recently, Tebēcis and Provins (1974) found no significant difference between hypnotized and non-hypnotized subjects in production of a 131-second duration. To my knowledge, no one has systematically investigated the remembered duration of a period of hypnosis. Since some people show partial amnesia for events that occurred during hypnosis—an effect that may be an example of a state-dependent retrieval effect—it is possible that the remembered duration of a hypnotized period would be shortened compared to a non-hypnotized period. When a suggestion is given to hypnotized subjects that they will not be able to remember events that occurred during hypnosis after being aroused from it, some subjects show a dramatic amnesia effect. Given such a suggestion, subjects would be expected to report a greatly shortened remembered duration of the hypnotic period.

A number of studies have investigated effects of specific "time-distortion" suggestions on temporal experience and behaviour. In their pioneering work, Cooper and Erickson (1959) gave deeply hypnotized subjects the suggestion that a short duration (e.g. 10 sec) would seem like a very long one (e.g. 1 h). They were told that sufficient time would be available for the completion of an activity, such as designing a dress, which ordinarily would require much more clock time. Subjects often reported completing the task, saying that the duration seemed greatly lengthened (e.g. "about an hour"). Cooper and Erickson claimed that these subjects actually experienced the duration as much longer than it really was. They also suggested that hypnotic time-distortion might be of practical benefit to a person wishing to engage in creative mental activity in an area of interest. Barber and Calverley (1964) challenged these assertions, claiming that details of the suggested mental activity might actually be constructed by the subject after the period of hypnosis, not during it. They compared hypnotized subjects given time-distortion suggestions, non-hypnotized subjects given similar suggestions, and non-hypnotized control subjects given no time-distortion suggestions. Both groups receiving the suggestions agreed that time seemed to go slowly during a 5-minute period, and both differed significantly from the no-suggestion control group. The difference between the hypnotized- and waking-suggestion subjects' retrospective duration estimates was not statistically significant, although mean estimates were 89·1 and 46·9 minutes, respectively; both were significantly greater estimates than the control subjects' mean estimate of 4·2 minutes. Barber and Calverley concluded that the induction of an apparent hypnotic trance state is not necessary to produce the time-distortion phenomenon. However, there appear to be effects of hypnotic time-distortion suggestions beyond what is implied by Barber and Calverley. Zimbardo *et al.* (1973) measured the behavioural consequences of hypnotic suggestions of altered personal tempo, which can be considered to be a manipulation of experienced duration. When it was suggested that they would experience time as either slowing down or speeding up, hypnotized subjects showed substantial effects on a behavioural response measure, while role-playing and control subjects did not. It seems reasonable to assert that experienced and remembered duration may be modified by suggestions given to a hypnotized person. Unfortunately, little or nothing is known about how cognitive processes are altered by such suggestions.

The practical consequences of hypnotic time-distortion suggestions have also been studied. Cooper and Erickson (1959) reported that hypnotic time-distortion produced a marked enhancement of learning ability; that is, memory for information processed under hypnotic time-distortion increased. In contrast, Barber and Calverley (1964) found a decrement in learning ability during hypnotic time-distortion. More recently, Krauss *et al.* (1974) conducted a well-designed experiment in which subjects attempted to learn a 60-word list. Hypnotized subjects who were allocated 3 minutes for the task and given the suggestion that it would seem like 10 minutes recalled about as many words as non-hypnotized subjects who were actually allocated 10 minutes. Both of these groups recalled more words than a control group given 3 minutes for the task. Krauss *et al.* suggested that "a hypnotic time-distortion procedure might ... increase the ratio of effective time to nominal time in free-recall learning" (p. 143). Further research is obviously needed in order to resolve controversies about the use of hypnotic time-distortion as an aid in learning and creating.

Hypnotism has also been used to observe the consequences of altered temporal perspective (Aaronson, 1972; Zimbardo *et al.*, 1971). Aaronson's experiments are the most extensive. In them, hypnotized subjects and non-hypnotized simulators were given the suggestion that one or two of the three temporal categories—past, present and future—either did not exist or was expanded. The behaviour and retrospectively reported experiences of hypnotized subjects under each condition were used to make inferences about the role played by each temporal category in normal temporal perspective. (It should be noted that non-hypnotized simulators often behaved differently from hypnotized subjects, so the results cannot be entirely explained in terms of demand characteristics.) The present is associated with "aliveness" and "attention to ongoing stimulation" (p. 307). Eliminating the present produced immobility, sleepiness and withdrawal; expanding the present produced emotionally positive reactions characterized by greater attention to ongoing events. The past gives "meaning and inhibition" to the present (p. 308). Eliminating the past produced confused, regressive behaviour, as well as loss of self-identity in the extreme case; expanding the past produced introverted disengagement from ongoing activities, although positive emotions dominated. Finally, the future is "the source of ambitions, goals, and anxiety" (p. 309). Eliminating the future reduced anxiety as well as motivation; expanding the future produced positive emotional states ranging from happiness to mystical euphoria. Aaronson concluded that "every mode of orienting to time has its existential consequences" (p. 310). These studies are valuable in pointing to the possibilities of different temporal perspectives, as well as suggesting how certain psycho-pathologies may be able to be understood and treated when viewed as disorders of temporal perspective.

3.6 Psycho-active Drugs

When discussing effects of psycho-active drugs on temporal experience, there is a tendency to refer to standard pharmacological categories of drugs and to make the simplifying assumption that all drugs within a given category induce a similar state of consciousness in all users. Actually, there are many variables that affect the nature of a drug-induced experience. The focus here is on typical experiences, drawing on both phenomenological reports and experimental observations of a variety of people. Reviews of relevant literature include those by Orme (1969), Ornstein (1969) and Doob (1971); these sources may be consulted for additional references.

It is frequently concluded that duration experience is altered by a wide variety of drugs. However, there is some disagreement on effects of specific drugs, with inconsistencies both between subjects and between studies. It is possible that some drugs increase the variability of temporal experience and behaviour. Orme (1969) concluded that "the work on the effects of drugs on time estimation is unsatisfactory" (p. 86). Nevertheless, duration experience is usually reported to be lengthened under the influence of stimulants (such as amphetamine and caffeine) and psychedelics (such as marijuana and LSD), while it is usually reported to be shortened under the influence of sedatives and hypnotics (such as secobarbital and alcohol) and tranquilizers (such as chlorpromazine). Some drugs produce relatively dramatic alterations in awareness of time and lengthening or shortening of duration experience, while other drugs produce only slight changes.

Although the specific physiological effects of some drugs are not yet understood completely, many drugs which alter duration experience probably have an effect on both autonomic and central nervous systems. Fischer (1971) proposed a "perception-hallucination continuum" of increasing ergotropic arousal (hyperarousal) and a "perception-meditation continuum" of increasing trophotropic arousal (hypoarousal). In his proposal, such drugs as psychedelics lead to a state of hyperarousal and cause lengthened duration experiences similar to those in creative, psychotic and ecstatic states; while such drugs as minor tranquilizers lead to a state of hypoarousal and cause shortened duration experiences similar to those in meditative states (such as Zen satori and Yoga samadhi). The controversy about internal-clock and cognitive approaches has been especially prominent in discussions of drug effects. Hyperaroused states can be described in terms of an acceleration of an internal clock, an increase in the rate of mental events, or both; hypoaroused states can be described in opposite terms.

Some drugs, most notably the psychedelics, apparently produce qualitatively different temporal phenomena at high doses than they produce at low or moderate doses. Effects at higher doses are often characterized as ineffable. Attempts to describe these kinds of temporal experiences include: loss of awareness of time, feelings of eternal or infinite time, awareness of only the present, feelings of archetypal time and feelings that time has slowed down so much that it has stopped (Anonymous, 1969; Hoffer and Osmond, 1967). According to Ornstein (1977), "the best the verbal-logical mode can do for these experiences is to term them *timeless*" (p. 108, his italics). Such phenomenological reports suggest that duration experience and temporal perspective might be intimately connected. Radical changes in duration experience may precede and, perhaps, cause radical changes in temporal perspective. Similar alterations in temporal perspective occur in mystical experiences (Pahnke and Richards, 1966), which are discussed in Section 3.7. These similarities support Fischer's (1971) notion that there is a similarity between extreme hyperaroused and hypoaroused states. Ornstein (1977) hypothesized that large doses of psychedelic drugs can "overwhelm the linear construction [of time] and allow 'an infinite present' to exist" (p. 109). This proposal is examined in more detail in the following sections of the present review.

3.7 Meditation and Mystical States

Temporal experiences resulting from meditation can be discussed in general terms without making distinctions among the varieties of meditation techniques. Indeed, different meditation techniques may ultimately produce similar alterations in consciousness. Further, some meditative states are similar to mystical states, in which there are "experiences of union with supernatural power" that occur "during a period of mental emptiness" (Zales, 1978, 254–255; Deikman, 1963, 1966). Mystical experiences are commonly reported by some practitioners of meditation, although a wide range of activities, such as physical exercise and scientific or artistic work, may promote mystical experiences.

Meditation typically produces a decreased amount of spontaneous mental activity, and it is commonly reported that the experienced duration of a meditation period is shortened compared to physical time. Attention to the passage of time is usually greatly minimized or absent, perhaps because concentrative meditation techniques involve attending to a single stimulus, such as a mantra or a physical movement. If an inexperienced meditator is unsuccessfully engaged in a struggle to concentrate, however, the experienced and remembered duration of the time period may be lengthened (Deikman, 1963).

A remarkable alteration in temporal experience of advanced meditators occurs in the state of samadhi, which is variously described as an experiencing of "voidness", "no-thingness" or "blankness" in which there is a paradoxical "pure" awareness without thoughts or "ego-involvement" (Capra, 1975; Naranjo and Ornstein, 1971). There is a qualitative change in temporal perspective in the state of samadhi, a change which is similar or identical to that described in both mystical experiences and psychedelic drug-induced experiences. This altered mode of temporal perspective has been characterized by the terms "timeless" and "eternal", where both terms refer to a shift in temporal perspective outside the ordinary range of duration experiences. There is a similarity with descriptions of the "Clairvoyant Reality" (LeShan, 1974) or "clairvoyant modes of being" (LeShan, 1976), in which the following laws, or limiting principles, operate: "Divisions of time, including divisions into past, present, and future, are errors and illusion. Events do not 'happen' or 'occur,' they 'are'" (LeShan, 1976, p. 92). Ornstein (1977) called this the "nonlinear mode", and he said, "In this mode, all action occurs in an infinite present. There is no attribution of causality or construction of sequence. All events occur simultaneously" (p. 111). A cognitive explanation of this kind of qualitative shift in temporal perspective might assume that ordinary human temporal perspective is stabilized by certain contents of consciousness (cf. Tart, 1975, 63–69)—reconstructions of past events, responses to present events and anticipations of future events. When there is a decrease or an elimination of these contents of consciousness during samadhi, ordinary temporal perspective is disrupted and replaced by a temporal perspective that may be more ontogenetically "primitive." Ordinary temporal concepts, which were learned during socialization with the development of the ego, cease to be maintained.

Capra, a "high-energy" (particle) physicist, identified similarities between the temporal perspective described by some mystics and the space–time views of some modern physicists (especially those instrumental in developing relativity theory). He said that:

> Because of the awareness that space and time are intimately connected and interpenetrating, the world views of modern physics and of Eastern mysticism are both intrinsically dynamic views which contain time and change as essential elements.
>
> (Capra, 1975, p. 173)

In comparison with the mystical experience of "timelessness", Capra asserted that the "space–time of relativistic physics is a similar timeless space of a higher dimension" (p. 186). Furthermore, the emphasis in Eastern mystical traditions on becoming free from the bondage of karma by transcending time is reflected in the "liberation from time" of relativistic physics, which may view interconnections between events (e.g. interactions of sub-atomic particles) as acausal. Capra's synthesis points clearly to the importance of investigating statements made by some explorers of altered states of consciousness. After all, it seems that certain viewpoints on the nature of physical reality must be at least partially credited to the much earlier Eastern mystical traditions.

3.8 Cerebral Hemispheres, Altered States of Consciousness and Temporal Experiences

Ornstein (1977) reviewed evidence suggesting that the two cerebral hemispheres are specialized to process information in different ways. He interpreted the evidence as indicating that the left hemisphere of most humans operates in a more linear way, processing information more sequentially; while the right hemisphere operates in a more holistic way, processing information more simultaneously. Several recent studies of experienced duration of very brief stimuli (Avant and Puffer, 1978; Polzella *et al.*, 1977) have explored the normal functioning of the two hemispheres in ordinary waking consciousness, but no broad implications can be drawn from these studies at present. Some older research, however, has clear implications for some of the issues discussed in this review. For example, Efron (1963) compared discrimination of temporal sequence in normal subjects and subjects with left-hemisphere damage. The relatively poor performance of subjects with damage in the left hemisphere supported his hypothesis that "temporal analysis of sequence . . . is performed in the left hemisphere" (p. 423). Based on this and other evidence, Ben-Dov and Carmon (1976) proposed a two-stage model of hemispheric asymmetry in information processing. In the first stage, the left hemisphere resolves temporal information, while the right hemisphere resolves spatial information. In the second stage, the left hemisphere codes information by extraction (analysis) of features, while the right hemisphere codes information by integration (synthesis) of features. In short, several theorists have proposed that the left hemisphere is ordinarily more intimately involved in temporal experience than the right.

Other theorists (e.g. Bakan, 1977–78) have suggested that the relative contribution of the hemispheres to conscious experience shifts from the left to the right hemisphere during certain altered states of consciousness. If this is the case, we can begin to appreciate the dramatically different temporal experiences and perspectives mediated by the functioning of the two hemispheres. The left hemisphere apparently plays the major role in "ordinary" temporal experiences by analysing events and temporal sequences of events. The right hemisphere apparently plays the major role in temporal experiences in some altered states of consciousness by synthesizing atemporal interconnections between events and by enabling humans to experience the timelessness of existence. An understanding of both modes of temporal functioning seems to be an essential pre-requisite to an understanding of consciousness.

4 Summary and Conclusions

Temporally-defined sequences of events permeate human consciousness, and temporal experiences originate in certain aspects and processes of consciousness. An internal-clock approach cannot adequately explain diverse influences on temporal experience, but a cognitive approach has few apparent drawbacks. The present review clarifies and extends a cognitive approach to understanding and explaining the origins of human temporal experiences in both "ordinary" and altered states of consciousness.

Experiences of simultaneity and successiveness, which form the basis of the notion of a psychological moment, do not reflect the operation of a pacemaker mechanism. Instead, such experiences are apparently derived from aspects of cognitive processes, although the nature of the processes remains obscure. Dynamics of sensory information storage may mediate very short duration experiences and underlie the notion of an indifference point. Both unconscious, pre-attentive processes and conscious, post-attentive processes are involved in very short duration experiences. The psychological present is a phenomenon that apparently originates in the maintenance of information in short-term memory. Outside the range of the psychological present, intervals between events are probably experienced as a result of a comparison of previous and present contextual aspects of consciousness. Longer duration experiences can be explained in terms of the encoding, storage and retrieval of changes in contextual information throughout an entire duration. The experienced duration of a time period might be affected mostly by processes involved in encoding contextual changes, while remembered duration might be affected mostly by processes involved in storing and retrieving contextual changes. The "ordinary" temporal perspective of most humans may arise as a result of conscious reconstructions of past events, responses to present events and anticipations of future events.

Temporal experiences may be altered in several categories of altered states of consciousness. The duration of sleeping and dreaming periods is usually able to be judged in a fairly veridical way, but distortions of temporal sequences and durations may occur in some dreams. The experienced and remembered duration of daydreaming periods is usually shortened. A shortening of duration experience may occur in sensory deprivation conditions, although the evidence is meagre. In hypnosis, specific time-distortion suggestions apparently can substantially modify duration experience, and suggestions regarding each of the three temporal categories—past, present and future—can alter temporal perspective and behaviour. Alterations in duration experience and temporal perspective typically accompany the use of certain psycho-active drugs, and psychedelics may produce an experience of "timelessness". Similar experiences occur in mystical states, which may result from meditation and a variety of other techniques and situations. Differences in the functioning of the two cerebral hemispheres may underlie the linear and nonlinear constructions of time.

In the future, theorists should pursue a unified cognitive approach to temporal experience in ordinary and altered states of consciousness, an approach that is sketched in the present review.

5 Acknowledgements

I thank Edward George for locating references and for commenting on the manuscript; Douglas Hintzman, Michael Posner and Sheldon Zack for commenting on parts of a previous draft; and Geoffrey Underwood for scholarly and editorial assistance.

6 References

Aaronson, B. S. (1972). Time, time stance, and existence. *In* "The Study of Time" (Eds J. T. Fraser, F. C. Haber and G. H. Müller). Springer-Verlag, Berlin.

Allport, D. A. (1968). Phenomenal simultaneity and the perceptual moment hypothesis. *British Journal of Psychology* **59**, 395–406.

Anderson, J. R. and Bower, G. H. (1973). "Human Associative Memory." Winston, Washington, DC.

Anonymous (1969). The effects of marijuana on consciousness. *In* "Altered States of Consciousness" (Ed. C. T. Tart). John Wiley, New York.

Avant, L. L. and Lyman, P. J. (1975). Stimulus familiarity modifies perceived duration in prerecognition visual processing. *Journal of Experimental Psychology: Human Perception and Performance* **1**, 205–213.

Avant, L. L., Lyman, P. J. and Antes, J. R. (1975). Effects of stimulus familiarity upon judged visual duration. *Perception and Psychophysics* **17**, 253–262.

Avant, L. L. and Puffer, J. A. (1978). Differences in prerecognition visual processing by left and right hemispheres. Paper presented at the meeting of the Psychonomic Society, San Antonio, November.

Bakan, P. (1977–78). Dreaming, REM sleep and the right hemisphere: A theoretical integration. *Journal of Altered States of Consciousness* **3**, 285–307.

Banks, R. and Cappon, D. (1962). Effect of reduced sensory input on time perception. *Perceptual and Motor Skills* **14**, 74.

Barber, T. X. and Calverley, D. S. (1964). Toward a theory of "hypnotic" behavior: An experimental study of "hypnotic time distortion." *Archives of General Psychiatry* **10**, 209–216.

Baron, J. (1971). The threshold for successiveness. *Perception and Psychophysics* **10**, 201–207.

Bell, C. R. and Provins, K. A. (1963). The relation between physiological responses to environmental heat and time judgments. *Journal of Experimental Psychology* **66**, 572–579.

Ben-Dov, G. and Carmon, A. (1976). On time space and the cerebral hemispheres: A theoretical note. *International Journal of Neuroscience* **7**, 29–33.

Berglund, B., Berglund, U., Ekman, G. and Frankenhaeuser, M. (1969). The influence of auditory stimulus intensity on apparent duration. *Scandinavian Journal of Psychology* **10**, 21–26.

Block, R. A. (1974). Memory and the experience of duration in retrospect. *Memory and Cognition* **2**, 153–160.

Block, R. A. (1978). Remembered duration: Effects of event and sequence complexity. *Memory and Cognition* **6**, 320–326.

Block, R. A. and Reed, M. A. (1978). Remembered duration: Evidence for a contextual-change hypothesis. *Journal of Experimental Psychology: Human Learning and Memory* **4**, 656–665.

Blumenthal, A. L. (1977). "The Process of Cognition." Prentice-Hall, Englewood Cliffs, New Jersey.

Boring, E. G. (1963). "The Physical Dimensions of Consciousness." Dover, New York. (Originally published, 1933.)

Boring, L. D. and Boring, E. G. (1917). Temporal judgments after sleep. *In* "Studies in Psychology". Wilson, Worcester, Mass.

Cantor, N. E. and Thomas, E. A. C. (1977). Control of attention in the processing of temporal and spatial information in complex visual patterns. *Journal of Experimental Psychology: Human Perception and Performance* **3**, 243–250.

Capra, F. (1975). "The Tao of Physics." Shambhala, Berkeley, California.

Cohen, J. (1954). The experience of time. *Acta Psychologica* **10**, 207–219.

Cohen, J., Hansel, C. E. M. and Sylvester, J. (1954). An experimental study of comparative judgements of time. *British Journal of Psychology* **45**, 108–114.

Cooper, L. F. and Erickson, M. H. (1959). "Time Distortion in Hypnosis" (2nd edn.). Williams and Wilkins, Baltimore.

Deikman, A. J. (1963). Experimental meditation. *Journal of Nervous and Mental Disorders* **136**, 329–343.

Deikman, A. J. (1966). Deautomatization and the mystic experience. *Psychiatry* **29**, 324–338.

Dement, W. and Kleitman, N. (1957). The relation of eye movements during sleep to dream activity: An objective method for the study of dreaming. *Journal of Experimental Psychology* **53**, 339–346.

Dement, W. and Wolpert, E. A. (1958). The relation of eye movements, body motility, and external stimuli to dream content. *Journal of Experimental Psychology* **55**, 543–555.

Doob, L. W. (1971). "Patterning of Time." Yale, New Haven, Conn.

Efron, R. (1963). Temporal perception, aphasia and déjà vu. *Brain* **86**, 403–424.

Efron, R. (1970). Effect of stimulus duration on perceptual onset and offset latencies. *Perception and Psychophysics* **8**, 231–234.

Efron, R. (1972). The measurement of perceptual durations. *In* "The Study of Time" (Eds J. T. Fraser, F. C. Haber and G. H. Müller). Springer-Verlag, Berlin.

Efron, R. and Lee, D. N. (1971). The visual persistence of a moving stroboscopically illuminated object. *American Journal of Psychology* **84**, 365–375.

Eisler, H. (1975). Subjective duration and psychophysics. *Psychological Review* **82**, 429–450.

Eisler, H. (1976). Experiments on subjective duration 1868–1975: A collection of power function exponents. *Psychological Bulletin* **83**, 1154–1171.

Fischer, R. (1971). A cartography of the ecstatic and meditative states. *Science* **174**, 897–904.

Forgays, D. G. and McClure, G. N. (1974). A direct comparison of the effects of the quiet room and water immersion isolation techniques. *Psychophysiology* **11**, 346–349.

Fraisse, P. (1963). "The Psychology of Time." Harper and Row, New York.

Frankenhaeuser, M. (1959). "Estimation of Time: An Experimental Study." Almqvist and Wiksell, Stockholm.

Gorman, B. S. and Wessman, A. E. (1977). Images, values, and concepts of time in psychological research. *In* "The Personal Experience of Time" (Eds B. S. Gorman and A. E. Wessman). Plenum, New York.

Hicks, R. E., Miller, G. W., Gaes, G. and Bierman, K. (1977). Concurrent processing demands and the experience of time-in-passing. *American Journal of Psychology* **90**, 431–446.

Hicks, R. E., Miller, G. W. and Kinsbourne, M. (1976). Prospective and retrospective judgments of time as a function of amount of information processed. *American Journal of Psychology* **89**, 719–730.

Hinrichs, J. V. (1970). A two-process memory-strength theory for judgment of recency. *Psychological Review* **77**, 223–233.

Hinrichs, J. V. and Buschke, H. (1968). Judgment of recency under steady-state conditions. *Journal of Experimental Psychology* **78**, 574–579.

Hintzman, D. L. (1970). Effects of repetition and exposure duration on memory. *Journal of Experimental Psychology* **83**, 435–444.

Hintzman, D. L. and Block, R. A. (1971). Repetition and memory: Evidence for a multiple-trace hypothesis. *Journal of Experimental Psychology* **88**, 297–306.

Hintzman, D. L. and Block, R. A. (1973). Memory for the spacing of repetitions. *Journal of Experimental Psychology* **99**, 70–74.

Hintzman, D. L., Block, R. A. and Summers, J. J. (1973). Contextual associations and memory for serial position. *Journal of Experimental Psychology* **97**, 220–229.

Hintzman, D. L., Summers, J. J. and Block, R. A. (1975). Spacing judgments as an index of study-phase retrieval. *Journal of Experimental Psychology: Human Learning and Memory* **1**, 31–40.

Hirsh, I. J. (1959). Auditory perception of temporal order. *Journal of the Acoustical Society of America* **31**, 759–767.

Hirsh, I. J. and Sherrick, C. E., Jr (1961). Perceived order in different sense modalities. *Journal of Experimental Psychology* **62**, 423–432.

Hoagland, H. (1933). The physiologic control of judgments of duration: Evidence for a chemical clock. *Journal of General Psychology* **9**, 267–287.

Hoagland, H. (1951). Consciousness and the chemistry of time. *In* "Problems of Consciousness" (Ed. H. Abramson). Corlies, Macy, New York.

Hoffer, A. and Osmond, H. (1967). "The Hallucinogens." Academic Press, New York.

Hylan, J. P. (1903). The distribution of attention. *Psychological Review* **10**, 373–403, 498–533.

James, W. (1890). "The Principles of Psychology", (Vol. 1). Henry Holt, New York.

Kahneman, D. (1973). "Attention and Effort." Prentice-Hall, Englewood Cliffs, New Jersey.

Krauss, H. H., Katzell, R. and Krauss, B. J. (1974). Effect of hypnotic time distortion upon free-recall learning. *Journal of Abnormal Psychology* **83**, 140–144.

Legg, C. F. (1968). Alpha rhythm and time judgments. *Journal of Experimental Psychology* **78**, 46–49.

LeShan, L. (1974). "The Medium, the Mystic, and the Physicist." Viking, New York.

LeShan, L. (1976). "Alternate Realities." Evans, New York.

Linton, M. (1975). Memory for real-world events. *In* "Explorations in Cognition" (Eds D. A. Norman and d. E. Rumelhart). Freeman, San Francisco.

Loehlin, J. C. (1959). The influence of different activities on the apparent length of time. *Psychological Monographs* **73** (4, Whole No. 474).

Ludwig, A. M. (1972). "Psychedelic" effects produced by sensory overload. *American Journal of Psychiatry* **128**, 1294–1297.

Michon, J. A. (1967). Magnitude scaling of short durations with closely spaced stimuli. *Psychonomic Science* **9**, 359–360.

Michon, J. A. (1972). Processing of temporal information and the cognitive theory of time experience. *In* "The Study of Time" (Eds J. T. Fraser, F. C. Haber and G. H. Müller). Springer-Verlag, Berlin.

Michon, J. A. (1975). Time experience and memory processes. *In* "The Study of Time II" (Eds J. T. Fraser and N. Lawrence). Springer-Verlag, New York.

Miller, G. W., Hicks, R. E. and Willette, M. (1978). Effects of concurrent verbal rehearsal and temporal set upon judgments of temporal duration. *Acta Psychologica* **42**, 173–179.

Mo, S. S. (1971). Judgment of temporal duration as a function of numerosity. *Psychonomic Science* **24**, 71–72.

Myers, T. I. (1969). Tolerance for sensory and perceptual deprivation. *In* "Sensory Deprivation: Fifteen Years of Research" (Ed. J. P. Zubek). Appleton-Century-Crofts, New York.

Naranjo, C. and Ornstein, R. E. (1971). "On the Psychology of Meditation." Viking, New York.

Noble, W. G. and Lundie, R. E. (1974). Temporal discrimination of short intervals of dreamless sleep. *Perceptual and Motor Skills* **38**, 445–446.

O'Hanlon, J. F., McGrath, J. J. and McCauley, M. E. (1974). Body temperature and temporal acuity. *Journal of Experimental Psychology* **102**, 788–794.

Orme, J. E. (1969). "Time, Experience and Behaviour." Illife, London.

Ornstein, R. E. (1969). "On the Experience of Time." Penguin, Harmondsworth.

Ornstein, R. E. (1977). "The Psychology of Consciousness" (2nd edn.). Harcourt Brace Jovanovich, New York.

Pahnke, W. N. and Richards, W. A. (1966). Implications of LSD and experimental mysticism. *Journal of Religion and Health* **5**, 175–208.

Polzella, D. J., DaPolito, F. and Hinsman, M. C. (1977). Cerebral asymmetry in time perception. *Perception and Psychophysics* **21**, 187–192.

Richards, W. (1973). Time reproductions by H. M. *Acta Psychologica* **37**, 279–282.

Robinson, C. E. and Pollack, I. (1971). Forward and backward masking: Testing a discrete perceptual-moment hypothesis in audition. *Journal of the Acoustical Society of America* **50**, 1512–1519.

Schaltenbrand, G. (1967). Consciousness and time. *Annals of the New York Academy of Sciences* **138**, 632–645.

Stalnaker, J. M. and Richardson, M. W. (1930). Time estimation in the hypnotic trance. *Journal of General Psychology* **4**, 362–366.

Stroud, J. M. (1955). The fine structure of psychological time. *In* "Information Theory in Psychology" (Ed. H. Quastler). Free Press, Glencoe, Ill.

Stroud, J. M. (1967). The fine structure of psychological time. *Annals of the New York Academy of Sciences* **138**, 623–631.

Sturt, M. (1925). "The Psychology of Time." Harcourt Brace Jovanovich, New York.

Tart, C. T. (1970). Waking from sleep at a preselected time. *Journal of the American Society of Psychosomatic Dentistry and Medicine* **17**, 3–16.

Tart, C. T. (1975). "States of Consciousness." Dutton, New York.

Tebēcis, A. K. and Provins, K. A. (1974). Accuracy of time estimation during hypnosis. *Perceptual and Motor Skills* **39**, 1123–1126.

Thomas, E. A. C. and Weaver, W. B. (1975). Cognitive processing and time perception. *Perception and Psychophysics* **17**, 363–367.

Treisman, M. (1963). Temporal discrimination and the indifference interval: Implications for a model of the "internal clock." *Psychological Monographs* **77**(13, Whole No. 576).

Tzeng, O. J. L., Lee, A. T. and Wetzel, C. D. (1979). Temporal coding in verbal information processing. *Journal of Experimental Psychology: Human Learning and Memory* **5**, 52–64.

Underwood, B. J. (1977). "Temporal Codes for Memories: Issues and Problems." Lawrence Erlbaum Associates, Hillsdale, New Jersey.

Underwood, G. (1975). Attention and the perception of duration during encoding and retrieval. *Perception* **4**, 291–296.

Underwood, G. and Swain, R. A. (1973). Selectivity of attention and the perception of duration. *Perception* **2**, 101–105.

Vernon, J. A. and McGill, T. E. (1963). Time estimations during sensory deprivation. *Journal of General Psychology* **69**, 11–18.

Vroon, P. A. (1970). Effects of presented and processed information on duration experience. *Acta Psychologica* **34**, 115–121.

Warm, J. S. and McCray, R. E. (1969). Influence of word frequency and length on the apparent duration of tachistoscopic presentations. *Journal of Experimental Psychology* **79**, 56–58.

Webb, W. B. and Ross, W. (1972). Estimation of the passing of four consecutive hours. *Perceptual and Motor Skills* **35**, 768–770.

Webster's New Collegiate Dictionary (1977). Merriam, Springfield, Mass.

Wheeler, J. G. (1969). Fantasy, affect, and the perception of time. Doctoral dissertation, City University of New York.

White, C. T. (1963). Temporal numerosity and the psychological unit of duration. *Psychological Monographs* **77**(12, Whole No. 575).

Wickelgren, W. A. (1974). Single-trace fragility theory of memory dynamics. *Memory and Cognition* **2**, 775–780.

Woodrow, H. (1951). Time perception. *In* "Handbook of Experimental Psychology" (Ed. S. S. Stevens). John Wiley, New York.

Zales, M. R. (1978). Mysticism: Psychodynamics and relationship to psychopathology. *In* "Expanding Dimensions of Consciousness" (Eds A. A. Sugerman and R. E. Tarter). Springer-Verlag, New York.

Zelkind, I. and Sprug, J. (1974). "Time Research: 1172 Studies." Scarecrow, Metuchen, New Jersey.

Zimbardo, P. G., Marshall, G. and Maslach, C. (1971). Liberating behavior from time-bound control: Expanding the present through hypnosis. *Journal of Applied Social Psychology* **4**, 305–323.

Zimbardo, P. G., Marshall, G., White, G. and Maslach, C. (1973). Objective assessment of hypnotically induced time distortion. *Science* **181**, 282–284.

Zung, W. W. K. and Wilson, W. P. (1971). Time estimation during sleep. *Biological Psychiatry* **3**, 159–164.

9 Hypnosis Considered as an Altered State of Consciousness

P. W. SHEEHAN

*Department of Psychology,
University of Queensland*

No matter what viewpoint one takes toward hypnosis, it is impossible to explain hypnotic phenomena without some appeal to the operation of intrapsychic, or internal subjective processes. James (1890) defined "psychology" as the description and explanation of states of consciousness, but for a while "behaviourism" took the stage and relegated the concept of consciousness to the world of meaningless statements. Today, psychology has returned to consciousness (McKeachie, 1976) and the discipline is now dominated by cognitive approaches to mental phenomena. The study of hypnosis reflects this Zeitgeist. Although altered state formulations are naturally biased towards viewing man in terms of intrapsychic systems, they do not deny the behaviours that are signs of that altered state. Whether such states cause, mediate, predict or simply correlate with behaviour, however, constitutes a matter for major debate.

It is impossible to argue whether or not hypnosis constitutes a shift in consciousness without examining the status of subjects' experience and whether that experience is uncustomary enough to merit the label "altered state". At the outset, this chapter will attempt to define the meaning of the term "altered state" and to outline its possible characteristics. Later sections will be concerned, however, to analyse more closely the evidence that suggests there may be behavioural increments or decrements of that state. The evidence that is available is, more often than not, equivocal as regards the existence of state, because its defining properties are nearly always inadequately specified in the first instance and the methods we adopt are not definitive enough in their consequences. We turn now to consider the specific theoretical connotations of the term altered state and its applicability to the field of hypnosis.

1 Theoretical Implications

1.1 Definitions of Altered State and Its Characteristics

Definitions of altered states of consciousness typically index the importance of psychological phenomena being recognized by the experiencing subject as a departure from normalcy where normalcy is taken to indicate experience that usually occurs during alert waking consciousness. Orne (1959) conveys something of the essential meaning of the position when he argues that "Any subject who has experienced deep trance will unhesitatingly describe this state as basically different from his normal one. He may be unable to explicate this difference but he will invariably be quite definite and certain about its presence" (p. 297). The alteration in the pattern of psychological functioning must be sufficiently different that the experience is judged to be a *significant* departure by the experiencing subject. There are subtleties involved in this distinction, however. For example a subject in hypnosis (just as in dreaming) may tell himself "this is being hypnotized" which, in a sense, identifies his role as an observer of the scene (c.f. Rapaport, 1957).

The concept of altered state is tied to the notion of hypnotic depth. Different degrees of state appear to correspond with different levels of hypnosis reached by susceptible subjects and the most radical alterations of reality in hypnosis—as indexed by the phenomena of amnesia, posthypnotic response and hallucination—are those that are precisely said to characterize its greatest depth. For example, a hypnotized subject may hallucinate and speak and interact with a person who doesn't exist without feeling embarrassed about the experience or considering it unusual in any way, and if he does so, he is said to be in deep hypnosis.

In hypnosis, as in other areas of study, the essential emphasis of definitions of altered state (Gill, 1972; Shor, 1959, 1962; Tart, 1972a, b) is on the qualitative rather than quantitative aspects of subjects' shifts in consciousness. It is not just a matter of subjects experiencing more anaesthesia in hypnosis, more imagery or more forgetfulness. Argument is made that the nature of mental processes themselves are changed. A subject does not just forget what he was told, for instance; if genuinely amnesic, he can't remember no matter how hard he tries—it is as if a barrier prevents the memories that are there from surging through to awareness. Gill (1972) further argues that the notion of an altered state conveys the implication of reversibility and that altered states of consciousness as seen in hypnosis should be viewed in terms of the person experiencing a transient reorganization of psychological functioning. It is necessary to recognize, however, that the phenomena that can occur in hypnosis (e.g. amnesia, hallucinations and posthypnotic compulsions) can and do occur in other states of consciousness as well (e.g. under medication, in psycho-pathological states and meditation).

The phenomena associated with altered states of consciousness frequently overlap, thus making precise classification of them difficult. The lines of definition easily blur, e.g. among a drug state, a drowsy or an intoxicated one, and a depressed or euphoric state. Ludwig (1969), however, has usefully outlined the general characteristics of altered states of consciousness; these include modifications in thinking that incorporate impairment of reality testing, time disturbance, loss of volition, perceptual distortions and increased susceptibility to accept and/or automatically respond to statements as they are directed. Hilgard (1965, 1969) has gone furthest to outlining the specific features of hypnosis as an altered state of consciousness. Characteristics that he mentions as relevant include (a) subsidence of planning function (the hypnotic subject lacks the desire to will action); (b) redistribution of attention (the subject demonstrates both selective attention and inattention to stimulus aspects of the environment); (c) heightened ability for fantasy production; (d) reduction in reality testing and a tolerance for persistent reality distortion (the subject, for example, may come to easily accept what he would normally find incompatible or incongruous); (e) increased suggestibility; (f) appropriate response to suit the demands of the situation; and (g) amnesia for what transpired within the hypnotic situation (a common though not necessarily distinctive phenomenon). Orne's (1959) emphasis on the discontinuity from waking experience, lack of volition, distortions of reality, and tolerance for incongruity substantially overlaps with this classification. There are secondary characteristics which are reported as well. Gill and Brenman (1961), for instance, talk of split-second hesitations, memory lapses, frozen postures and slow body movement where hypnotized subjects indicate changes in bodily awareness, even in the absence of specific suggestion.

Although theorists substantially agree in a descriptive sense on the various features of hypnosis that match the term "altered state", they differ quite markedly in the concepts around which they hang the state characteristics. Gill (1972), for instance, conceives the changes in reflective awareness, voluntariness and reduction in reality testing as "regression in the service of the ego". Hilgard (1973b, 1975, 1977a), Hilgard and Hilgard (1975) and Bowers (1976) appeal to the relevance of the process of "dissociation", while Orne (1974) highlights the concept of "delusion" as the most significant intrapsychic process for understanding hypnotic phenomena.

1.2 Theoretical Conceptions of Hypnosis

Theories of hypnosis which appeal to the concept of an altered state of consciousness usually argue that the concept is a theoretically and empirically viable one, which is useful both for co-ordinating data and for generating hypotheses for test. Nonstate theorists reject this viewpoint and argue essentially that the evidence can be more simply explained in terms of concepts or mediating variables that tap ordinary processes of social control and cognitive influence such as expectancies, attitudes and imaginative involvement.

1.2.1 *State theories of hypnosis*

It is beyond the scope of this chapter to review in full those theories which emphasize the concept of altered state in the sense that has been outlined above. They are many and varied in nature. Attempt will be made to sample only a few.

Gill and Brenman's (1961) systematic attempt to describe hypnosis in terms of regression in the service of the ego offers us an especially broad and useful explanatory framework within which to view hypnosis. Regression excludes aspects of ordinary ego functioning, the exclusion implying "a separation, a lack of integration of what might otherwise be synthesized" (Gill, 1972, p. 228). According to regression theory, hypnosis is a condition in which a general alteration of consciousness takes place, the subject's behaviour becoming not only a function of his state, but also of his interaction with the hypnotist. The viewpoint further acknowledges that manifestations observed in hypnosis can be evident in other states as well. For example states such as fugue, traumatic neurosis and multiple personality can be seen as altered regressive states which overlap in the phenomena that they manifest, but are nevertheless distinct in the nature of the organization of the phenomena that they display.

For Hilgard (1973b, 1975, 1977a), the differences in hypnotized subjects' behaviour and experience are due to cognitive reorganization resulting from the operation of dissociation. Hypnosis is one way (among many others) in which multiple cognitive control systems are ordered hierarchically, and the arrangement of these cognitive controls is modified in hypnosis so that some of them become demarcated from others. The concept of *neo*-dissociation is specifically invoked by him, his notion recognizing explicitly that effort is required to keep a task out of awareness while it is being performed. Like regression theory, dissociation theory acknowledges the need to conceive hypnosis as incorporating a reality separate from, but concordant with, ordinary everyday waking consciousness and the dissociation is always considered partial rather than complete. In an important sense, Hilgard's theory substitutes the concept of neo-dissociation for altered state. His theory recognizes implicitly, if not explicitly, that hypnotized subjects experience significant alterations in consciousness and that these alterations in consciousness have far more than a descriptive role to play in our understanding of hypnotic events.

As Hilgard stresses the relevance of dissociation, Orne (1974) and others (Sutcliffe, 1961) focus specifically on the process of delusion. Delusion, for instance, directly incorporates one of the major features said to characterize hypnosis as a special state, the subject's ability to tolerate incongruity or paradoxical response. How else, says Orne, can one really explain the apparent absurdity of the hypnotized subject who acts as if he is 5 years old but tolerates his being able to spell correctly as an adult? The delusion permits the subject to be convinced he is a child while it at the same time allows him to write complicated sentences without error. According to this account, the extent to which the hypnotized individual is able to distort his perceptions and memories so as to become subjectively convinced of the truth of the hypnotist's suggestions indexes a transient (i.e reversible) cognitive-delusory state.

1.2.2 *Nonstate formulations of hypnosis*

Spanos and Barber (1974) view hypnosis in terms of "involvement in suggestion-related imaginings" where the subject thinks along with and vividly imagines events as they are suggested by the hypnotist. Sarbin talks also of "believed-in imaginings"; here, hypnosis is similarly described in terms of internal process variables involving an alteration in subjective experience (Sarbin and Coe, (1972). State and nonstate theory merge almost indistinguishably, together when we consider concepts such as those offered by Barber and Sarbin. There are many who would argue that role playing at a non-conscious level where the subject comes to believe in his imaginings explains hypnotic events in the same way as does the process of delusion; in these terms, state simply becomes self-role coalescence (Sheehan and Perry, 1976) and is merely reformulated as an issue.

The difference between state and nonstate theories is largely one of emphasis regarding particular variables of influence: e.g. Sarbin would look to the influence of situational variables to a degree that state theorists normally would not and focusses integrally on the concept of role enactment. As one sifts through alternative theoretical formulations of hypnosis, however, it becomes increasingly evident that theorists translate terms used by others into their own preferred conceptions. It is hard to argue essential differences between "susceptibility" and "role skill", or even between "altered state of consciousness" and "self-role congruence". Further, arguments that concepts such as believed-in imaginings should substitute for concepts invoking the notion of altered state really require that data be produced to demonstrate why internal processes of these kinds are more fruitful and valid than the state construct itself. What makes subjects' internal imaginative processes believable? Similarly, in what way is experience sufficiently altered to justify invoking the process of delusion?

1.2.3 *Convergence*

All the theories that have been reviewed above argue cogently for the relevance of subjects' experience to the explanation of hypnotic events—whether those experiences are attributed to the influence of an altered state of consciousness, person characteristics, situational factors or all three in combination. It is clear, as Spanos and Barber (1974) have noted, that the cognitive processes chosen by contemporary theorists to explain hypnotic phenomena have much in common. Theorists agree, for instance, that genuine changes in experience occur among hypnotized subjects and that they are not simply shamming, faking or complying in a simple voluntary manner. No theorist of any sophistication now asserts that hypnosis achieves any supranormal level of functioning and it is no longer embarrassing for state theorists to admit that unique effects of hypnosis will not be found. State theory, however, does still argue that *distinctive* effects will be evident. If hypnosis is an altered state of consciousness, then the consequences of hypnotic induction ought to differentiate susceptible hypnotized subjects from unhypnotized subjects who are highly motivated in other ways—e.g. by task motivational instruction or by waking exhortation to perform well. Studies using motivated controls have, in fact, demonstrated differences for phenomena such as hallucination (Spanos and Barber, 1968), trance logic (Sheehan, 1977) and analgesia (Hilgard, 1977a).

Even though theorists have generally converged on the importance of subjects' imaginative involvement in their trance experiences (Hilgard, 1975; Spanos and Barber, 1974), state theorists continue to look for qualitative indications of differentiation between hypnotized and unhypnotized subjects while nonstate theorists are more content to demonstrate that hypnotized subjects' behaviour can be matched in ways which do not involve hypnotic induction. State and nonstate theory, then, appear to emphasize different aspects of the total hypnotic setting (e.g. person v. situation) as well as pursuing different research questions in search for qualitative differences among hypnotized and unhypnotized subjects. The two accounts of hypnosis co-exist amicably now where much friction existed previously, but differences in viewpoint are nevertheless apparent.

1.3 Conditions for Arousal

Regardless of how one attempts to explain hypnotic events, it is clear that altered states of consciousness may be produced in any situation by a variety of methods and techniques. Argument has been made that the basic criterion for the effectiveness of such methods is that they should be able to change or modify the ordinary flow and organization of experience, and techniques known to alter experience in this way include hypnosis, drugs, fatigue, meditation, sensory deprivation and yoga. The term hypnosis, however, is normally associated with a specific set of procedures labelled "hypnotic induction". Standard induction procedures typically reduce subjects' attention on external stimuli and specifically aim to focus attention narrowly on what the hypnotist is communicating. The reduction in sensory input, the change in patterning of stimulation, and the constant repetitive stimulation of the hypnotist's voice and communication are favourable for establishing the state-like features of experience that have been outlined above. Under such conditions the subjects can be easily led to demonstrate decreased alertness and relaxation of their critical faculties.

It is difficult to be precise about what defines "hypnotic induction" since techniques of induction vary so widely. As Gill (1972) asserts, hypnosis can arise without any apparent set of procedures having been administered; we can be faced with the dilemma of comparing an allegedly non-hypnotic state—which may be hypnosis—with an allegedly hypnotic state following induction—which may not be hypnosis. Further, the fact that, after a set of procedures is given, one person can be hypnotized while another cannot seems totally inconsistent with the idea of defining an altered state in terms of any particular set of techniques. Specific sets of procedures cannot really be tied to the occurrence of hypnosis.

1.4 Conclusion

Hypnosis may be aptly conceived as an altered state of consciousness especially if that label is used to classify radical changes in experience where the hypnotized subject experiences a qualitative shift in functioning from the normal waking state. Different theoretical frameworks may also account for that shift, but the changes that are most significant would appear to relate to ideational processes, reality testing, volition and tolerance of incongruity. The state itself may be induced in a variety of ways and hypnosis may arise following or not following the specific set of procedures traditionally labelled in the literature "hypnotic induction".

A concept that generally integrates state characteristics rather well is Shor's (1959, 1962) notion of "Generalized Reality-Orientation". Shor argues that in hypnosis our normal orientation fades into the background so that current experiences come to be isolated from their everyday frame of reference. The temporary giving up of this normal orientation corresponds to a regression to primary process levels of mentation and psychological functioning. Hypnosis so reduces alertness and critical thinking that this reduction facilitates a flow of associations thus bringing the hypnotized individual into contact with more primary forms of ideation and thinking.

In agreeing on a definition of the concept "altered state" and its salient features, however, it is important to stress the major assumptions that lie behind the concept, especially as they apply to hypnotic phenomena. First, hypnosis ought not to be viewed as a unitary or consistent state. Just as other states of consciousness are continuously in alteration (viz. stages of sleep), hypnosis involves shifts in consciousness as the subject experiences different hypnotic phenomena. Although the notion "altered state" is seen in its most obvious manifestation in deep hypnosis, it is conceivable, however, that suggestion items not requiring gross distortions of reality may also illustrate qualitative shifts in psychological functioning. Subjects can problem solve and think critically in trance situations, if it is necessary to do so, and are known to bring considerable cognitive effort to bear on their reactions (Dolby and Sheehan, 1977; Sheehan, 1977). It would appear that only a concept of shifting levels of consciousness can adequately incorporate the phenomena as they exist. Such a notion is compatible with the discussions of Ornstein (1977) who argues that states of consciousness are not discrete but, rather, shift according to the influence of situational factors illustrated by needs and training.

In concluding on a definition of hypnosis as an altered state of consciousness it is necessary to distinguish between process and content. The point is well taken by Tart (1972a) who comments that states of consciousness result from the interaction of a number of separate sub-systems (e.g. identity, memory, cognition, etc.) and such modes of organization constitute the distinctiveness of the state in question.

States, then, should be differentiated not in terms of their content (e.g. the objects that are hallucinated, or the specific memories that are forgotten), but in terms of the altered configuration or interaction among the sub-systems—which result in a new organization. The distinction between process and content fully acknowledges the fact that content may actually be equivalent across widely varying stages (e.g. memories can be ablated in hypnosis as well as following the administration of drugs); it is the process changes that are important. Under LSD, for example, loss of awareness of self may indicate an identity change just as in hypnosis one's sense of identity may also be profoundly altered. In hypnosis, though, as opposed to the drug state, the change may be distinctively in the attention sub-system; here, the subject simply doesn't come to focus attention on the question of his self-identity (Tart, 1972a, p. 450) and normal feelings of identity fail to remain intact.

We turn now to review briefly some of the empirical evidence that bears upon the concept of hypnosis as an altered state of consciousness. Comment will be made on physiological and psychological (i.e. internal process) indicators, in turn, and on the evidence supporting the validity of subjective report as an indicant of hypnosis.

2 Evidence Related to Concept of Altered State

2.1 Physiological Indices

Comprehensive reviews conducted in the literature (Sarbin and Slagle, 1972) reveal no evidence for an independent physiological criterion of hypnosis. Nothing comparable exists to the REM activity that accompanies dreaming, or the blood level changes which index intoxication states. Results on evoked potentials (Ulett *et al.*, 1972) yield quite confusing results. Hilgard (1975) makes the point, though, that the hypnotized subject is capable of a wide range of activity while responding in hypnosis—activity which ranges from relaxed acquiescence to active and sustained physical effort—and it might well be unreasonable to look for stable indicators of physiological functioning when so many simultaneous activities of various organ systems are involved. Undoubtedly, our knowledge of hypnosis would benefit from the isolation of stable indices, but the presence or absence of them is not crucial to our acceptance of the notion of altered state. If firm indices were found we could simply be more persuasive about the scientific value of that concept and its inherent testability.

2.2 Internal Processing Correlates

The evidence which best supports the viability of the altered state concept can be drawn from the data available on the operation of internal process variables such as imaginative involvement, dissociation, delusion and hypnotized subjects' motivated cognitive commitment to their tasks.

2.2.1 *Imagination*

The role imagery plays in altered states of consciousness has generally been very well indexed (Ludwig, 1969) and detailed evidence is reviewed elsewhere on the question of the role imagination processes play in altered state formulations of hypnosis (Sheehan, 1972). Suffice to say that current work on operation of processes such as believed-in imagining (Sarbin and Coe, 1972), involvement in suggestion-related imaginings (Spanos and Barber, 1974) and goal-directed fantasies (Spanos *et al.*, 1977) all attest the relevance of this internal process to the explanation of subjects' experience of hypnotic events.

2.2.2 *Dissociation*

The process of dissociation clearly relates to the state/nonstate issue in that it implies a definite shift in cognitive controls. When dissociations are substantial, as indicated by the behavioural responses of a highly susceptible person when hypnotized and by his self report, a description of that change in terms of a hypnotic state is regarded by the proponents of this view as particularly appropriate. The viewpoint as a whole has gained substantial empirical support from studies on the "hidden observer effect" where hypnotized individuals indicate through automatic writing (or talking) that pain is experienced, even though neither pain nor suffering is indicated in the analgesic state by the usual method of verbal report (Hilgard, 1977a). This effect has been studied with real and simulating subjects and data show differences in response when subjects are asked to be honest about their reactions (Hilgard, 1977b). In the study in question, susceptible subjects showed no change in their response when requested to be truthful about their pain reactions; a sizeable number of simulating subjects, on the other hand, reported under the same request that they had actually felt pain equivalent to that experienced by them during waking analgesia.

The classical concept of dissociation asserts that dissociated activities will not interfere with each other, in the sense that performance of one will not adversely affect the performance of the other. Data indicate, however, that when tasks are performed out of awareness through hypnotic suggestion, then more rather than less interference will result between tasks than when both are performed with full awareness (Knox *et al.*, 1975). The concept of neo-dissociation specifically recognizes the effort that is involved in taking the task out of awareness. The notion of effort is important to the understanding of hypnotic phenomena in other ways. The fact that it differentiates hypnotized persons in the quality of their response has been observed in studies bearing upon the relevance of the process of delusion to hypnosis.

2.2.3 *Delusion*

The workings of imagination in hypnosis do not implicate the notion of altered state with the same strength as does the process of delusion; e.g. appeal to the latter process suggests a more marked qualitative shift in mentation from the waking to the hypnosis setting. Evidence which supports the relevance of delusion has come most recently from work showing that hypnotized subjects behave with conviction in ways that suggest they are registering and processing stimulus information quite differently from other highly motivated waking subjects. The processes of attention that are obviously involved may lead a small sample of highly susceptible subjects to be quite deluded about what they are perceiving. Working with ambiguous stimuli (Boring's "Wife/Mother-in-law" figure) that can be resolved to be seen one way (as an old woman) or another (a young woman), Dolby and Sheehan (Sheehan and Dolby, 1975; Dolby and Sheehan, 1977) found that hypnotized subjects quite distinctively overrode strong task constraints which led other subjects to structure ambiguous information in the same way as they had done previously in the waking state. For some susceptible subjects, the expectancy behaviour was so strong that they mismatched completely the figure that was actually shown to them, deeply hypnotized subjects indicating in quite unreal fashion that the figure they had seen was the one they had been led to anticipate would appear. Hypnotized subjects, in fact, were also able to switch from seeing one kind of figure (the old woman) to seeing an altogether different one (the young woman), again depending on what the hypnotist led them to expect—such behaviour was never shown by task motivated or control waking subjects. Both these groups were consistently bound by the compelling stimulus constraints that existed in the test situation for subjects to perceive the figure differently from what was expected. Further, for selected samples of susceptible subjects this pattern of results was replicated over independent studies. Susceptible subjects consistently expressed a mistaken belief in the veracity of what the hypnotist said in the face of quite contradictory evidence emanating from the real world.

The cognitions of hypnotized subjects are obviously quite complex. The misperception of ambiguous information which indexed delusion was accompanied for some, but not all, deluded subjects by extensive time taken to explore the ambiguous figure before the expected response was given. Subjects' mistaken convictions were accompanied in some instances by extensive cognitive construction of the information they received, while in other instances they were not. As argued in detail elsewhere (Dolby and Sheehan, 1977), such data imply that active cognitive processing and delusion present alternative paths to subjects' acquiescence to hypnotic demands and that the two routes may be taken either conjointly, or in isolation. The data, in all, highlight not just the relevance of delusion, but also the fact that situational influences obviously shape hypnotic subjects' behaviour in different ways.

In assessing the data on internal processes and their operation in hypnosis it is necessary to draw a distinction between the imaginative involvement that hypnotized persons may display and their *motivated cognitive commitment*. Subjects may accept the suggestions given to them and translate them into imaginative terms, but some hypnotized subjects appear to work cognitively to construct the response that they consider is most attuned to what the hypnotist wants. The structuring of information according to expectancy was demonstrated, e.g. in Dolby and Sheehan's (1977) study by the introspective reports of subjects who indicated that they worked carefully through the ambiguous information presented to them, building up the desired response in clearly schematic fashion. In similar fashion, hypnotized subjects have been shown to resolve conflicting information about appropriate hypnotic response in favour of the wishes of the hypnotist when other unhypnotized subjects (faced with the same conflict) opted to be influenced less by the hypnotist than by information they had received outside hypnosis (Sheehan, 1971). The motivated commitment of some susceptible subjects to what the hypnotist personally requests suggests a degree of positive (often effortful) striving not implicated in the term "imaginative involvement". Further, the subtleties of these aspects of subjects' consciousness in the hypnotic setting appear to be evident across a range of phenomena. As far as cognitive effort is concerned, brief mention of amnesia illustrates the point.

Suggested amnesia is currently defined as a reversible inability to remember events that have been associated with instructions to forget

(Kihlstrom, 1977; Nace *et al*., 1974), and recent work has indicated that hypnotic amnesia involves a temporary breakdown of the organizational techniques used by subjects to help them in their recall. Employing both hypnotic and task motivated subjects, Spanos and Bodorik (1977) administered amnesia suggestions to subjects for a previously learned list of categorized words; the number of words remembered and the extent to which they were remembered in clusters were compared before, during and after the amnesia suggestion was lifted. Data supported Evans and Kihlstrom's (1973) contention that amnesia involves a temporary breakdown in organizational strategy. Full understanding of the amnesia demonstrated by subjects, however, requires extensive exploration of the cognitive effort expended by them to remember. As in other studies concerned with internal processing in hypnosis, Spanos and Bodorik demonstrated that subjects processed the amnesia suggestion with a considerable degree of intersubject variation in effort and attention; effort was expended by some subjects far more obviously than by others in their attempts to recall.

2.2.4 *Tolerance for incongruity*

Theorizing about the capacity of some subjects to tolerate incongruity argues that it is not just an anomaly of behaviour that is involved. Subjects who demonstrate this characteristic illustrate a peculiar quality of consciousness that is said to be related to trance depth and hypnotic involvement, and it reflects an attribute of behaviour that contemporary theorists of hypnosis claim is distinctive to the hypnotic state (Orne, 1959; Orne and Hammer, 1974). The most widely known instance of the phenomenon is the subject's report of the co-existence of a real and hallucinated object, and his or her unsuggested transparency report of the hallucinated stimulus.

A series of studies has been conducted recently (Sheehan *et al*., 1976; Obstoj and Sheehan, 1977) to examine Orne's (1959) original claim that trance logic is a primary, distinctive feature of hypnosis. Preliminary data supported the claim for transparency, but not double hallucination, report. Later work showed, however, that subjects who were not hypnotized, but who were motivated highly for their report, could nevertheless report seeing an object in diaphanous fashion. The evidence clearly indicates that search for the presence of unique behaviour among hypnotized persons is not a credible goal. Tolerance for logical incongruity did distinguish hypnotic from task motivated subjects on a number of tasks, but no incongruity behaviour was unique to hypnotic subjects. Although aptitude for hypnosis was insufficient to explain all of the data, the evidence showed that a substantial degree of aptitude for trance was nevertheless necessary for subjects to behave in a paradoxical fashion.

A common problem relating to all of the processes we have considered is the difficulty of indexing intrapsychic events in an unequivocal manner. One could, for instance, look for measurable psycho-physiological changes in the hypnotized person, or behavioural increments (or decrements) in performances as well as taking reports at first hand when they indicate that experience in hypnosis is somehow different to what it is out of trance. Unfortunately, no distinctive physiological index of hypnosis exists and there are no unique behaviours, or performance enhancements. The main reason for utilizing the state construct is that it does appear to adequately classify the reported experiences of hypnotized subjects and acknowledges explicitly that the essential departure from normal experience is radical in character—involving not just quantitative changes of experience but qualitative alterations as well. There are definite risks, however, in the breadth of explanatory power of such a concept when it relies integrally on the accuracy of what subjects report. There are difficulties also in establishing the limits of the concept in an operational sense. Waking suggestions of a certain kind, for example, are as much a part of the domain of hypnosis as suggestions given following trance induction (Hilgard, 1973a), and if hypnosis is to be considered as a distinctive alteration in consciousness then the limits of that waking consciousness must be more clearly demarcated empirically from the boundaries of the hypnotic domain.

2.3 Status of Subjective Reports

If any hypothetical mental state is to be inferred to explain hypnotic phenomena then the ultimate index of this inference is the subjective report of experience offered by the hypnotized subject.

Empirically speaking, one of the most important indications of the need to study subjects' testimony of trance is that verbal reports often appear to be out of phase, as it were, with the objective concomitants of suggestion. Subjective and objective scores following hypnotic induction normally correlate highly together with one score replicating the other, but verbal reports of hypnosis can at times correct or rectify assessments made on the basis of objective data where the latter are misleading (Hilgard, 1973a; Ruch *et al.*, 1974). Objective scores can, for example, be influenced unduly by pressures for compliance (Bowers, 1967; Sheehan and Dolby, 1974) and may be modified when the experimenter specifically requests honest and truthful reports (Spanos and Barber, 1968). At times also, test conditions can show appreciable inconsistencies in the effects of hypnotic treatments while subjective evidence demonstrates near-perfect stability (Connors and Sheehan, 1978). It is clear that items failed objectively are not necessarily failed subjectively and subjects may have very genuine feelings of responsiveness even though the motor action indicating conformity to the suggestion is not actually demonstrated (Ruch *et al.*, 1974). It is not just on theoretical grounds, then, that verbal reports are important. The extent to which subjective scores may correct objective scores index their primary and significant nature in a strictly empirical sense.

2.3.1 *The accuracy of reports*

Where confirmation of the existence of an altered state of experience relies heavily on the status of verbal testimony it is essential to explore the question whether such reports are accurate, in fact. Testimony can depend on what subjects believe is proper and appropriate to report and what is and what is not the case may not match what hypnotized subjects assert about the real world.

Nisbett and Wilson (1977) provide a searching critique of subject reports that has important implications for the analysis of hypnotic phenomena. They offer the radical thesis that subjects report falsely rather than truthfully most of the time and that if correct reports do happen to occur then they do so incidentally because the subjects correctly employ *a priori* causal theories about the behaviour they have just shown. According to this thesis, subjects in experiments will work to formulate appropriate theories to explain their actions and, more often than not, they do not formulate the correct ones. Subjects in dissonance studies, for instance, often can't report correctly about the existence of motivational responses produced by the complex manipulations of the experimenter. The risk of hypnosis research is that it would appear relatively easy for subjects to formulate similar conceptions about explaining their trance behaviour to those held by the hypnotist–experimenter who tests them. The implications of hypnosis being an altered state of consciousness are perhaps too readily apprehended by subject and investigator alike.

3 Trait, Situation and Relevance to State

A wide variety of data tapping quite different hypnotic phenomena (e.g. amnesia, Kihlstrom, 1977; expectancy response, Dolby and Sheehan, 1977; analgesia, Hilgard, 1977a, b; regression behaviour, O'Connell *et al.*, 1970; and trance logic, Sheehan, 1977) have demonstrated that aptitude for trance is a critical factor in determining the nature of response that hypnotized subjects display. Only very few subjects, for example, eliminated pain entirely and felt nothing following analgesia suggestions after they were requested to place their hand and forearm in circulating ice water for a short period of time. Even subjects who kept pain at a tolerable level in those circumstances typically required a high level of aptitude to demonstrate the phenomenon. Success on this task as on others that we have considered normally requires a high level of hypnotizability. The relevance of aptitude compels us to consider, then, whether hypnotizability constitutes a stable personality trait or set of characteristics.

3.1 The Influence of Trait

On standard hypnotic phenomena hypnotized subjects reliably report that their response to hypnotic suggestions is different from ordinary subjective experience and their pattern of responsiveness to suggestions appears to be relatively consistent across time. The nature of the regularity of individual differences in hypnotizability leads us to have considerable confidence, in fact, in the inference that hypnotizability is a stable durable trait. Recent literature on the modifiability of hypnosis has challenged that conclusion (Diamond, 1974, 1977) but in the studies that have been cited the criteria for modifiability have tended to be poorly specified. It is not at all clear, for example, that low susceptible subjects can be transformed into highly susceptible subjects as the modifiability position tends to imply (Perry, 1977).

The conception of hypnosis in terms of a single trait has led to a long and frustrating search for the correlates of the hypnotizable "personality" (Deckert and West, 1963). Work has focussed lately on the imaginative capacities of the susceptible subject and it appears that the role played by subjects' imagination and fantasy abilities is a most significant one (Sheehan, 1972; Spanos and Barber, 1974). With all the evidence to indicate the relative stability of individual differences in susceptibility, though, it is somewhat surprising that data support so particularly the relevance of subjects' imagination capacities and related correlates such as absorption (Tellegen and Atkinson, 1974). The influence of the trait characteristics of the hypnotized person would appear to be quite pervasive in other respects. For example, subjects will respond to waking suggestions without prior induction and the correlation of waking and hypnotic suggestibility is particularly high among susceptible subjects (Hilgard, 1973a). The aptitudes and skills of the susceptible subject maintain responsiveness just as specific procedures like hypnotic induction do, and hypnosis is very clearly a function of the person as well as of the treatment that person receives.

3.2 The Hypnotic Situation and Its Impact

Just as one may focus on the trait attributes or person characteristics of the susceptible subject, one may also focus on the impact of the hypnotic test situation as a complex setting that involves the operation of a host of variables of a social–psychological kind. Hypnosis can be viewed as an attitude change situation where the hypnotist is an agent of influence working through the social communications that he administers to the subject. Barber (1969, 1972) and others (Sarbin and Coe, 1972) have long drawn attention to the motivations, expectancies and attitudes that hypnotic subjects bring with them to the hypnotic setting. For example, subjects will demonstrate catalepsy of the dominant hand when there is no reason that they should do so by the nature of hypnosis itself, simply because they believe it is expected of them by a hypnotist who leads them to that belief prior to induction (Orne, 1959; Sheehan, 1971).

3.3 Trait and Situation in Interaction

The question of what influence situational factors actually have on hypnotic subjects has not been clarified fully by research. Proponents of the trait position have tended to stress that aptitudes and skills relating specifically to hypnosis are the prime determinants of hypnotic responsiveness and that situational factors have relatively minimal impact on the behaviour of the persons being hypnotized. Closer analysis of the issue of trait and its interaction with situation as determinant, however, helps to put the two sources of influence in proper perspective.

The trait position does not argue that behaviour is stable in any absolute fashion. The social influence of prior expectancies or attitudes will quite definitely shape and modify subjects' responsiveness in important respects (Sarbin and Coe, 1972). The trait position, however, really argues that behaviour will be *relatively* consistent across different situations. This is to say that although situations will influence subjects to perhaps alter their response, their behaviour will still be stable in the sense that two subjects differing in amnesic ability across two contexts of testing will be differentiated comparably in each setting even though the settings themselves may have a noticeable impact on both subjects' memory performance.

The true meaning of the term "relatively stable" is not fully appreciated in the hypnotic literature, since argument about the impact of trait is frequently premised on the implicit assumption that hypnotic performance will be stable in an absolute sense across settings varying in social complexity. Such a position is naïve. Outside the area of hypnosis, the importance of talking about traits and person characteristics operating in interaction with the environment is fully acknowledged. It is *person-in-context* that shapes behaviour and experience and if individual differences in hypnotic susceptibility clearly exist, their importance is not at all diminished by recognizing at the same time that the social characteristics of the hypnotic setting may interact dynamically with these characteristics to shape the detail of subjects' final hypnotic response. As Ekehammar (1974) argues elsewhere, the interaction between the two sets of variables should be seen as one involving mutual, bi-directional causality. Hypnotic responsiveness is a function of both susceptibility and the social influence character of the specific hypnotic setting and each may operate on the other to determine actual response. In the work on trance logic, for example (Sheehan, 1977), the nature of an object to be hallucinated determined whether the object would be viewed in transparent fashion, but only susceptible subjects took the opportunity to respond in that way.

3.4 Trait, Situation and State

It can be misleading to ask whether hypnotic responsiveness is more a matter of the trait characteristics of the susceptible person than either setting characteristics, or the state produced by hypnotic induction. It is deceptively easy to take sides on the issue and to polarize by emphasizing one dimension to the exclusion of another. State theorists inevitably underemphasize the situational aspects of hypnosis, while nonstate theorists over-accentuate them. Barber (1969, 1972) gives prime emphasis to the social psychological processes accruing to the hypnotic context while paying relatively little attention to the person characteristics of the hypnotic subject. Assuming an altered state exists in hypnosis, then it is entirely conceivable that some persons may achieve or reach that state more easily than others by virtue of their particular trait characteristics. There is nothing inconsistent with the concept of altered state, for example to argue that if enhanced imagery is experienced in hypnosis or a radical alteration in reality achieved through hallucination, then the subject behaved in that way for reasons partly due to the fact he or she had the necessary aptitudes or skills to do so in the first instance.

Empirically speaking, it is important to be able to differentiate the consequences of the three components: trait, situation and state; and discussion of a number of different studies serves to illustrate the point.

McGlashan *et al.* (1969) argued that there are two components involved in analgesia—one that can be explained in terms of non-specific or placebo effects resulting from using hypnosis as a technique of treatment, while the other can be conceptualized as a distortion or modification of perception consequent upon hypnosis itself. In the study which they conducted, changes in pain threshold and tolerance (compared to an initial base level performance) were positively related to changes in subjects' subjective ratings of pain intensity. Data highlighted an analgesic response that was quantitatively and qualitatively different from a placebo response among those deeply hypnotized subjects who had the positive experience that hypnotic analgesia worked for them. The study can be interpreted as one that differentiated the relative contribution of state and situation for a particular level of trait.

In another study, reported above (Dolby and Sheehan, 1977), subjects demonstrating expectancy behaviour—i.e. performace in accord with what the hypnotist wanted rather than external task constraints—were influenced differently by stimulus structure depending on the level of their susceptibility to hypnosis. Only those subjects who were susceptible to hypnosis were able to switch their behaviour to match the changing wishes of the hypnotist, but the precise nature of subjects' response was clearly dependent on the stimulus features of the object they were considering. In a third study (Perry and Sheehan, 1978), susceptible and insusceptible, simulating subjects were tested in standard fashion, but within this mode the interpersonal nature of testing was varied systematically. Fifty per cent of the subjects were tested impersonally and 50% were tested personally. Varying the personal nature of testing had relatively little effect on high susceptible subjects; where aptitude for trance was not high, however, the extent of ability present appeared to be a definite limiting factor—here, the effects obtained were closely related to the social characteristics of the testing situation that was employed. Results indicated that situations were influential in their impact, but the nature of their influence depended on the level of hypnotic susceptibility of the groups of subjects who were studied.

4 Conclusion: the Utility of the Altered State Conception of Hypnosis

In this chapter we have reviewed the concept of altered state as it relates to the field of hypnosis. There seems little argument that the concept can be used to classify hypnotic events and can be embedded within a number of different conceptual frameworks. Any theory of hypnosis, however, must ultimately attempt to explain the kinds of alterations that can be brought about in the hypnotic setting and should explain the ease with which they appear to be accomplished (Orne, 1967). The concept of altered state has no difficulty in assimilating the extent of change that is evident for some hypnotized subjects, but the very ease of that assimilation reflects the risk of over-generalization and the breadth of the concept's explanatory power.

The real utility of the notion of hypnosis as an altered state of consciousness lies in the kinds of differences between hypnotized and unhypnotized subjects that state theorists pursue. The concept is useful in that it orients investigators to look for radical alterations in perceptual and cognitive functioning, and qualitative shifts in consciousness that reflect subtle cognitive effects. Appeal to concepts such as imaginative involvement, absorption and believed-in imaginings do not go far enough in orientating researchers either to the extent of some subjects' alterations in experience or the qualitative nature of their consciousness. The definition of altered state of consciousness that has been pursued in this chapter recognizes the utility of viewing hypnosis as forming subjectively and objectively distinct cognitive organizations. Following this account, one therefore tends to look for the operation of processes such as dissociation, delusion and motivated cognitive commitment so as to explain the extent of the alterations in experience that are countenanced in the first instance.

The tenability of state theory basically depends on differences being isolated between hypnotized and unhypnotized subjects. Data tell us that the differences emerging from comparison with traditional groups of non-hypnotic controls are not unique, but there appear to be a sufficient number of differences resulting in distinctive patterns of behaviour to support the maintenance of the state concept—at least until such time that other explanations can be demonstrated un-equivocally to be better. As the conceptual boundaries between state and nonstate accounts of hypnosis blur, the onus is as much on the proponents of the latter framework to show it can accommodate the differences that are apparent as it is on the advocates of the former account to yield testable predictions to further substantiate their theory. For example, one half of good hypnotic subjects demonstrate the hidden observer effect, suggesting multiple levels of cognitive control (Hilgard, 1973b, 1975); some susceptible hypnotic subjects interpret hypnotic events in ways which lead them to counter previously held preconceptions about appropriate patterns of response (Sheehan, 1971); and very good susceptible subjects can continue to respond to unterminated suggestions (Duncan and Perry, 1977), respond incongruously (Orne, 1959; Sheehan et al., 1976; Obstoj and Sheehan, 1977), and override the cognitive influence of previous perceptions so as to behave in the ways that are expected of them (Sheehan and Dolby, 1975; Dolby and Sheehan, 1977). Appeal to subjects' aptitude for trance is relevant but that factor alone is obviously insufficient to account for the data. Close analysis of the performance of control subjects in these studies also shows that situational factors are influential, but cannot themselves solely account for the effects that have been found.

Strictly speaking, the status of an altered state conception of hypnosis is that it poses an alternative explanation of hypnotic events—albeit one that is imperfectly indexed by subjects' verbal reports. The notion of "alternative account" specifies that it cannot lay claim to being the only possible explanation of events; rather, it is a plausible substitute for other accounts at this stage of our fact gathering. In summary, its special usefulness lies in the extent to which it orientates us to look for distinctive, rather than unique, differences between hypnotized and unhypnotized subjects, especially as those differences are associated with qualitative shifts in experience—varying among hypnotized subjects themselves. Where such an account is invoked, however, it is important to stress that the altered state of awareness of the hypnotized subject necessarily interacts with the influence of situational factors adhering to the hypnotic setting and the person characteristics of the individual who is hypnotized; and the concept of altered state is not at all falsified by the demonstration that trait characteristics and situational cues are both operative.

It is not yet clear what functions consciousness actually serves (Ornstein, 1977) and many questions remain to be asked, and answered, with respect to the application of altered consciousness theorizing to hypnotic events. We do not know what precise processes are involved when changes in subjects' states of awareness are affected by hypnosis, and what changes in hypnotic behaviour are associated with variations in conscious activity itself. Research has yet to determine how delusory conviction is actually communicated by the hypnotist, and what turns the imaginative involvement of some susceptible subjects into their believing in the truth of the events that are being suggested. As Rapaport (1957) noted some time ago, academic psychology has failed to account for the structure of consciousness. Simple constructs cannot handle the data and many would argue that it is still time to give the concept, "altered state of consciousness", a turn.

5 References

Barber, T. X. (1969). "Hypnosis: A Scientific Approach". Van Nostrand, New York.

Barber, T. X. (1972). Suggested ("hypnotic") behavior: The trance paradigm versus an alternative paradigm. *In* "Hypnosis: Research Developments and Perspectives" (Eds E. Fromm and R. E. Shor), 115–182. Aldine-Atherton, Chicago.

Bowers, K. S. (1967). The effect of demands for honesty on reports of visual and auditory hallucinations. *International Journal of Clinical and Experimental Hypnosis* **15**, 31–36.

Bowers, K. S. (1976). "Hypnosis for the Seriously Curious." Brooks Cole, Monterey, California.

Connors, J. and Sheehan, P. W. (1978). The influence of control comparison tasks and between- vs. within-subjects effects in hypnotic responsivity. *International Journal of Clinical and Experimental Hypnosis* **26**, 104–122.

Deckert, G. H. and West, L. J. (1963). The problem of hypnotizability: A review. *International Journal of Clinical and Experimental Hypnosis* **11**, 205–235.

Diamond, M. J. (1974). Modification of hypnotizability: A review. *Psychological Bulletin* **81**, 180–198.

Diamond, M. J. (1977). Hypnotizability is modifiable: An alternative approach. *International Journal of Clinical and Experimental Hypnosis* **25**, 147–166.

Dolby, R. M. and Sheehan, P. W. (1977). Cognitive processing and expectancy behavior in hypnosis. *Journal of Abnormal Psychology* **36**, 334–345.

Duncan, B. and Perry, C. W. (1977). Uncancelled hypnotic suggestions: Initial studies. *American Journal of Clinical Hypnosis* **19**, 166–176.

Ekehammar, B. (1974). Interactionism in modern personality from a historical perspective. *Psychological Bulletin* **81**, 1026–1048.

Evans, F. J. and Kihlstrom, J. F. (1973). Posthypnotic amnesia as disrupted retrieval. *Journal of Abnormal Psychology* **82**, 317–323.

Gill, M. M. (1972). Hypnosis as an altered and regressed state. *International Journal of Clinical and Experimental Hypnosis* **20**, 224–237.

Gill, M. M. and Brenman, M. (1961). "Hypnosis and Related States." International Universities Press, New York.

Hilgard, E. R. (1965). "Hypnotic Susceptibility." Harcourt, Brace and World, New York.

Hilgard, E. R. (1969). Altered states of awareness. *Journal of Nervous and Mental Disease* **149**, 68–79.

Hilgard, E. R. (1973a). The domain of hypnosis: With some comments on alternative paradigms. *American Psychologist* **23**, 972–982.

Hilgard, E. R. (1973b). A neodissociation interpretation of pain reduction in hypnosis. *Psychological Review* **80**, 396–411.

Hilgard, E. R. (1975). Hypnosis. *Annual Review of Psychology* **26**, 19–44.

Hilgard, E. R. (1977a). "Divided Consciousness." Kaufmann, Los Altos, California.

Hilgard, E. R. (1977b). The problem of divided consciousness: A neodissociation interpretation. *In* "Conceptual and Investigative Approaches to Hypnosis and Hypnotic Phenomena" (Ed. W. E. Edmonston). *Annals of the New York Academy of Science* **296**, 48–59.

Hilgard, E. R. and Hilgard, J. R. (1975). "Hypnosis in the Relief of Pain." Kaufmann, Los Altos, California.

James, W. (1890). "Psychology." Holt, New York.

Kihlstrom, F. (1977). Models of posthypnotic amnesia. *In* "Conceptual and Investigative Approaches to Hypnosis and Hypnotic Phenomena" (Ed. W. E. Edmonston). *Annals of the New York Academy of Science* **296**, 284–301.

Knox, V. J., Crutchfield, L. and Hilgard, E. R. (1975). The nature of task interference in hypnotic dissociation: An investigation of hypnotic behavior. *International Journal of Clinical and Experimental Hypnosis* **23**, 305–323.

Ludwig, A. M. (1969). Altered states of consciousness. *In* "Altered States of Consciousness" (Ed. C. Tart), 9–22, New York.

McGlashan, T. H., Evans, F. J. and Orne, M. T. (1969). The nature of hypnotic analgesia and placebo response to experimental pain. *Psychosomatic Medicine* **31**, 227–246.

McKeachie, W. J. (1976). Psychology in America's Bicentennial year. *American Psychologist* **31**, 819–833.

Nace, E. R., Orne, M. T. and Hammer, A. G. (1974). Posthypnotic amnesia as an active psychic process: The reversibility of amnesia. *Archives of General Psychiatry* **31**, 257–260.

Nisbett, R. E. and Wilson, T. D. (1977). Telling more than we can know: Verbal reports on mental processes. *Psychological Review* **84**, 231–259.

Obstoj, I. and Sheehan, P. W. (1977). Aptitude for trance, task generalizability and incongruity response in hypnosis. *Journal of Abnormal Psychology* **86**, 543–552.

O'Connell, D. N., Shor, R. E. and Orne, M. T. (1970). Hypnotic age regression: An empirical and methodological analysis. *Journal of Abnormal Psychology: Monograph Supplement* **76**, No. 3, Part 2, 1–32.

Orne, M. T. (1959). The nature of hypnosis: Artifact and essence. *Journal of Abnormal and Social Psychology* **58**, 277–299.

Orne, M. T. (1967). What must a satisfactory theory of hypnosis explain? *International Journal of Psychiatry* **3**, 206–211.

Orne, M. T. (1974). On the concept of hypnotic depth. Paper presented at 18th International Conference of Applied Psychology, Montreal (August).

Orne, M. T. and Hammer, A. G. (1974). Hypnosis. *In* "Encyclopaedia Britannica", 133–140. William Benton, Chicago, Illinois.

Ornstein, R. E. (1977). "The Psychology of Consciousness." Harcourt Brace Jovanovich, New York.

Perry, C. W. (1977). Is hypnotizability modifiable? *International Journal of Clinical and Experimental Hypnosis* **25**, 125–146.

Perry, C. W. and Sheehan, P. W. (1978). Aptitude for trance and situational effects of varying the interpersonal nature of the hypnotic setting. *American Journal of Clinical Hypnosis* **20**, 256–262.

Rapaport, D. (1957). Cognitive structures. *In* "Contemporary Approaches to Cognition" University of Colorado Symposium, Harvard University Press.

Ruch, J. C., Morgan, A. H. and Hilgard, E. R. (1974). Measuring hypnotic responsiveness: A comparison of the Barber Suggestibility Scale and the Stanford Hypnotic Susceptibility Scale, Form A. *International Journal of Clinical and Experimental Hypnosis* **22**, 365–376.

Sarbin, T. R. and Coe, W. C. (1972). "Hypnosis: A Social Psychological Analysis of Influence Communication." Holt, Rinehart and Winston, New York.

Sarbin, T. R. and Slagle, R. W. (1972). Hypnosis and psychophysiological outcomes. *In* "Hypnosis: Research Developments and Perspectives" (Eds E. Fromm and R. E. Shor), 185–214. Academic Press, New York.

Sheehan, P. W. (1971). Countering preconceptions about hypnosis: An objective index of involvement with the hypnotist. *Journal of Abnormal Psychology: Monograph* **78**, 299–322.

Sheehan, P. W. (1972). Hypnosis and the manifestations of "imagination". *In* "Hypnosis: Research Developments and Perspectives" (Eds E. Fromm and R. E. Shor), 293–319. Aldine-Atherton, Chicago.

Sheehan, P. W. (1977). Incongruity in trance behavior: A defining property of hypnosis? "Conceptual and Investigative Approaches to Hypnotic Phenomena" (Ed. W. E. Edmonston). *Annals of the New York Academy of Science* **296**, 194–207.

Sheehan, P. W. and Dolby, R. M. (1974). Artifact and Barber's model of hypnosis: A logical-empirical analysis. *Journal of Experimental and Social Psychology* **10**, 171–187.

Sheehan, P. W. and Dolby, R. M. (1975). Hypnosis and the influence of most recently perceived events. *Journal of Abnormal Psychology* **84**, 331–345.

Sheehan, P. W., Obstoj, I. and McConkey, K. (1976). Trance logic and cue structure as supplied by the hypnotist. *Journal of Abnormal Psychology* **85**, 459–472.

Sheehan, P. W. and Perry, C. W. (1976). "Methodologies of Hypnosis: A Critical Appraisal of Contemporary Paradigms of Hypnosis." Lawrence Erlbaum Associates, Hillsdale, New Jersey.

Shor, R. E. (1959). Hypnosis and the concept of the generalized reality-orientation. *American Journal of Psychotherapy* **13**, 582–602.

Shor, R. E. (1962). Three dimensions of hypnotic depth. *International Journal of Clinical and Experimental Hypnosis* **10**, 23–28.

Spanos, N. P. and Barber, T. X. (1968). "Hypnotic" experiences as inferred from subjective reports: Auditory and visual hallucinations. *Journal of Experimental Research in Personality* **3**, 136–150.

Spanos, N. P. and Barber, T. X. (1974). Toward a convergence in hypnosis research. *American Psychologist* **29**, 500–511.

Spanos, N. P. and Bodorik, H. L. (1977). Suggested amnesia and disorganized recall in hypnotic and task-motivated subjects. *Journal of Abnormal Psychology* **86**, 295–305.

Spanos, N. P., Rivers, S. M. and Ross, S. Experienced involuntariness and response to hypnotic suggestions. *In* "Conceptual and Investigative Approaches to Hypnosis and Hypnotic Phenomena" (Ed. W. E. Edmonston). *Annals of the New York Academy of Science* **296**, 208–221.

Sutcliffe, J. P. (1961). "Credulous" and "skeptical" views of hypnotic phenomena: Experiments in esthesia, hallucination, and delusion. *Journal of Abnormal and Social Psychology* **62**, 189–200.

Tart, C. T. (1972a). Measuring the depth of an altered state of consciousness, with particular reference to self-report scales of hypnotic depth. *In* "Hypnosis: Research Developments and Perspectives" (Eds E. Fromm and R. E. Shor), 445–477. Aldine-Atherton, Chicago.

Tart, C. T. (1972b). States of consciousness and state-specific sciences. *Science* **176**, 1203–1210.

Tellegen, A. and Atkinson, G. (1974). Openness to absorbing and self-altering experiences ("absorption"), a trait related to hypnotic susceptibility. *Journal of Abnormal Psychology* **83**, 268–277.

Ulett, G. A., Akpinar, S. and Itil, T. M. (1972). Quantitative EEG analysis during hypnosis. *Electroencephalography and Clinical Neurophysiology* **33**, 361–368.

Subject Index